MURDER ON THE
WHISKEY
GEORGE

D1565717

A Novel

by

JJ Brinks

PRAISE FOR JJ BRINKS AND
MURDER ON THE WHISKEY GEORGE

"JJ Brinks' debut novel, Murder on the Whiskey George, is an absolute smash, a terrific tale with superbly written prose and edgy dialogue that spin a web of intricate deception in a riveting read that picks you up and sets you smack down in the sultry sway of a sun-drenched Florida. Brinks' characters are intelligent, genuine, and unforgettable. The story is spine-tingling, the novel, sensational. Let's hope the tales yet to be told by JJ Brinks come fast and often in what promises to be a superlative series!"

Kim LeMasters, Los Angeles, CA
Former President, CBS
Entertainment and Executive Producer,
Steven J. Cannell Productions

"I read your novel with great pleasure. You write extremely well, indeed on a high professional level. The book is far better than many of those currently on the market."

Richard (Dick) Marek, New York, NY
Editor of nine Best Selling novels by Robert Ludlum

"JJ Brinks has the start to a great series with his book "Murder on the Whiskey George." His characters are engaging, his plot interesting and suspenseful with enough twists and turns to keep us turning pages. I look forward to reading future additions to this series."

Doris Brogan
Kindle Edition

"JJ Brinks crafts a fast-paced thriller with finely drawn characters who are rich in texture, believable and interesting. Spanning Boston and New York City to the sandy beaches and Gulf waters of Florida, one can smell the salt air and feel the sun and water. Good work!!! This book held my attention with its many twists, turns and reasoning...... so I read it all in one day!!"

JB King
Kindle Edition

"I was taken in almost immediately. Such wonderful writing. I didn't want to put the book down. Thank you, Mr. Brinks, and I look forward to reading all the books in the series."

Kim Stiles
Kindle Edition

"This book kept me awake all night long! Loved the character development. I recommend this book without qualification."

Greg Reddick
Kindle Edition

"This book was hard to put down. The plot twists, fully developed characters, dramatic revelations, action, mystery, were all top notch! This is a great read!"

D.Dobler

"Loved the book, the characters, the plot twists, and the end! Who could ask for anything more?"

Janie G.
Kindle Edition

"Attention holding, interesting story, would recommend it to anyone. Couldn't put it down, looking forward to the next book. Keep them coming!"

Norma McInturff
Kindle edition

"Great read. Highly recommended. Enjoyed the plot, the characters, the writing technique of the author. Left me wanting more of the story. Didn't want it to end!"

R. Keslinger
Kindle Edition

To Barbara. For this, and for everything.

ISBN 978-0-9836784-2-7

Copyright JJ Brinks 2015. All rights reserved.

Empire Mystery Press

This novel is a product of the Author's imagination. Any resemblance to any person, living or dead, is coincidental. Names of characters, places, and/or other incidents or events that may exist or have taken place are used fictitiously.

Any reproduction, re-publication, or other use of the material contained herein, either in whole or in part, is expressly prohibited without the written consent of the author.

PROLOGUE

THE AIRBOAT SKIMMED the calm black surface of the winding creek, running deep into the recesses of the North Florida night, its propeller droning like the beating wings of some titanic prehistoric insect long since entombed beneath the muck and decay of the vast swampland. Nocturnal creatures scurried from the boat's path, or died trying.

The pilot swung the craft into a left turn, slowed to an idle then maneuvered forty yards along a narrow tributary where he cut the engine and let the boat's momentum carry it through a stand of tall grass, the sound like sandpaper being drawn in a single long stroke against the underside of the aluminum hull.

The bow came to rest against the edge of a small hummock. From a distance the boat and the land form would appear as one—a dark construct cut from opaque material, pasted in silhouette against a backdrop of pine, oak, and cypress.

The pilot climbed down from his seat, crouched for a moment on the flat deck listening to the night-sounds, then positioned himself behind his passenger who sat as motionless in the bow chair as a man anticipating the first snip of the barber's scissors.

Moonlight played off the shaggy blond flop of the seated man's hair and painted the ragged sweatshirt he'd had since college in a soft glow. His face was masked by a slick of sweat although the air was cool.

Several hours had passed since he'd been drugged—sufficient time to sober his brain so that he was aware first of the cessation of motion, then to a change in the stillness as the narcotic fog continued to dissipate.

He marveled at his predicament with a weird detachment, as if he were a spectator, not a participant, pondering a question that came to him like a recorded voice not fully his. *Why hadn't he just walked away and taken his chances?*

In answer, an image of Samantha formed of fog and light appeared in the blackness before his eyes.

For me, Billy. You did it for me.

Then as quickly as it had appeared, her face swirled and vanished into the pitch of a black vortex; he was overcome by a frantic need to survive—to be with her, to protect her.

He strained at first with rag doll-force against the cord that bound him to the chair, then began to buck and gyrate as a surge of adrenaline coursed through his blood. The veins in his neck bulged with the effort as his eyes filled with rage.

The pilot moved in quickly, certain that the muscular man was about to break free. He shoved the muzzle of the big Ruger against the back of the man's head and jerked the trigger.

The round entered low behind the right ear, ripping away in a bloody spray of teeth, bone, and tissue the Duct Tape that had covered his victim's mouth.

The shooter stumbled backward as a mushy cry escaped the gaping hole where his target's jaw had been only an instant before. Near panic, he took aim and fired again, then dropped to the deck, kneeling in his own vomit, sucking in brief gasps of air as he waited for the nausea to pass, wishing the asshole had simply stopped breathing hours before. But he hadn't. And that had left no option. He had his orders. Dead meant *dead.*

In time he forced himself into action, cutting the body loose from the chair, dragging its weight over the bow and onto the small patch of ground.

He stepped back onto the deck, gathered up lengths of cord and moved aft where he opened a locker, tossed in the gun and the pieces of rope, then grabbed a bucket and washed down the deck and chair, flushing away the gore and his own spew.

That done, he jumped into the water and pulled the boat free of the hummock, swung it around and hopped aboard where he climbed to the pilot's seat and hit the ignition. The engine roared to life, the propeller wash throwing the rudder from side to side until it steadied under his grip.

He worked his way slowly through the tangled overhang of moss-hung limbs and snake-like vines to the main creek, then made his course back along the familiar stretch of swampy waterway, the wind in his face seeming to blow away any fear he'd had about being caught. Everything had turned out okay, even with the change in plans.

As the boat gathered speed he reached beneath his seat for the flask filled with Jack, his thoughts turning to the money he'd earned for a day's work—more than he'd made in the past six months. With any luck—and he was due some—he'd triple it in no time at the Greyhound track.

He took a long pull of the smooth, sweet bourbon, throttled back and made a few lazy turns, reliving the moment, feeling his finger on the trigger, a proud sneer tugging at his mouth.

Maybe he deserved more money, what with the unexpected problems and all. Sort of a bonus.

The more he thought on the idea, the surer he was.

A big one at that.

ONE

A man's dying is more of the survivor's affair than his own.

—*Thomas Mann*

CHAPTER 1

ACHEERLESS DECEMBER SKY leaden with clouds holding moisture like dirty sponges had begun to drip rain on the city by the time I'd slogged my way through a half-hearted noon workout at the New York Athletic Club. For decades the place had been Mecca to the male ego—still was, although the membership caved to social and media pressure a few years back and began admitting women. I'd thought it appropriate; my father hadn't lived to see it; Jamie, my live-in Irish lady loved it, even gloated a little.

I showered and dressed, then caught the elevator down to the lobby and headed toward the main entrance on Fifty Ninth Street.

The desk manager wished me a good day with that stylized, reserved compassion the genteel dole out to those who've suffered the recent loss of a family member or close friend so that after a while it becomes more an annoyance than a kindness.

I pushed through the door and crossed Central Park South in the drizzle on a nearly hopeless mission to hail a cab. Umbrella in one hand, I used the other in the traditional New York manner— waving with growing frustration at the passing hacks already occupied, and those whose humor it was to go *Off Duty* as soon as the weather turns.

As I stood there with my arm thrust upward into the air, a faint vibration in my pocket signaled an incoming call; with some difficulty I dug out my Blackberry. "Cage Royce," I said, tucking the device under my chin and again raising my hand to the passing world as though I were eager to share the answer to some trivial question no one seemed to care about.

"Cage, Luke here."

"Counselor. How's everything in the sunny South?" I asked from my dreary spot on the globe.

"Oh, just dandy. Seems I got a client who's about to lose the farm. I'm at fault, naturally, even though the Missus's got a nifty snapshot of him all cozied up and lip locked with Little Miss Sand Bunny."

"You'll think of an angle," I said, glancing impatiently at my watch.

"Doubtful. Truth is, he's a real putz, so I don't feel all that badly. Anyway, somethin's come up."

"Problems with the contract?"

"No, no problems. Everything's cool. The place is yours and Jamie's." There was a short silence before he spoke again. "You at the office?"

"On the curb. Running late for a meeting. Why?"

Another pause, as if he were debating something. "Go take care 'a bidness. Call me at the house tonight. It'll keep."

"You're sure?" I asked as a cab miraculously pulled to a stop in front of me. I got in and pulled the door shut.

"Yeah, I'm sure."

He didn't sound it, but I'd learned not to push him.

"Will do," I said.

With my brief conversation ended, I gave the cabbie the address of my destination then sat back and gazed through the windshield where the wipers clicked back and forth with the hypnotic effect of a metronome, marking the beat of Luke Carey's words in four-four time.

It'll keep . . . It'll keep, he'd said.

I'd met Luke two months earlier on a directive from my brother Billy who was at the time jailed, waiting to get out on bail and for me to come to his rescue.

Now, as the cab driver fought his way into the jam of traffic, I felt again the single brand of bewilderment that comes packaged with the realization and shock that death has taken someone unexpectedly—someone who was alive one minute, and by all rational counts should be still.

I sorted through an abstract memory of a teacher explaining to a room full of third graders sitting attentively at their desks the loss of a classmate's mother and why it was that we needed to be exceedingly kind and show special understanding when our jocular friend returned after a three week absence, solemn and sullen and inconsolable.

The upshot of that experience had not been to aid in the development of a child's unformed sensitivities, but instead to send each of us home to look at our own mothers in the frightening new light of vulnerability.

I thought back on the death of our mother and father when an accident took their lives at a time when Billy and I were young adults. In that instance, the pain of loss was more measurable, my mind more capable of comprehending and accepting the random order of a chaotic world.

Now this—a premeditated act of homicide, a footnote in the chronicles of a society numbed to violent crime by the frequency of the act itself and the incessant coverage of the media.

Still, when the victim is someone you love, in this instance a brother lost forever to a murderous act, a void is created, and thicker bones and darker thoughts move in with a certainty of purpose to fill the emptiness—in my case, into the black hole left by Billy's death.

I'd heard nothing from Luke in days; now came a call that he'd casually tabled until evening. Excluding a pending real estate transaction—a by-product of my brother's murder that left me the benefactor of a bar and grill in Florida—our common ground was Billy. So the call, I reasoned, had to be related to his case, not the closing on the property Jamie and I were about to take on.

The driver turned north on Central Park West where we crawled along in the snarl of cabs and cars and buses.

Soon the dark emptiness returned and I was snared by the rhythm of thought and found myself floating back across the span of recent weeks to the trip I'd made, bent on helping my brother. Back to memories as fresh as newly turned earth.

I'D BEEN IN my office, a bland space in a bland building just north of Fifty-Third and Lex drafting some equally bland piece of corporate correspondence when Billy called.

My brother was a sun seeker, a free-spirited water rat. I kept track of him through occasional phone chats and sporadic post cards, the tasteless kind that appeal to tourists—pink flamingos, sea shells, oiled women in tiny bikinis.

The last I knew, he'd been in Florida's Panhandle working fishing charters out of a Panama City marina. He was still there when he called, but in jail, not on a boat.

I was nonplused. "What the hell'd you do, catch too many grouper?"

"I broke some guy's jaw. He's pressing charges. But that's the least of it." His words were tight, at odds with the Jimmy Buffet devotee who'd been my unflappable sidekick growing up—a natural politician who'd kept me out of more fights than I could remember.

"What happened? Who started—?"

He cut me off cold. "I'm in some serious shit, Cage. You've got to get me out of here before it gets any worse."

"Slow down. What are you talking ab—?"

"Listen to me, goddamnit! Call my attorney. His name is Luke Carey. He's in Panama City Beach. Then get down here as soon as you can. I'm not answering questions until you do. Just tell him that it's— Say it was a fight over a girlfriend so he doesn't rag me about it."

"Okay, okay. Stay cool," I said. "And don't talk to anyone. I'll be there tomorrow."

"I need your help, big brother." His voice became choked, and it rocked me. "I really fucked up this time."

WHEN I STEPPED off the plane in Panama City the following morning, the day was bright and balmy, counterpoint to my mood and the crappy weather I'd left behind in the Northeast.

I'd wasted no time in contacting Billy's attorney, downplaying my concern and wiring him the funds for the bail bond and his fee for representing my brother at the arraignment. He'd assured me that the advance wasn't necessary. Said believe it or not, he trusted lawyers.

I told him I'd be coming down—not that I doubted his ability: I had an unexpected break in my schedule and it was as good a time as any to catch up with my brother. It was a crock and I sensed in his silence that he knew it.

As I entered the terminal and headed for the rental car counter, I heard someone calling my name. A big man was crossing the lobby in a direct, purposeful line, the few people in his path moving aside as if the compression of air preceding him had pushed them away. His easy strides quickly closed the distance between us; he extended a massive hand as he took the last long steps that brought him to a stop in front of me. He was taller by four inches than my six-two, and I'd have needed at least forty pounds of hard ballast to even the scales. He had a full head of unkempt brown hair streaked with silver. His eyes were sharp as lasers and set deeply into his tanned face.

"Cage Royce," he said, a statement of fact, not a question that required a confirming answer.

There was no mistaking the voice I'd heard on the phone. It belonged to Luke Carey, Attorney at Law, and nothing at all resembling the short, bald man I'd pictured. I followed with questions asking why he was here and not waiting at his office as we'd arranged, and how he knew who I was.

"I needed to come this way on some errands," he said. "Anyway, it'll give us a chance to catch up on a couple details on the way back to the Beach." Almost as an afterthought he added, "And I made a bet with myself soon as I laid eyes-on that if you weren't kin to Billy, I'd give up beer 'n cigarettes. And trust me on this . . . I'm not about to do either."

I cancelled the rental car and followed Luke out to his illegally parked pickup.

I tossed my bag in the back and climbed in among a collection of tools and assorted litter.

"Sorry about the mess," he said. "Nothin' toxic, last I checked." His words tailed off in a chuckle that played shallow in his throat. The humor didn't reach his eyes. "Cage, let me get right to it. Billy's not where he's supposed to be. Never made it to the office for our meetin'."

"You're not suggesting that he skipped bail, are you?"

He merged left into the exit lane. "I'm a decent lawyer and a fair judge of character. I doubt the thought ever crossed his mind. No, he was countin' on seein' you." He glanced in my direction. "Wound mighty tight, though. Could be somethin' besides this girlfriend bidness you told me about that was troublin' him."

No comment.

We'd stopped in a short line of traffic. Carey looked at me. "Truth is, somethin' spooked him pretty good and I'd say without much warnin'." The traffic began to move. "I had him stay with us rather than at a motel after he got out on bail. He'd quit his job the day he got arrested and lost his bunk. When LuAnn and I left the house this mornin' he was up and dressed for a run. Said he was gonna do a few miles on the beach. When he was a no-show at the office, I called the house. No answer. So I went back to see if I could get a sense of what was goin' on. Saw right away that he'd checked out. He didn't come with a full-packed set of Louis Vuitton, you understand, but what he had looked to be gathered up and gone."

"No note?"

"Nada. Checked all around. More I did the fuzzier it looked. LuAnn'd made him give up some things to be washed this mornin'. That stuff was still on top of the machine. Nothin' else to do so LuAnn stayed put at the office and I came to get you. Thought maybe you'd have some insight on the subject."

I didn't. But a knife twisted in my gut, a pained feeling that something was seriously wrong. "Maybe he'll be there by the time we get back."

"We'll know before then. LuAnn'll call us here in the truck if he turns up."

We took a steel bridge across the bay that separates Panama City from Panama City Beach, and within a few minutes turned onto a two-lane ribbon of asphalt lined with T-shirt huts, daiquiri bars, tattoo parlors, bike rental shops and cut-rate motels that looked like big painted shoe boxes sitting parallel to the Gulf of Mexico.

"Front Beach Road. The main drag. Pretty as Park Avenue, idn't it?" Luke said as he pulled into an alleyway and parked behind a white, single-story cinder block house.

We entered through the back door and walked down a short hall to what I guessed had once been a living room but now served as a reception area. Seated behind a desk was a woman several years younger than Luke, auburn-haired with eyes as green as Jamie's, if that were possible. She came around to greet me.

"Cage. I'm LuAnn. Luke's wife." In answer to my question she said that, no, she was sorry but she hadn't heard anything from Billy. "But that doesn't mean he isn't coming back. In fact, he left some—"

"Already told Cage about the clothes," Luke said.

"No, not that," LuAnn said. "I remembered something else, so I stuck a note on the door and dashed home for a look. He'd put some things in the storage room under the house—foul weather gear, some expensive tackle. It's still there. He'll want that too, don't you think?"

Luke nodded, but without much conviction. "He just might at that." He turned to me. "Meantime, what say you cancel out on that motel 'a yours and bunk at the house? Got twins in the guest room and cold ones in the fridge. Y'all don't snore, do ya?"

I wasn't feeling particularly social and tried saying thanks, but no thanks.

He was insistent.

And while I would have much preferred my privacy just then, I wasn't up to the argument. I was tired, worried about Billy and building nicely on a shit pile of a mood. "That would be just fine," I managed. "Thanks."

LuAnn covered the office while Luke and I left for their house, hoping that Billy would eventually call or show up at one place or the other.

Ten minutes after setting out, Luke pulled his truck under a weathered-cedar, two-story house built atop telephone poles sunk deeply into the sandy earth, providing the place a foundation in the form of pilings.

We climbed a flight of stairs that led to an entry door ten feet up and went inside.

Glass doors covered the width of the rear of the main room providing access to a large deck. Beyond that lay a blazing stripe of white sand and the limitless expanse of the Gulf of Mexico, post card perfect.

Luke slid open a screen; I followed him out into the face of a cool breeze that blew in off water as iridescent as the Caribbean, then down a flight of wooden stairs to the beach. I took in the smell of the salt air as I bent and scooped up a handful of sand and let it run through my fingers.

"Sugar Sand. Goes clear to the border lookin' this way," Luke said, "and you can walk nearly every foot of it. Best beaches in Florida—maybe the whole damn world. Only way I'll leave this place is in a box."

A chord sounded. New York is a one-and-only, an intensely vibrant city. You thrive on its energy, or fight to survive it. Lately I'd been losing rounds, become bored and complacent and half-joked with Jamie that we should take Billy's advice—give it all up and head south. She was always game for a new adventure. I professed the same, but desire and determination are spoken in different dialects; the conversation would invariably become lost in translation.

Now, standing on the beach, the possibility that I was too given to compromise seemed a dispiriting reality, one that begged an exorcism before I became hopelessly trapped by my own indecision. I realized suddenly how much I'd missed the years away from Billy. How irretrievable they were.

The day seemed to darken a shade.

"Then again, city's got its benefits, too, I imagine," Luke said.

"Do you, now? But not like here, right?" I said, tasting the sarcasm in my words as they left my lips.

Luke seemed bemused. "We manage to get by."

"Great place to retire–dabble in the law now and then?" I added for seasoning.

He picked at a fingernail. "There a rule says you gotta be cooped up in a big city box all day coverin' Wall Street butt in order to do your lawyerin'?"

"Cooped up. Right. Thanks so much for the insight."

He closed one eye against the sun and squinted at me. "Wasn't you in particular I was referrin' to. Nothin' intended." He smiled—a great big friendly one—and it grated on me. "Still," he said, "it's amazin' the number of folks who window shop their lives away."

I started to say something but was stopped by the thought of how easily I'd been read, and how I'd just insulted a man who'd offered his help.

We walked back to the house in silence.

"Think I'll go have a talk with Wesley Harland. He's police chief here—a friend 'a mine. He'll have a thought or two on what we might do at this point. Why don't you grab a nap or catch some rays. Food and brew in the icebox if you're hungry or thirsty or both. You hear anything from Billy, you call LuAnn at the office. I'll be back in an hour or so."

When Luke returned he had to shake me awake. The sun was low in the sky. It took a minute to clear my head. I'd been out cold. Mix one part early morning flight on no sleep with a couple of beers and the warmth of a sunny day, add in a heaping measure of worry and stress and you can down a bull elephant.

"Wesley'll give us a little time to look for your brother if we want, but he'll have to say somethin' to the court before long. Anyway, I don't think waitin's best."

Neither did I.

BY THEN LUANN had given up her vigil and returned from the office. She took drink orders and in a minute returned to the deck with a tray of martinis, joining us where we stood leaning on the rail. She made a stab at encouragement as we clinked glasses all around. "You watch," she said. "This whole thing will turn out to be some silly misunderstanding."

"Sure," I half-mumbled as I turned and looked out over the Gulf where the sun was sinking low on the distant waterline. Thin layers of color stretched along the horizon like wet streaks of spilled pigment. Reds and oranges spread in a crown across the sky, intensifying by the minute until the last sliver of the burning sphere slid from view and a firestorm paid out. Puffs of clouds erupted in brilliant flame, some appearing to be seared on their underbellies, others completely charred as though they'd borne witness to Armageddon and all that remained beneath them was an illusion.

"Piece a' work, idn't it?" Luke said. "One of the few things in this world of ours we mortals haven't figured out how to fuck up. Not a lot left that we haven't, in some fashion or other."

THAT NIGHT I lay awake for hours, alone, in a strange bed, puzzled by my brother's disappearance, Luke's assessment of the state of man's condition gnawing away at any hope I harbored that everything would be okay.

I relived the day Billy'd called me with the news that our parents had died in the crash of a private plane. Heard again the questions he'd asked about our future.

Now the questions were mine to ask. Only this time they were about Billy, the kid brother I'd die for.

Finally, mental and physical fatigue drew me down into a fitful sleep—one where a storyteller whose kicks were found in the terror of small children waited with a special dream.

I was on the Careys' deck. Billy was inside the house. We were kids again—nine or ten. I wanted him to see the sunset.

"C'mon man. You're gonna miss it!"

I heard him call my name and went in to find him. It was dark in the house. I couldn't see.

I called out to him—again and again.

"Cage!" he cried, but only once, the sound of his voice cut short, deadened like a radio fried by a lightning strike in a terrible storm.

Deep in the recesses of a room without definition or dimension, I saw a figure with no face dressed in ragged clothes that hung from its small body in smoldering strips.

I ran back out to the deck, alone and frightened.

The waters of the Gulf were boiling and hissing, the sky consumed by billowing flames that licked the sand and turned it black.

CHAPTER 2

B Y SEVEN THE next morning I was on the beach, running close to the water's edge. A scattering of people jogged at a leisurely pace, some alone, others tethered by leads to their canine companions. It took some getting used to but I finally got the idea and began returning their greetings. I was a long way from Central Park.

With the exercise and fresh air a touch of false optimism edged in next to the remnants of the previous night's dream. For a moment the illusion was that of the kind of day taking shape where everything should be right in the world.

But it seldom is.

Luke was on the deck drinking coffee as I returned from my run, a cigarette protruding from the corner of his broad mouth. "Beats me as to why a fella'd go wearin' himself out to start the day." He flipped the butt of his cigarette over the rail. "Anyway, let's you and me go in for a bite and get you a cup 'a LuAnn's finest. And there's somebody here who'd like to meet you."

I followed him inside. A man was seated at the breakfast bar eating scrambled eggs and sausage—a bookend for Luke in physical dimension, only with skin as black as the coffee that filled the glass mug next to his plate. He put down his fork and wiped his mouth and hands on his napkin, his wide smile exposing two rows of brilliant white teeth.

"You'd be Cage Royce," he said. "Wes Harland. Police Chief."

He glanced at Luke. "More so, I'm a friend to this big tub with the bad haircut."

We shook hands.

"Luke tells me you're a lawyer," the chief said to me, "so you understand the issue of the bail bond—assuming Billy took it upon himself to skip out for the hell of it."

"If he took off, something or someone forced him into it," I said.

"Maybe somethin' to do with the fight," Wes said. "I was hoping Billy might have told you what set it off."

Luke answered before I could, edging a sausage patty onto a biscuit half with the study of a man building a house of cards. "A misunderstandin' involving some woman."

Wes shot eyes at Luke then picked up a file from the counter next to his plate and opened it. "Maybe," he said with more than a little skepticism. "We have statements from three witnesses: the waitress, the bartender, and the guy who pressed the charges." He perused the documents for a minute, then summarized:

When Billy arrived at the restaurant, he'd joined a man who appeared to be about his age who'd stood and waved him over to a table.

Billy ordered a beer. When the waitress brought it to him the two men seemed to be involved in a serious discussion. When she returned a few minutes later to offer another round, the discussion had become an intense argument that seemed about to end.

Both men stood. The man with Billy threw a fifty on the table and told the waitress to keep the change.

The bartender watched as they walked out to the parking lot, then called the police on the hunch that it was about to get ugly.

"Who was the guy at the table?" I asked.

Wes shrugged. "We don't know. By the time the patrol car got there he was gone."

"And the one with the broken jaw?"

"Local contractor. Rough and tumble type. Says he saw your brother pounding on this guy, stepped in to break it up and Billy tagged him. About then the patrol car showed up. Meanwhile the guy your brother was hammering took off—never contacted the police. Didn't seem important then. Now with Billy's disappearance, we're checking to see if maybe he sought medical attention that night or the next day. So far, nothing."

Wes closed the folder. "That's all we know."

I choked down the last of my coffee along with the temptation to share what Billy had told me, not yet willing to give up hope that I'd learn the truth of what this was about from him. "I wish there was something I could add. But there isn't."

Wes stood, his eyes searching my face for the truth that I held poorly hidden. "Anyway, I better head for the station before everybody thinks I came to my senses and quit this damned job. Maybe that coffee'll jog your memory, Cage. Let me know if it does."

LuAnn came into the kitchen. She gave Wes a quick hug and me a piece of paper.

"What's this?" I asked.

She glanced at her husband then looked uncertainly at me. "Jamie called for you while you were on your run. We chatted a bit, and she asked about Billy. I sort of told her that—"

"Sort of told her *what?*" I'd left Jamie a message the evening before telling her where I'd be staying and that I'd call her again today but said nothing about Billy's disappearance. I'd been stalling, not wanting to set off alarms that might only prove false. That option was now apparently gone.

Luke eyed me. "No harm intended, Cage."

"I'm sure not. Anyway, there's nothing I can do about it now, is there."

"You could have said something to her from the git go."

"That's my business, don't you think?" I looked at the scrap of paper in my hand as though it contained bad news I didn't want to read.

"Flight information," LuAnn said as she stiffened and turned away. "She'll be here tomorrow."

JAMIE'S PLANE ARRIVED early the next morning; I drove LuAnn's Jeep to the airport and met her at security.

Her stare was icy.

"LuAnn shouldn't have said anything."

"I *asked*," Jamie snapped. "Why was that, I wonder. Maybe because your message was clipped so damned short that it raised a flag? The way you treat me when you decide to cut me out of your troubles?"

"That wasn't it."

"Then, what was it, Cage?"

I took her carry-on and her hand as we began to trudge down the corridor toward the exit. "Can we not do this? Billy's the main issue here."

She slumped against me, softening. "You're right. It's just that— I mean, all the times we've talked about coming to see him, and it takes this? What *happened* to us? How did we get so . . . disconnected?"

"Because there'll always be another day, Jamie. Always time to catch up. No need to rush. Pay attention to our own little problems first. Someone else's can wait."

"Human nature, Cage. Don't blame—"

"Then, one day it's too goddamn late. We go looking, and they're no longer around. Worse, we wake up but maybe they don't."

She squeezed my arm. "Like you just said, not the time for this."

"No? Then when is?" I said as we left the building and headed for the Jeep.

We said little on the drive back to Luke and LuAnn's, stopping first to check into the motel I'd booked then cancelled for the night before. We needed time and space to bang out the dents of the last few hours.

Our assigned room was small with sand ground into the damp carpet, the view of the Gulf obscured by a salt-crust that covered the lone window like a cataract.

Jamie sulked around, unpacking the few things she'd brought, taking too long in the cramped, musty bathroom. "So why didn't you say something?" she asked finally as she came over and sat next to me on the bed.

"No defense." I looked at her for a long moment, seeing in her face the worry and hurt that I had caused at the expense of some inherent need to protect Billy, as if we were still the young brothers who'd exchanged blood from small cuts on the backs of our hands one summer afternoon, pledging to lie to the death to cover each others butts when the heat was on. A pact that after all these years now seemed pointless.

"Something seriously bad has happened here," I said.

She took my hand. "You don't know that. You can't."

I felt a burn in my eyes as I looked at the hope in hers. "No, Jamie. It has. I only hope I have the strength to face whatever it is."

As we left the motel the rain stopped, but the skies still threatened.

I PARKED THE JEEP under the Careys' house, took Jamie's hand and led her up the stairs.

Luke was hunched over the fireplace adjusting the logs. LuAnn was in the kitchen and came around the corner of the breakfast bar that separated the two rooms. She exchanged quick eye contact and a wordless embrace with Jamie, a silent introduction shared on a sensory level of plaintive communication between two women who had only just met, but in that instant were no longer strangers.

Luke replaced the poker in its rack then came over. I introduced him to Jamie. His grin was forced, his words divorced from their intended levity. "What I wanna know is, why you hang around with this no-count Royce fella?"

Jamie's smile could not hide the trepidation in her eyes. "My calling in life was to become a child psychologist," she said. She turned and patted my cheek. "I like to keep one around for practice."

LuAnn offered coffee; she and Jamie went into the kitchen.

Luke turned to me. "What say we get a breath of fresh air before the rain kicks back up and washes the whole damn day away."

I followed him out to the deck, a buzz growing in my head, knowing the essence of what he was about to tell me before he'd spoken the first word.

"I heard from Wesley after you left for the airport to get Jamie. Sheriff over in Franklin County—east 'a here—called. They recovered a body early this mornin'. Christ a' Mighty, Cage, I'm truly sorry, but from the sound of things, they've found your brother."

Luke's words struck my ears as if spoken from a great distance. My eyes shifted mechanically back into the house.

Jamie stood on the other side of the glass door, a look of unbearable grief frozen on her face.

I turned back to Luke. "They're sure?"

"Gonna take you to confirm it, but it looks that way, yes. Wesley's got it all set up for us. Wish there was another way. I truly do".

CHAPTER 3

WE MET CHIEF Harland at the Panama City Beach Police Station where he waited in the parking lot leaning against the fender of a white Jeep with a light-rack and the blue and green logo of the department stenciled down its sides. He shook hands with Jamie then said, "We'll be meeting at a local mortuary over near to where it happened. These small counties don't have their own medical examiner. All that's done up in Tallahassee."

I opened the back door on the driver's side for Jamie, closed it once she was inside then went around behind the Jeep to climb in next to her.

Luke stood at the door, his thick fingers hooked through the handle, eyes watching me as I approached.

"What?" I said.

He lowered his gaze. "Nothin', partner. Other than if it's Billy, your world is about to change in ways you can't imagine." His voice was flat as the calm that warns of the coming of a straight-line storm in the heat of summer.

My look was one of question, as if he were speaking in words just beyond my comprehension.

"This is no accident we're talkin' about, Cage. From what I'm hearin' this was a killin'. One with a great amount of damage done. So stack it up, partner. You're gonna need it for your sanity."

I stared at him, my thoughts bent and contorted by anger and fear. It seemed in that moment that his eyes became dark windows that opened on a place I knew nothing about, where humpbacked shapes moved in pained steps, beaten down and disfigured by the burden of malevolence.

***

THE TRIP TOOK ninety minutes.

No one said a word as we pulled in behind the low brick building, a place that held promise of nothing beyond the confirmation of death.

Inside, the air felt heavy. Breathing took thought and effort. Fluorescent lights robbed the space of any warmth and the smell of disinfectant erased any scent of the living.

Half-way down the corridor the door to an office stood open. Inside, two men sat on opposite sides of a large desk talking amicably. They stood as we entered, cutting short their conversation. We were introduced to Melvin Hough, owner of Hough and Sons Funeral Home, and Sheriff Enis Shine.

"Mr. Royce. Ma'am," Hough said as we moved to a grouping of a couch and high-back chairs, "I realize how difficult this must be for you. Unfortunately, I'm unable to intervene, to do anything to assuage your level of anxiety. Not with a criminal investigation in the offing. An autopsy, if you will." He spoke with a deep Southern accent in words that were soft yet penetrating. "It appears the deceased fell victim to severe head trauma—that perhaps multiple gun shots were inflict—"

I threw a look at Luke and cut Hough short. "I'd like to get on with it as quickly as possible and without any narrative, if you don't mind."

Enis Shine cleared his throat. The sheriff had a simple face, an overweight man with thinning hair and a shyness about him, the buttons of his shirt stretching the dark synthetic fabric over his belly, exposing the undershirt beneath in small, evenly spaced blossoms of white cotton. "We got a good fix on when this happened," he said. "Pretty much exact. A touch of dumb luck's what it was. Even so, the body was on that patch a' ground for near-on thirty-six hours. Couldn't help but make things worse than they already was." He pulled a handkerchief from his back pocket and wiped his face and eyes. "Been at this a long time. This one's downright hard to look at's what Mr. Hough meant.

Old Tate's Hell had a hand in the damage for sure. Think y'all need to be ready's what we're sayin'."

"I'll keep that in mind," I said in words chipped from ice.

Jamie shifted her weight as I stood. She took my hand and squeezed hard.

"I'll only be gone a minute," I said, then followed Wes, Luke, and Melvin Hough into the hall, the weight of each footfall as heavy as if I'd been walking in deep mud instead of on thick carpeting the color of dried blood.

The room was stark. White paint and metal cabinets, the light too harsh. Coldness seeped from the floor and wormed its way into my bones. My pulse quickened, my breath liquid in my chest.

By then I'd accepted the fact that the body I was about to identify was my brother's. But as I looked at the motionless shape beneath the thin white sheet, I wished the ill-fortune unfairly on someone else—someone I didn't know. Someone whose life meant nothing to me.

Let it be a mistake. Don't let it be Billy.

As Hough moved in measured steps toward the table, my eyes fell on a hand protruding from beneath the sheet, palm-up, pale and fleshy. A band of gold encircled the ring finger. "Turn it over," I said.

"I'm sorry, I don't—"

"The *hand*, Mr. Hough. Turn . . . it . . . over."

Hough did as I requested, revealing the red stone and embossed crest of Boston University.

I turned my head to one side and stared at nothing. When I looked back the hand had been tucked beneath the white linen; Hough had positioned himself at the head of the corpse. Our eyes met. One more body, I thought without justification. Another payday. What did he care?

He lifted the sheet in fat, pinched fingers by the corners and turned it back in a neat fold, keeping his eyes on me all the while.

I stepped to the head of the table, into the circle of air that carried the faint smell of decayed earth and looked down into the mire of skin and bone and nameless sinew that was the death-face of my brother.

A wordless sound formed in my throat, the cry of an ache so intense that it nearly drove me to my knees. I reached toward Billy's ruined face with a trembling hand, caressed the cold skin of his one remaining cheek, smoothed back the blond hair that lay against his left temple and ear.

To my horror, the shape of something with a thick black carapace emerged from the depths of my brother's skull. The beetle settled on my hand. The floor began to spin. My head pounded. I flung the insect against the wall then lunged past Wes Harland and bolted from the room, sprinting the length of the hallway, nearly colliding with Jamie as she came out of Hough's office.

She grabbed at my shirt sleeve. "Cage? Cage!"

I never slowed.

I banged through the exit, running with all my strength, grunting and pumping my legs—ran until I tripped and was sent sprawling across the lawn, my face plowing into the earth, the smells of grass and dirt filling my nostrils. I struggled to sit up, then lowered my head and retched on the ground in front of me in grieving spasms that wracked my body and clutched at my heart.

In a moment I felt a hand on my shoulder.

Luke's voice came from behind me. "Not much I can say that'll help. Only that I know how you feel."

I raised my head in warning like a panting, diseased dog and glared at him. "That's my *brother* in there! How the hell would you know how it feels? And I don't want your fucking pity."

His eyes passed over my face, then seemed to lose their focus. "This idn't the time or place to get into it," he said evenly. "But you're wrong. And pity's the last thing I'll offer."

JAMIE HUDDLED AGAINST me in the back seat of the Jeep on the return trip to the Beach.

"Will someone explain to me what Enis Shine meant about *Tate's Hell*?" I blurted after miles of silence that had me struggling to process feelings and thoughts that seemed as indecipherable as Sanskrit while those two words played as an unbearable riddle in my head. "What the hell are we talking about here? Some kind of Southern Voodoo?"

Luke's eyes caught mine in the mirror. "Tate's Hell is a *place*, Cage, no hocus-pocus about it." He lit a cigarette with a tarnished and battered Zippo, blowing the first drag out through his partially lowered window, the faint scent of burned tobacco floating on the air. "Years ago a settler in these parts—fella name of Tate—wound up lost in the big area of swamp n' woodlands that stretches between the Apalachicola and Ochlockonee Rivers just north of the road we're on.

"One version of the story says he was never found. But the one that became legend is that he staggered out after spendin' too many days and nights with the 'gators and snakes and said to the first person he saw, 'My name's Tate and I just been to Hell and back.' After a time, the name became official."

"And that's where they found Billy," I said.

"In a small corner of it, yes," Wes said. "We're talking about two-hundred thousand acres all told—maybe eighty-thousand or so at the true heart. Back in the fifties the timber companies cleared a good part of the swamp to grow pine to feed the paper mills—changed the water flow from there to the Gulf and messed up the shrimp and oyster beds in the East Bay. Now the state's trying to straighten it all out. That's where the luck that Enis was talking about comes in.

"Team of scientists and a guy from Water Management were camped up the Whiskey George Creek. They'd turned in for the night when they heard an airboat coming at a good clip. It moved on past. Few minutes later they heard the engine stop. Then nothing for a while. Then came what sounded like two gun shots. Awhile after that, the boat came back down the creek and ran off in the distance."

"And they didn't bother to go *look*? Jesus," I said.

"Figured it was poachers after 'gators. No sense in tangling with that sort. Planned to report it after they'd finished," Wes said as he drove. "Until early this morning, that is. They were working the area when they scared up some buzz . . . you know, some birds, up a small branch of the Whiskey George. They decided to check it out. They called it in on the cell phone and Enis and his deputies went out to set up a crime scene and bring in the body."

Wes looked at me in the rearview mirror. I held his eyes. "The manner of the killing, where it took place and all suggests something other than a random act—like a robbery" he said. "Fact is, it almost looks like . . . ." He turned his eyes back to the road ahead. "Sorry. You don't need to hear this just now."

"An execution is what you're thinking, isn't it," I said, stunned by the inference. Even so, the possibility was undeniable.

It looked like someone had put a hit on my brother.

CHAPTER 4

"A PROFESSIONAL KILLING–EXECUTION, HIT, whatever you want to call it. That's the first impression," Wes said as he unlocked the door to his office.

We'd dropped Jamie at the house then gone to the station to retrieve Luke's truck only to find ourselves quickly caught up in the question and answer game–the cold dissection of the history and character of the deceased necessary for the elimination, inclusion, or confirmation of the elements, circumstances, and motives surrounding the act of murder. That's the classroom definition.

In real life, it stinks. As the son of a high-powered criminal defense attorney, a high schooler interested in a legal career who often watched his father at work, I've seen families come apart over innuendo and the unfounded accusations of cops and lawyers alike. It's easy to kick the dead around if it benefits your case then offer an apology after the damage has been inflicted. Nothing personal. No offense. I discovered early on that I had no stomach for it and wondered more than once if what he did for a living eventually drove my father to the bottle.

The same tension I'd detected on my father's face at times was on Wes's face now, there in the rhythmic flexing of jaw muscles. "This can hold," he said. "Not long, but it *can* hold."

"You have a job to do," I said. "It's not my intention to drag it out or make it more difficult than it already is. For any of us."

Wes nodded, drew in a deep breath. "I appreciate that." He picked up a yellow legal pad and a pencil from his desk. "Okay. To start, then. Cage, do you have any reason to believe that your brother was a user. That he was in involved with drugs somehow?"

A popular place to begin. "No," I said.

"Any depression? Talk of money problems?"

"My brother was upbeat. And I'm sure a check of his accounts will show that he had plenty to live on—his inheritance from our parents' estate. Not a fortune, but enough."

"Any known enemies? Did he gamble? Mess with anyone's wife?"

"Not that I'm aware of. And no, he didn't gamble," I said. "As to the last, I couldn't say. But it would be way out of character."

Wes tossed the pad back onto his desk. "So he goes to a bar. Has a of couple beers. Chats for a while then tears this guy a new asshole. Soon thereafter he disappears and winds up dead in the fucking middle of East Jesus. All for no reason?"

"'Course there was a reason, " Luke said.

Wes cut his eyes. "No shit."

"Fine. But Cage's brother wadn't a heavy."

I suspected that Luke believed the story about a fight over a girlfriend to be a fabrication. He'd telegraphed as much when I'd first met him, but hadn't questioned it directly. Now it seemed that he was covering for Billy. But why? Did it have something to do with his relationship with my brother?

I'd held my cards long enough. I saw no advantage in doing so any longer. "When Billy called me from the lockup he told me that he was in some serious trouble," I said. "I'd say his murder supports that premise, wouldn't you?"

Luke's eyes narrowed almost imperceptibly.

Wes looked at me as if I'd pissed on his camp fire. "Damnit! Why'd you keep this from us 'til now?"

"Because I wasn't sure what he was talking about. He was my brother, for Christ's sake, not some felon. He deserved the chance for me to hear him out first." I shot out of my seat. "And in case you forgot, he wasn't fucking *dead* yet, okay?"

"Foreign territory, Cage." Luke said softly. "Understandable. Hard to tell who to trust."

I looked at him but didn't respond. Not verbally.

Wes watched the exchange then eyed me with considerable caution. "No one's saying he was a criminal."

I dropped back into my chair.

"When I said that it looked like a professional hit, that's what I meant—that it *looked* that way, not that it was," Wes said, watching me as though I might explode at the wrong word or inflection. "I'm not the FBI or an expert on hit men, but here's what I see:

"First, why would a pro go to the trouble of doing the killing in the middle of the night in a God-forsaken place like Tate's Hell? Nothin' wrong with the miles of back road around here. No one to take notice of a shot being fired, and a body buried out in the scrub would stay buried. There's a bunch of reasons why it doesn't make sense. What if the boat broke down, for instance?

"That means the place was familiar to the shooter. Figured he was safe on his own turf. He would've been, too, except he was heard instead of seen and the body *was* found. He shit where he sleeps. No experienced killer would risk it.

"So we'll assume that our shooter's no Einstein. I'd say he's a local. Franklin County probably. We'll check out boat registrations but most people don't bother—not in the back woods. They do any poaching or illegal trapping, forget it." Wes began to pace. "Next there's the choice of weapons. This guy used something big and loud. With a pro you'd see a small caliber pistol—just as effective. Or a knife. My guess is he used what he had or got something that he thought he needed. Either case says he's an amateur.

"Then there's the physical evidence. From the few pieces of rope left at the scene it looks like the shooter tried to clean up.

Maybe he felt like he had to, even way out there. Nerves. No, I'm convinced that we've got us a local bad boy. *That's* the easy part."

Wes's private line rang. He answered, then handed the receiver to Luke who spoke briefly then hung up. "We should get a move on. I think it's best if Cage is with Jamie right now. And supper's waitin'."

Wes checked his watch. "Time flies, huh? I oughta do the same myself. One divorce is quite enough, thank you. Anyway, we should have some preliminaries available from the medical examiner by tomorrow afternoon. Let's pick it up then. And Cage? Stay cool, man, okay?"

D INNER CONVERSATION WAS at first sparse and stilted. But with wine as the lubricant and Billy's murder the black hole of topics that kept us focused on random stories that would under different circumstances lay untouched and unexplored for weeks or months, we eased into social discovery with a sense of casualness.

Luke had been married once before; the rigors of law school and the early years of establishing a practice in Atlanta had not been appreciated by his first wife. They'd split up after five years.

He'd met LuAnn fifteen years ago on a weekend trip with friends to Panama City Beach. He'd taken immediately to the sand and the sun and within days, to his future wife, eventually coming to stay, buying the house that was now his office, hanging out his shingle and offering LuAnn a job and a ring. She'd accepted both, placing her faith in someone she barely knew but instinctively trusted. A giant of a man, gentle and complex, protective, with a power that hummed like a high tension wire deep within a place not easily probed.

Jamie and I had been together since Boston. There was no particular reason why we hadn't married, she explained, other than the fact that our respective parents were all dead and our collective families, small. With Billy's murder the sum total of siblings had been eradicated: Jamie was an only child.

My contribution to the conversation had been no more than a few words spread out between gulps of Merlot—little puffs of wind with about as much substance. Try as I might, I could think of little other than Billy.

A T MIDNIGHT LUKE drove us back to the motel. Jamie stripped the blanket from the bed, took my hand and led us onto the beach.

The sky was clear and black, the moon high and full, its light reflecting off the Gulf, turning the water's flat surface into a sea of obsidian.

Jamie looked up as we walked barefoot along the shoreline. "The stars. They're so bright," she said. "I remember my mother telling me one night that each was the soul of a lost person— someone who'd died alone—and that in Heaven they all became angels with flaming wings. I'd almost forgotten they existed. Can't remember the last time I even thought to look. For all I know they might not shine over Manhattan anymore. Pretty sad, huh?"

We walked for several minutes without words, the blanket draped over our shoulders in defense of the brisk night air then stopped a hundred yards from the motel at a clump of small grassy dunes.

"Rough day," I said. "I'm sorry for the way I acted."

Jamie pressed her fingers against my mouth, knelt and spread the blanket at our feet and pulled me down to the sand.

And there under countless stars that were Jamie's angels, we made love with urgency, overwhelmed by the intense need for the confirmation of life that commands physical contact— to perform the animalistic, instinctive act of self-preservation when all mortal defenses are lost, and the raw vulnerability of death and extinction seems all too real.

CHAPTER 5

MONDAY MORNING WE rented a car. I was tired of being shuttled everywhere. We drove along Front Beach Road until we found a public stretch of sand where we could plop down in solitude under blue skies in our newly-purchased aluminum and plastic-strapped chairs, a venue away from our damp room and a temporary refuge from damper spirits.

Jamie's face was buried behind the newspaper when suddenly she lowered it and handed me a section. "Bottom half," she said.

I found the article:

FRANKLIN COUNTY MURDER HAS BEACH CONNECTION

Staff Reporter

Panama City Beach– Beach Police confirmed late last night that the body of a man found in a remote area of Franklin County is that of William T. Royce, age 35, an area resident reported missing Friday by his attorney, Lucious Carey. The death is a suspected homicide.

According to sources, Royce had been arrested late last week on assault charges stemming from an altercation at the Sea Goddess Tavern, but had since been released on bail.

Police refused to speculate on any connection between the discovery of the body, and the circumstances surrounding Royce's arrest.

I crumpled the paper and tossed it onto the sand. "So much for a few fucking minutes of distraction."

Jamie reached for my hand. "They'll be tough to find anywhere, babe. For a long time, I think." Tears marked her cheeks, glistening in the sun. "It's so hard to accept that he's gone."

Impossible was more like it. It's both unworkable and futile to assess the weight of a tragedy in present terms while words and images and special memories crowd into the same space, without choreography, and the door will not close on the chaos.

I have never considered myself to be a complicated man. More to the point, like most I have not examined at close range the human complex of self. Dreams, fears, wants and wishes? I suppose. But never in the context of confronting a catastrophic event. The mind is too protective, the aversion to accepting that we might one day find ourselves at the core of such an eventuality, too pronounced.

I'd been totally unprepared to deal with the matrix of Billy's death—the event, the circumstances surrounding it, the people involved with and affected by it. Or to know or recognize how its impact would play out in the remaining stages of my life. But without question something was at work inside of me— old circuits closing, others opening for the first time. Fractions of light and motion, hints of things taking shape without my consent or concurrence. What was yet to come was as uncertain as an unwritten page.

But through it all, I would face the age-old questions: Given the chance, what would I have done differently? Would anything have changed the course of events? What had I missed? What more might I have said or done to impact the direction of my brother's life?

IT WAS DURING his junior year at Boston University—my second year in law school and Jamie's last in grad school— that things began to change.

Billy became more distant and from what I could tell, hadn't a clue as to where his life was going. I'd brought it up too often, had become a pain in the ass on the subject. But I couldn't let go, and finally pushed it to the limit on an otherwise perfect spring day.

We'd been running along the Charles River and slowed to a walk to cool down.

Billy eyed me. "You've got that look."

"I only want to help. I don't—"

"What's with you, Cage? You rag me constantly about getting my shit together. I try to explain myself but you don't want to hear it. You don't listen. So why ask in the first place?"

"Forget it," I said, wiping the sweat from my face onto my shirt.

"That's fucking perfect, you know? A classic. Another special evening at the dinner table with you and—"

"*Don't*," I warned. "That's out of bounds, and you know it."

"Fine. Then so is this conversation."

Before I could say another word, he took off at a dead run.

For the next two days my calls were taken by his answering machine. Finally, I went looking and found him at one of our less-frequented spots.

I stood inside the door letting my eyes adjust from late afternoon sun to smoke-filled, near-darkness before going to the bar where he sat with a lady I didn't recognize.

As I approached, she kissed his cheek and drifted away.

"You been drinking, big brother?" Billy asked without looking at me.

"Checked a lot of places before I thought of this one."

"It's not all your fault," he said. "My line about you and Dad was uncalled for. It just . . . came out."

"Maybe it needed to," I said, recalling the alcohol-fueled lectures that progressed to all-out battles by the end of my high school years.

"The two years after you left for college were the worst," Billy said. "The Old Man needed a new target. His drinking got worse. He'd go on about you as if you were still there then lay into me about 'motivation, excellence, responsibility'—the whole bit."

"And you just sat there and took it." But then he would have, I thought. Always the peacemaker. I began to connect the dots. "The phone calls, the weekend visits. But you never *said* anything."

He downed the rest of his beer.

I signaled for the bar tab. "Come on, let's get out of this hole."

We ended the night at a seedy dump near Fenway Park. By then I was drunk—partly by volume, mostly by design. Even so I whipped Billy repeatedly at Nine Ball, teamed with him at Foosball where we held our own, then lost three in a row to him at darts.

"One more," I said.

He moved to the board to gather up the little hand-held spears. "Not your game, ace," he said. "Not gonna happen."

In four rounds, it was over. I never got close.

We stood at the bar for last call. "It's a stupid game, anyway," I said.

"Not if you understand it."

I offered a little drunken nod. "And so, my good man, I am learning impaired."

"That's not the problem," he said. "It's a matter of style."

I looked at him but he avoided my eyes. "This isn't about darts, *or* style, is it, Billy."

He said nothing.

"Don't shut me off. I want to hear it."

He measured my sincerity. "No, it isn't. It's about growing up—about realizations."

"Monosyllables, little brother. I'm slightly shitfaced here."

"Then I'll make it simple. I'm not you. There was a time I wanted to be. But not anymore. All I can do is be who I am."

I fumbled. "Yeah? . . . and . . . what's so wrong with that?"

"Nothing. But it means disappointing you. Letting you down."

"Jesus Christ! Have I been that big a prick? That fucking insensitive that you thought you needed my *approval* to get on with your life?"

"Basically? . . . yeah. And the bitch is, I don't know what I want so I *can't* answer your questions. I can't see into the future and map out my goddamn life the way you can. I'm a fringe player, Cage. Like at darts. It's more interesting that way. Maybe you should give it a try sometime instead of always going for whatever bulls-eye it is you're aiming at."

I felt dazed. "I never looked at us as competitors. I always—"

"What you did was look out for *me*. And that was terrific. I'm not laying the whole thing off on you. It was my problem, too. I'd watch you then look at myself to see how I stacked up. I can't let myself do that any longer."

"The last thing I meant to do was direct your life the way Dad did mine."

"It's history, Cage. It's okay. I learned a lot of things from you. Now I've got to make it on my own." His hand fell on my shoulder. "I'll figure it out. And if I fall flat on my face along the way? What's the big deal? Look who I've got to pick me up."

I stood there looking at him. Brothers become men. It happens. I wrapped my arms around him and hugged him. It was a send-off, not an ending as I'd feared.

"Out of the way, ladies." It was a big Irishman from a group to Billy's left. He pushed his way past us. "If you're all done dancin', I gotta piss—standin' up, not sittin' down like one of you fuckin' steroid homos."

I started after him.

Billy stepped between us. The guy spun and threw a punch. Billy caught his wrist in mid-swing. "Not worth it, pal. My brother's had a couple too many."

"Beers? Or *boys*?"

Billy released his arm. "Let it be. We'll pay up, then we're gone."

Irish jabbed a finger in Billy's chest. "Oh, you'll leave, all right—or what's left of you will."

Billy held the Irishman's stare. "Cage, I think you'd better—"

Something exploded against the back of my head, driving me against the bar.

To this day what happened after that remains a blurred sequence of fists and kicks, bodies smacking into tables and rolling around on the pub's floor.

I regained my senses in the back of a cab, shirt torn and spattered with blood, knuckles bruised. Billy sat next to me looking much the same. "So, how were we?"

He laughed. "Hell of a lot better than they expected, my man."

It was the last of the times we'd stood shoulder to shoulder—in a way, the best of all.

By his senior year, Jamie and I saw less and less of Billy. He graduated—barely—then spent the summer cruising with friends down the Intracoastal Waterway to Florida.

And there he'd stayed, happy in a nomadic, adventurous sense, but still nowhere near settled on his life.

I told him I thought that was just fine. I worried about him, and missed him, but was no longer his shepherd.

"**H**EY," JAMIE SAID, "you're getting fried kiddo." I poked a finger against the skin of my chest—pink turning to white as I cleared my head of old memories. "Hadn't noticed," I said.

We gathered up our beach chairs, grabbed a quick shower at the motel then drove to the Careys' in response to the message Luke had left on our phone: Luke and I were to be at the police station to meet with Wes again at two.

Jamie and LuAnn went to shop for a few things Jamie had neglected to pack in her rush to catch her flight from New York.

Luke said that he had some business to tend to before our scheduled meeting and asked if I'd mind going along.

"It's not far," he said. "Let's hoof it."

We walked the beach eastward for fifteen minutes, then crossed the sand to a set of stairs that took us up over the low dunes and onto the deck of a battered looking eatery.

The deck was packed with tables; the tables packed with people. We picked our way around the maze and went in through a glass door of a vintage newer than the building itself. A hand-carved sign that read, *The Ship's Hatch Cafe* was nailed above it. Picture windows ran the length of the deck.

Inside, we were greeted by a waitress who flashed a brilliant smile in my direction then planted a kiss fully on Luke's mouth.

"How they hangin'? And who's the handsome—?"

"Already spoken for, darlin'," Luke said. "Now go on and get the boss for me before I report you for harassin' the customers."

Off she went with a waggle of hips and a bounce in her step.

A moment later a squat man of about seventy came through the kitchen door carrying a thick folder. He headed in a hobbled gait toward the table where we sat. When he spoke I knew without question that he came from Brooklyn, his accent distinctively heavy with a glue-like quality making it sound as though his words were being processed through a meat grinder.

"Jesus H. and all the Holy Saints, Luke. I'm sorry about Billy. I really liked that kid, ya know? He . . . ." His words evaporated like steam from a boiling pot as he looked at me.

Luke started the introduction. "Vinnie, this is—"

"Yeah, yeah . . . no shit. Billy's brother. Gotta be." He stuck the folder under his arm and wiped his hand on his apron.

"My name's Cage," I said as we shook."

"Vinnie," he said. "Vinnie Garafolo. Jeez Louise. What can I say? This is terrible." He glanced at Luke, then back at me. He seemed at odds with something. "The loss. A brother, yet. Jeez."

"Quite a shock, yes. So tell me, how did you come to know Billy?"

"Billy? Oh, he was—"

Luke cut him off like a switch. "Through me. We'll get to that later." He turned to Vinnie. "Everything in the file?"

Vinnie appeared perplexed as he handed Luke the folder. "Yeah. Sure. Tax stuff, contracts, agreements—the whole shabang."

"That's fine," Luke said, getting to his feet. "I'll let you know as soon as I hear from the buyer."

"Yeah. Sure," Vinnie said again, the uncertainty lingering in his eyes. "Meantime, sit down, okay? I got a double order of grease on the way out. Burgers, fries, rings—the whole barrel. You'll stay and chow down, huh?"

"Couldn't think of anything better, " I said.

"So why is he selling?" I asked Luke as we drove to the police station for our appointment, the food weighing on my stomach like wet sawdust. "And what was the chop off about when Billy's name came up?"

Luke looked at me with some uncertainty, or perhaps in watchful appraisal. I couldn't tell which. "Then you didn't know?"

"Didn't know what?"

"That Vinnie sold the place to Billy."

I took a second to let the news sink in. "No, I didn't know. Billy never said anything about it to me. But I guess I'm not all that surprised. He was a social hound, drawn to the bar and grill scene. Daycare for adults, he called it. And then there's the beach, of course. So I suppose it was a perfect combination. Yeah. I can see him doing it." After a beat I added, "But you still haven't answered my question as to why Vinnie sold. Books going bad on him?"

Luke chuckled, a poor attempt at hiding his exasperation, or an effective way to make a point of it. "No, the place turns a good buck. Probably better with an owner who pays more attention to business and less to givin' away handouts. I just didn't want to get into it in front of Vinnie. The whole thing's been hard enough on him as it is.

"Anyway, Gina—Vinnie's wife—lost her best friend after Hurricane Opal hit a few years back. She was a widow. No insurance. Storm water sucked out the sand under the slab. House slid off like an egg off a hot skillet. Lost everything. When old Doris saw it, she fell over dead on the spot. Stroke, I think it was. Gina never could shake the memory of her friend droppin' dead at her feet.

Couple more big storms set in over time. Few months back she sorta gave up and passed away. Vinnie decided to stay on 'til he got The Hatch sold and the deal was done. Now, there's a problem. It's a bit complicated—somethin' I need to talk with you about. But first let's wrap up our date with Wesley," he said as we pulled into the lot and parked next to a police cruiser.

I followed Luke into the station, then down a drab corridor to Chief Harland's office.

"Afternoon, gentlemen," Wes said, lowering his bulk into a brown vinyl-covered chair worn through on the armrests. He spoke without preamble. "Tallahassee confirmed the obvious: Two gunshot wounds. Large caliber. They also found a little something that might help explain how Billy got himself overpowered and trussed up. There were fresh needle marks in the crook of his left elbow—several punctures, like he had trouble finding a vein. He was baked to the teeth well before the time of death. Drug of choice was heroin."

My anger blew like an old flashbulb. "You're accusing Billy of being an *addict*?"

"Give me a chance here, okay? Your brother had to piss in a jar at the jail like all new arrivals. His was negative, Cage. Not a chemical in his body."

My apology was in my silence.

"What we're dealing with here is the abduction of a physically powerful man. If they wanted him drugged it would have taken more than one person to do it. Someone he knew to draw him out and set him up. Maybe he thought he was being asked to another meeting on whatever disagreement he had that caused the fight. Anyway, my guess is that it was a faked overdose that didn't work. Not enough dope for his size. Somebody improvised the rest."

"It's speculation," I said.

Wes's look was a study in patience. *"Reasonable speculation, and all we have to go on."*

"Fine," I said. "So now what?"

"So now we do everything we can to find the man Billy beat up. And we see if we can't get a line on our shooter." Wes handed me a slip of paper. "Your brother's body is being released at five today. Friend of mine with the Medical Examiner's office gave me names of some funeral homes to pass on to you. You'll have to call one to authorize the transfer."

Luke dropped me at the motel and headed back to his office.

I hadn't pursued the issue of Billy and Vinnie. At this point, the big question was why Billy hadn't shared the news of his new business venture with me, asked for free advice as he always did when an idea that meant dipping into his financial reserve popped into his head Or, maybe he was going to—that *The Hatch* had something to do with his troubles. I figured that Luke wouldn't know, not the way Billy had me try and snowball him regarding the fight he'd gotten into.

I plugged my near-dead Blackberry into the charger, then picked up the oily room phone and made calls to the funeral home in Tallahassee and the Medical Examiner's Office to approve the arrangements for the transfer of Billy's remains.

I followed with a conversation with a friend of mine in the travel business in Connecticut who was sorry to hear what had happened and would make all the arrangements for the transport of the coffin and tickets home for Jamie and me.

The last call went to the funeral home that had taken care of my parents years before. It was owned by a couple who'd known Billy forever and were deeply saddened, they said, by the bad news of his death.

Was this in contrast to the *good* news that someone *else* had passed away? I let the sarcastic comment drown in better sense before it had a chance to surface.

I changed to a swimsuit, grabbed a couple of beers from the bar and carried a lounge chair from the motel's patio onto the sand.

At first I was surprised that the beach was so deserted; it took me a minute to remember that it was Monday and like anywhere, people were at work or off tending to the various things that comprised a normal day in a world organized by ritual and routine.

My corner of the planet felt anything *but* normal. The unnatural energy brought on by the shock of Billy's murder was spent. I felt an internal deflation, like an inner tube losing its buoyancy and sagged heavily into the chair, mood shifting back and forth—anger giving way to sadness, sadness to a run at philosophical insight, then anger again.

And that's where it stayed.

Jamie worries that I internalize too much where sorrow is concerned because of the way I'd reacted to the sudden death of my parents.

Let it all out, she says, *let it run its course. If you don't, someday you'll pay the price.*

I'd mourned, of course; it was a terrible loss. But even so what I'd felt most was bitterness and resentment, much of it unfocused but all of it centered around my father's drinking—how it changed him—and how my mother seemed to blindly accept it as part of 'for better or for worse'. The way I saw it, near the end there *was* no 'better.'

I popped open the second beer and ambled knee-deep into the water where I stood watching a freighter until it disappeared over the horizon like a fly over the edge of a table, then without thought waded further out and submerged myself completely, holding my beer over my head.

There I was, bobbing up and down like a fool, feeling a strange vitality as if I were drawing strength from the heat of the sun while receiving absolution from the cold depths of the Gulf.

Cage the Baptist.

When I finally stopped, every thought had left my head but one: Track down Billy's killer or killers and deliver them into the next world. Personally.

But it was more than an emotional moment of bravado.

A sudden chill blanketed my skin as I waded toward shore.

CHAPTER 6

W E PACKED UP Tuesday morning, then made a stop at the Careys' before heading to the airport in Tallahassee for our flight home. We'd be accompanying Billy's casket back to Connecticut.

I pulled Luke to the side. "I owe you an apology for what I said at Hough's on Sunday. It wasn't directed at you." I drew in a deep breath of salt air as though it had the power to cleanse the soul. "While I'm at it, let's toss in my whole attitude these past few days."

"Not a problem. There'll be rough times ahead," Luke said. "You find yourself taken by the need to lash out, be sure whoever's on the receivin' end's up to it. I can absorb a hefty blow. Not everyone can. Remember that.

"Now . . . this other matter. The Hatch. Fact is, that's how I met Billy. I do a good job of lawyerin' and don't ask needless questions. It was a cash deal on the down stroke. Vinnie held the paper. No banks. Complication is, there's a blind minority partner—SG Investments, a Michigan sole proprietorship. Don't know who it is. It's the way Billy wanted the deal structured. Lawyer up there handles everything from that end. I was hopin' you'd be able to enlighten me on just who this SG Investments might be."

"Not a clue."

Luke eyed me for a long beat. "Okay. So here's the bricks of it. With Billy dead, the place is yours to buy—first option, two hundred fifty-thousand cash. The fifty goes to the minority owner, this SG Investments. The rest to Vinnie." He handed me an envelope. "It's all here in Billy's will. Thing is, he had me re-draw it this way only a couple of months before he died. Place would be goin' cheap at three times the price, you ask me. Gift from Billy's what it is. I already contacted the Michigan attorney. Said I had a buyer ready to sign. If you don't want it, then I lied. Not the first time or the last, I suppose. Have to look somewhere else to peddle it."

A glance passed between us, a shared thought. "It's all tied to Billy's murder, isn't it."

"That's the big question," Luke said. "We don't know that for certain. But I guarantee you Vinnie's totally in the dark if it is. Whatever, one thing's for sure—the show's off to a bad start, and I got a feelin' there's more shit flyin' around behind the curtain than we might care to know."

"May be," I said. "Or maybe he was just determined to get me out of New York."

A network of lines contracted at the corners of Luke's eyes. "Could be he's tryin' to help you."

"From the grave?" I said.

"Maybe so. Maybe on more than one count. Maybe for both of you."

Something snagged in my mental net—a thought that I knew I should ignore but for some reason couldn't. I looked at Luke. "Or maybe after Billy got into trouble you asked one of those 'needless' questions and found out he was dealing out of bounds—figured I'd know what it was and that there'd be something in it for you."

Luke gazed out over the water, thick forearms resting on the deck rail. "If that's your belief, then get out of my face and find somebody else to handle the details. Better yet, might be you should get the fuck out of here altogether and not bother comin' back."

I leaned in next to him and spoke in a secretive way, as though my words might be caught by the wind and carried to the wrong ears. "My brother's dead," I said. "This whole thing stinks. I know nothing about you. You're asking me to deal solely on trust yet for some reason you've held back on this juicy little bit of information about The Hatch until now."

He lit a cigarette, then tapped the old Zippo on the wood of the deck rail next to my arm. A long flume of smoke escaped his nostrils and floated away on the breeze. His laugh was deep and unnerving. "What I knew of your brother, I liked. What I knew of you when you stepped off that plane, I coulda' crapped into a Baggie. But your suspicion—wrong as it is—tells me a great deal about your smarts, and your character. And how deeply you'd go to protect your brother. Even in the hereafter. Thing is, it's *both* of us who need to deal on trust." He flicked the cigarette butt over the rail and onto the sand. "There was really no reason to tell you before this. You had more than enough to deal with, losin' Billy the way you did. Truth is, I thought maybe you'd need a bit of space and think time before you made a decision. Back in New York, maybe."

We eyeballed one another for a good ten seconds.

"If you weren't a decent lawyer," I said, smiling for perhaps the first time in days, "you'd have made a great salesman."

Luke extended his hand in my direction. "We got all the belly bumpin' out 'a the way?"

I took his hand, feeling a sense of relief, a heavy measure of embarrassment. "Yeah. We do. Sorry."

"Don't be," he said. "I'd 'a been worried if you hadn't brought it up. This way I know my back's covered. I'll start the paperwork if that's okay by you?"

"Fine by me. And . . . thanks for caring about Billy."

"Go on home and put your brother to rest. I'll be in touch in a day or two."

***

WE LEFT TALLAHASSEE on time, landing in Atlanta with ninety minutes to burn before our connecting flight was scheduled to depart for New York.

Reflexively, I glanced at my watch. Only my watch wasn't on my wrist. I saw it lying on the sink in the guest bath at the Careys' house. I punched the Careys' name on the contact list on my Blackberry.

It was LuAnn who answered. "Ah, yeah, sure, Cage. He's . . . ."

Luke came on the line. "Right here is where I am."

"Everything okay?" I asked, alerted by something odd in LuAnn's voice.

"Reasonably so. Considerin'."

"Considering what?"

"In a minute. Your nickel," he said.

Doesn't miss a trick, I thought. I knew a lot of clever attorneys in New York who would not want to come up against Luke's shrewdness, the sort of mental auto pilot that culls out the best from the average. "My watch. In the guest bath. But that's not—"

"Hold on," he said, and was gone for a few seconds. "Yep, here it is. I'll send it off tomorrow."

"Thanks. I lose another one those overpriced numbers, next one's a Timex."

"Well then, lucky you didn't," he said, "seein' as how we had a tag team snoop the place while we were on the way to dinner. You got a minute, you might want to hear about it."

I shifted slightly away from Jamie. "Plenty of time."

***

L UKE AND LUANN had left the house to go eat then returned to retrieve a dinner coupon.

"You and your two-fer-ones," Luke said to his wife. "I swear."

"It'll save us twenty bucks, for your information. I think it's on the . . . ."

Luke slowed as he approached the house, then without explanation drove by and pulled LuAnn's Jeep into a neighboring driveway, killing the headlights.

"Luke? . . . what is it?"

"My imagination, most likely," he said to LuAnn. "You sit tight while I check it out." He opened the center console and retrieved the stubby automatic he'd given her a year earlier in the wake of a series of local carjackings.

She laid a hand on his shoulder. "Honey, please . . . let's call Wes."

"Keep the doors locked," he said, then got out of the Jeep knowing that imagination had nothing to do with it: He'd seen the beam of a flashlight move across the slats of the blinds in the guest bedroom window.

Luke moved quickly down his neighbor's side yard and onto the beach, then broke into a sprint that brought him to the base of the stairs that led up to his house. The interior lights were off, the drapes drawn across the glass sliders, the fabric billowing in and out of the partially open door as though the house were breathing.

He crept up the wooden stairs, nerves crackling with anticipation. He was neither fearful nor foolish; he was instead sure of the ingrained military skills he'd mastered years before, at ease with the thought of taking whatever action was warranted in the preservation of his territory—of his belongings, of his life, if it came to that.

As he reached the door he drew the pistol tightly against his chest. The opening was barely wide enough to accommodate his bulk as he turned sideways and slid silently into the blackened room.

This was his turf—at the moment, his hunting ground. Intuitively he knew every inch of it, every shape and shadow.

A thickening in the density of the dark hollow to the right of the kitchen marked the location of the intruder.

In a micro-second Luke assessed his bad judgement: He'd been too confident—a little rusty, maybe. His entrance had been witnessed. Whoever was there was no quick hit artist. No punk thief. The door had been left open for a rapid escape. The slowing of the car had been noted. Had he pulled into the carport under the house clearly signaling their return, they would have fled—*they*, because while one had been searching, another had been on watch.

He was in serious trouble.

The most effective and deceptive way to reach the ground is by vertical drop, not the anticipated dive. With practice, hips, knees, and ankles can be trained to unwind in unison as though all tendons have been severed simultaneously and without warning. What follows is a roll to the left or right—a fifty-fifty chance of escaping the first bullet and returning fire.

As he collapsed to the floor, Luke heard the double pop of a silencer and felt a tug at his left sleeve. He rolled hard and came immediately to his knees, squeezing off a shot into the depths of the shadow by the kitchen.

In the strobe-flash of the muzzle he saw a man clutch his shoulder and spin to his left; in the bang of the exploding cartridge, the sound of the door behind him being ripped from its track was nearly lost as the second burglar launched himself at the opening.

Luke scrambled for the door only to be caught in the incoming rush of drapery, costing him precious seconds.

Finally free, he vaulted the deck rail, absorbing the shock of the ten foot drop to the beach with his powerful legs, his gun hand involuntarily impacting the sand as he sought to maintain his balance. *Shit!* he said under his breath.

The night sky was thickly overcast. He opened his eyes to their widest, looked straight ahead but focused his attention at the edges of his vision as he simultaneously strained to hear any sound.

The intruder was thirty feet away, hunkered down in a stand of sea grass.

Luke had no choice. The automatic was most likely clogged with sand. By now the enemy had him in his sights. He sat down heavily and grabbed his ankle, lowered his head and moaned.

His adversary waited for a moment, then broke into a run and disappeared into the night.

Luke crawled under the deck. Going back into the lightless house was not an option. He had no idea how badly hurt the man he'd shot might be—or if he was dead.

Then the deck boards over his head sighed under weight, and he had his answer.

He listened as the footfalls moved to his right; when they started slowly down the stairs, Luke edged further back under the support beams where he tested the gun's slide.

Frozen. The weapon was useless.

The wounded man stopped at the bottom of the stairs. Luke could see his legs through the open risers ten feet away. He calculated his chances of closing on him and dragging him down from behind. Risky, but—

An air horn sounded. Two short blasts. The man took off toward the water, hunched over and clutching his shoulder.

Luke heard muted voices followed by the sound of a small outboard revving up, then heading away from shore.

"It's happened in the past that way," Luke finished, "beachfront homes hit by thieves with a little getaway boat they pull ashore. But this has a way different air to it. The muffler on his pop gun kinda says so, dudn't it? Anyway, Wesley'll be here any minute. He'll dig a pair of slugs out of the wall. The one tore a hole in my shirt and never nicked a hair. Whoever it is is still carryin' the .25 I hit him with. Didn't go through. Not much blood around. No real power in the damned thing."

My mouth had gone dry. "Jesus. You could've been—"

"Yeah, but I wadn't. Christ, you sound like LuAnn. Forget all that. The important thing is figurin' what they were after. Might be it's with you."

I wet my lips. "You mean if it was something of Billy's."

"I doubt it was the Hope Diamond they were after."

"There was nothing other than his clothes. Nothing out of the—" Then it hit me. "The storage room. Didn't LuAnn say something about a box of things Billy'd put in there?"

The phone bounced on the kitchen counter. I pictured Luke lumbering down the stairs. He was back in less than thirty seconds.

"It's gone. God*damn*! If there was anything important, it's history."

I heard voices in the background.

"Wesley and his cavalry just rode in. Travel safe. I'll call."

I turned and looked at Jamie, an uneasiness boring its way into the pit of my stomach. "Watch your back, Luke," I said into the dead phone, then clicked it off.

***

A S THE 737 rose into the night sky en route to New York City, Jamie studied my face in the dim cabin light. "The break-in wasn't just coincidence, was it. There's something deeper behind Billy's death than someone getting even for being beaten up."

I couldn't deny it. "Yeah. There is. He was planning to tell me about it. A little late for that now."

"You could have said something earlier."

"Guess that makes me oh-for-two in the disclosure department." I considered telling her about Billy's buying *The Ship's Hatch Café*. But I needed to sort that one out for myself first—needed to be absolutely certain that I'd go through with it. Oh-for-three. I was pushing it.

She might have sensed that there was more to talk about but let it pass and changed the subject. "LuAnn's really sweet," she said.

"But not Luke," I answered. Guilt by exclusion. I recognized the trick she used to avoid saying anything bad about someone.

"It's in his eyes. He seems nice enough and all. It's just that there's . . . . I don't know, it's like a darkness. I can't think of another way to describe it."

"You're imagining things. These were not the best of circumstances. He's fine."

"I'm not so sure it's the kind of *fine* I feel good about."

In truth, I wasn't at all sure what 'fine' meant in terms of defining Luke Carey. I considered his warning that things could get rougher; the inferred offer to help find the killer of someone he hardly knew; his comment about my covering his back. Defending him just then was not a case I particularly wanted to argue.

When I looked again at Jamie, she'd fallen asleep.

Small blessings: I wondered how she would have felt about him had I bothered to tell her that Luke had just shot someone.

Oh-for-four. Not a good average.

CHAPTER 7

WE LANDED IN New York shortly before midnight. At Ground Transportation I spied the sign with my name scribbled in back-slant black marker, a piece of cardboard torn off a box and held by a driver named Mikhail with drooping eyelids and heavy eyebrows that looked like caterpillars glued to his forehead. He spoke fluent Russian but little useable English.

After a lengthy exchange of fractured words, Mikhail had me convinced that he understood the route I wanted him to take to our apartment on the Upper West Side. But I was wrong, and three blocks short of our destination we wound up stuck in the snarl of a late night water main project that had stretched out for weeks beyond its completion date.

Out of patience, tired, and generally pissed at the world, I directed him to pull to the curb; Jamie and I would lug our bags—and ourselves—the rest of the way.

It happened fifty feet from the entrance to our building.

Two men emerged from the shadowy stairway of a basement apartment and blocked our path. Both wore dark sweatshirts with large hoods pulled over their heads, their faces lost to us in shadow.

"All of it, motherfuckers! Now! Watches, rings, wallets. The bags, too. Be smart. Do it!"

Every muscle tensed.

Jamie clutched my arm. "Honey, do what he says. *Please.* You know the rules. It's not worth—"

Screw the rules. I'd had it.

"Run!" I yelled at Jamie as I shot out my right foot and caught the nearest mugger flush in the groin. I flung my bag at the face-hole of the other, followed with my body weight and plowed him hard into the metal railing of the staircase that descended below street level.

Something cracked. He drew in a sharp breath, arched his spine and reeled away clawing at his back in a comical, flailing motion.

I spun quickly to be sure Jamie was on the move and was caught mid-section in the grasp of the man with melon balls who'd regained his balance but not his strength.

A sharp blow to the side of his head and he was down on all fours; a kick to his gut and he was flat on the ground.

I sprinted behind Jamie as she ran toward the door to our building—pulled even as we reached the stairs. "Keys, babe, and fast."

But a quick look back told me that neither man had cared to follow. One was nowhere in sight; the other was on the move in the opposite direction, a garment bag dangling from each hand.

We bolted the door and collapsed together on the living room sofa. Jamie was fuming.

"Jesus, Cage, what the *hell* were you thinking? What about your 'give-it-up-and-don't-get-hurt' speech, huh? What about *that*?"

"Calm down. We're okay," I said.

"No. *You're* okay. I was scared shitless. Still am. Pardon-fucking-me while I go change my panties!"

I waited until Jamie had showered and gone to bed, then called and left a message at Luke's office telling him about the attempted mugging. Was it happenstance? Or was there a connection with the break-in at his house? I was a New Yorker and knew better than to walk the neighborhood streets at that time of night no matter how safe they appeared to be. Anyway, if they'd been after something specific, all they'd gotten was dirty laundry.

I slid in next to Jamie, trying not to disturb her. She'd sleep off her anger. She always did.

"It was a stupid thing to do," she said softly.

"Yeah, it was."

She coiled up in a ball. I drew her tightly against my stomach.

"Nite, Batman," she said in the dark. "I still love you, you crazy idiot."

I slept soundly and without dreams until I was awakened at four-thirty by the sound of the garbage collectors in the street below. Noise is one of the curses of living in Manhattan. But after enough time your system learns to block it out. At least on the surface.

On a deeper level, Jamie says, the perpetual din makes a significant contribution to the stress quotient. After the events of the last few days, the crashing sounds that floated up through our windows were particularly grating.

They awakened Jamie as well.

The rest of the early morning hours were a loss. Once awake my mind refused to shut down. After thirty minutes of Ninety-nine Bottles of Beer in the Wall I got out of bed and went into the study to read.

As I picked my way through a stack of magazines I was struck by a thought and went to one of the windows that faced West 82nd Street. I removed the screen, then angled it back through the window and sat my ass on the sill.

After a time I heard Jamie calling me. With my head thrust out into the night her voice seemed distant, ethereal.

"Hon? What are you doing?" She spoke from the doorway.

I ducked back inside. "Nothing." I closed the window feeling foolish. "Let's go to bed."

We started down the hall, my arm around her waist.

"Couldn't see them, could you," she said.

"Not even one," I answered as we got under the covers.

But sleep wouldn't come. I lay awake, unable to shake the image of Billy's face or recall what I'd said to him the last time I'd seen him alive. Nor could I understand why he'd said nothing to me about Vinnie's place or the terms of my inheritance outlined in his will.

"A penny . . . ?" Jamie said.

I studied the light on the ceiling as it moved in random patterns, the curtains in our windows fluttering in the rising heat of the steam radiator beneath them. "Just thinking," I said.

"About . . . ?"

"About how there's nobody in line ahead of me, or behind. About the fact that up until now I've never really had to pay any heavy dues in my life."

"Survivor's guilt. There's no set number of lashes we're expected to endure for whatever good fortune we have in our lives."

"I suppose not."

She was quiet for a time. "I often wonder what it would have been like if my mother had lived. How it might have changed my life. Or if it would have changed it at all. Then again, I suppose it really doesn't matter does it? What's past, is done. *This* is where we are—*who* we are."

I rolled on my side to face her. "I thought you helped people interpret the past in order to straighten out their heads and move on in life with a better understanding."

"I do. But I'm not immune to being a cynic. I've got a few rough spots of my own that I'd much rather forget than try to sort out."

"I never considered that the doctor and the patient might share the same disease."

"Not many people do. That's why so many psychiatrists and psychologists jump off bridges. But that's not me. So don't worry."

"And why shouldn't I?"

"Because basically," Jamie said, "I'm pretty well balanced."

"Debatable," I said.

"Very funny."

We fell into an uneasy silence. The early years after her mother's death remained clouded. We'd touch on it from time to time but Jamie would dismiss it quickly, leaving the impression that there was something unpleasant she kept locked away, something she feared might work its way between us, bringing distance or doubt to our relationship. Now she'd brought it up again—*offered* it up.

I rested my hand on the deep curve of her narrow waist. "Tell me, what happened after your mother died?"

At first she lay there so still and so silent that I thought she'd drifted off to sleep, or intended to give that impression. Then, slowly, tentative as a shy child learning to dance, she began.

THE FIRST FEW months had been difficult but with time she'd begun to cope with her loss. Jamie moved in with her aunt and uncle who treated her like a member of their own family.

She'd been through a lot, losing both parents in a short period of time and in such difficult ways, her mother to ovarian cancer and her father a year earlier to alcohol.

She lacked for nothing. Her uncle was a wealthy man and while a bit formal, was nevertheless kind and caring. Her aunt lavished her with clothes and gifts—and love. Jamie became the daughter she never had.

She'd gotten along reasonably well with her cousins. But as they grew the older of the three boys began to tease Jamie. She took it good-naturedly in the beginning. But as the teasing turned more often to sexual innuendo, she began to be bothered by it.

Then one night, it turned serious.

Jamie's aunt and uncle were out of town for the weekend. The other boys were off on a sleep-over at a friend's.

Jamie and her cousin popped some popcorn, swiped a couple of beers out of the refrigerator and spent the evening watching TV. When Saturday Night Live was over, Jamie went off to bed.

"Something awakened me. When I opened my eyes my cousin was standing there staring at me. At first I had no idea what he wanted. In the second it took me to figure it out he was on me. I tried to fight him off. He was a strong kid. I screamed, and he hit me, then grabbed my throat with one hand while he freed himself with the other. He drove his knees between my legs and tried to penetrate me. I bit him and I hit him. But I was losing ground fast.

"Then all at once he stopped and collapsed on top of me. He was drunk. I thought that maybe he'd passed out."

Jamie turned her back toward me as if recoiling from the memory.

"He just lay there, his full weight on me. I couldn't catch my breath. But I was afraid to do anything.

"Finally, he got off me—said that if I ever told a soul about what had just happened, he'd hurt me. He made me promise. Over and over. Then he called me a *fucking bitch* in the most hateful voice I'd ever heard and ran out of the room.

"All I wanted was for my mother to hold me, to tell me everything was all right. I'd never felt so alone. I got up and went into the bathroom. I saw what had happened, why he'd stopped. It was all over me—on my legs, my nightgown. I locked the door and showered until my skin felt raw. I slept on the floor the rest of the night."

Jamie turned to me, the worst now said. "Neither of us ever brought it up. But I believed his threat. He would have hurt me—badly—if I ever told anyone. And I never have. Not until now."

"You never so much as *hinted* about it to your aunt or uncle?"

"Where would I have gone? Nope, I toughed it out until I left for college. I made sure we were never alone together after that but I never felt totally safe."

"Where is he now?" I said. "I'd like to meet the little fuck."

She sat up. "Cage, I'm a big girl. Way beyond needing my boyfriend to avenge my honor by beating up the bad guy. Besides, he's a grown man. You'd only end up in trouble over it and it wouldn't change anything. Honest, I'm fine with it. I'm sure he's long since justified it or doesn't even remember it. It's the last secret I had. Now I've shared it with you. That's important to me. Leave it alone, okay?" She kissed me, then worked her way deep under the covers. "I mean it. You didn't even know me back then. You'd only cause problems with my aunt and uncle. Now come over here and show me how much you love me."

But in that moment I could not master my own body, and for the first time in our relationship Jamie's need was one I could not fulfill.

"This is on me, not you," I said as I struggled toward sleep, feeling shame for the uninvited thoughts that had entered my head.

Jamie pressed against me in reassurance, much as a mother might seek to comfort a feverish child. "Don't worry, babe. I understand."

Her gentleness only served to hone the edge of a rage so sharp that it cut to the core of my dreams that night with a scene of extreme violence as I watched the attack her cousin had made on her person, and saw what I would do to him to defend her honor.

These were the childish thoughts of an over-tired, emotionally wrung out man whose brother had been brutalized in death—whose Madonna had had her perfect persona tarnished unreasonably in his mind by a drunk cousin at a time when he'd not yet known that she walked the same earth.

By the first light of morning I'd managed to drive the images out of my head, knowing in truth that they were far from fully erased.

CHAPTER 8

FRIDAY WAS A day meant for a funeral, the sky a dull shade of gray that matched the centuries-old low fieldstone walls that crisscross the Connecticut countryside—rocks that had been culled from the earth and piled atop one another to mark one man's field from that of his neighbor, not to shut one out nor confine the other.

It was to be a simple graveside service followed by lunch with a few close friends at Mario's, a favorite hangout of my father's across the street from the Westport train station.

Jamie's Aunt Giselle and her Uncle Michael came down from Boston for the day. She reminded me again of my promise to say nothing of her past dealings with her cousin.

When the last words were said and the formal service that committed his soul to a Higher Power was over, I placed a flower on Billy's coffin, wondering as I did how it was that you said farewell to your kid brother.

Images of our years together passed before me. I let myself go back in time to the hot summer days when school was out and we'd pal around with not much to do other than pick on each other. It was there that I imagined my hand atop his head, and ruffled his hair for a final time.

As Jamie and I turned to leave, I felt a tingle in my arm where he'd punched me a thousand different times—for no reason, and for every reason.

Just because that's what brothers do.

Jamie's aunt and uncle were standing at the curb as we exited the cemetery, their stretch limousine parked several yards away.

"We're so sorry," Jamie's aunt said, resting a hand on my forearm. "Jamie tells us your brother was a fine young man."

It was an awkward moment. I'd met the Monahans only twice before and felt no real kinship. "He was, yes," I managed. "Thanks for coming."

"Nonsense," Jamie's uncle said. "It's the least we could do." Michael Monahan stood to my right, a tall, striking man attired in a tailored black cashmere topcoat and matching short-brimmed hat. He took my arm and deftly guided us a few paces away from Jamie and her aunt, leaving them to talk.

"How's our little girl?" he asked, as if we were a chummy duo ambling along the sidewalk. For some reason I couldn't quite identify his attitude piqued my nerves.

"Jamie's doing well, Mr. Monahan, although this has been hard on her, too. She and my brother were like family to each other."

He adjusted the scarf around his neck as we walked. "You and I have something in common—aside from Jamie, that is. We've both lost brothers. It's not easy but we learn to cope. My loss was perhaps not as difficult as yours. My brother and I were . . . estranged at the end. Frankly, in his last years I hardly knew him. Still, we'd had many good times growing up together and I cherish the memories of those days. You and William—"

I stopped walking. "Billy."

"I'm sorry. Of course. You and . . . *Billy* were close?" Monahan asked.

His tone had become too familiar, somehow intrusive. "I don't see where that has anything to do with—"

There was a look in his eyes and an edge to his voice that stopped me cold.

"How we play the hand life deals us, Cage, may well determine not only how we *live* but how we die. My brother chose the bottle. Yours? Well, let's not mar the occasion with conjecture. But whatever his undoing, let it be. Consider instead my niece's happiness. Nothing else matters to me. Do you understand what I'm . . . ?"

His demeanor suddenly softened; his static smile becoming one of convincing compassion and concern. "In any event, life as they say is for the living." He extended his hand, and I took it. Our eyes locked. "Be happy. God's speed to you both."

"Can you and Aunt Giselle join us for lunch?" Jamie asked from behind her uncle.

I marveled at Monahan's timing. Or had he somehow sensed their approach?

"Your aunt and I are due back in Boston. Business. You understand."

"Sure. Maybe some other time, then," Jamie said.

We watched silently as they strode to their waiting limousine and got in.

The fog from the exhaust obscured the dark shape of the Cadillac as it pulled away but in the oval frame of the rear window, I saw clearly the hard look on Michael Monahan's face as he glanced back over his shoulder and waved a farewell.

"What were you and my uncle talking about?" Jamie asked.

"You. And I said not word one about your shithead of a cousin."

"And that's it?"

I mulled over Monahan's words. "I'm really not sure."

***

THE PHONE RANG at ten on Saturday morning, my hangover a harbinger of the hard day ahead. We'd been too intoxicated to drive and with encouragement from our friends had left the car in Westport and taken the train back to Manhattan.

"Yo," I croaked into the receiver.

"Cage?" Luke's voice seemed to reverberate in my ear.

"What's left of me."

"How'd the service go?"

"Connecticut's out of beer. Anything new?"

"Wes idn't thrilled about losin' the stuff in the storage room, I'll tell ya. Other than that they pried a pair of .38's out of the plaster, got zero on fingerprints, got pissed at me for playin' Peter Gunn and came up with A negative for a blood type. In other words, zip."

I propped myself up against the headboard. Jamie slid out of bed and went into the bathroom. "You get my message about our muggers?"

"If it's connected, it's disturbin'."

"Don't see how we'll ever know," I said.

"Any case, accordin' to LuAnn what happened down here should be enough to tell me to mind my own bidness."

"And will you?"

"Like hell. Enis is workin' through the airboat registrations. Gonna take some time. Not a lot of deputies over there. Cooperation, either. Still, somethin' this big? If a local's holdin' anything back Enis thought a bit a' grease might do the trick."

"A reward," I surmised.

"Normally he wouldn't advise it—says it only creates a bunch of false leads and stirs up fights between neighbors. But considerin' the poverty level in the area he and Enis hope that if you'll put it up, then it might do some good."

"Five thousand enough?"

"No need for more."

I heard the shower come on. The idea of soothing hot water running over my head called to me like a Siren. "Let me go do some damage control," I said. "Consider the funds posted."

We caught an afternoon train out to Connecticut to retrieve my car. At Jamie's suggestion we'd packed a small duffel and planned to stay the night at a bed-and-breakfast in Southport. On the way to the inn I made an unplanned stop.

A gusty breeze swirled through the small cemetery carrying fallen leaves restlessly from place to place among the headstones as we stood silently at Billy's freshly covered grave, my eyes fixed intently on his headstone.

"Honey? Are you okay?" Jamie asked.

I was about as far from it as you could get. The fact was, I was getting worse with time, not better, outraged at the whole situation. "No, Jamie. Not really. Not at all. Truth is, all I can *think* about right now is fucking up whoever did this."

She held my hand until I'd calmed, then let go and stepped over to Billy's headstone where she said a few words not meant for me to hear before returning to the car, leaving me time alone.

I sat on the fall-brown grass next to the mound of raw dirt and rock that covered my brother's coffin opposite the final resting place of our mother and father. I whipped a handful of small stones at a scrap of paper that had come to rest against the base of an old oak tree a few feet away.

"I'm sorry for all the time we missed together, little brother. Sorry as hell. Whatever it is you wanted me to do, I will. Somehow, I'll figure it out." I got up after several minutes, anger finally dissipating like the last smoke of a fire, brushed the dirt from the back of my jeans then laid my hand on the cold granite of Billy's marker. "Stay with me, Billy. We're a hell of a lot better that way, you know? Do that and I swear I'll finish this for both of us."

A T SIX, WE checked into our room then dressed and went to a favorite waterside bistro for dinner. The waiter brought our drink order. Jamie watched with a look of concern as I sipped a straight-up vodka.

"I feel like the rest of the world's on a different plane than I am. One minute I'm okay, then the next I sink into one of these moods," I said.

"You're angered and hurt by what's happened, Cage. I don't expect you to just shut it off. But . . don't think that you should . . . ."

"I know. Let the police handle it."

"I'm sure they're capable, hon." She held her wineglass suspended in front of her eyes and studied me over the rim. "There's something more you're not telling me, isn't there— something you've been wrestling with ever since we left Florida."

"It's nothing," I said.

"Not true."

"I haven't sorted it out yet."

"So again, I'm excluded," Jamie said. "Am I sensing a pattern here?"

"No, you're not. I'm just a bit fucked in the head lately. You're very much a part of it—if you can still hustle drinks, that is."

And with that I outlined Billy's ownership in *The Ship's Hatch Café*, and the buyout provision in his will.

Jamie's reaction was framed in a mix of annoyance for my not having said something earlier, her uncertainty about my commitment, and real excitement at the prospect. "And you're sure about your law practice? That you can just toss it away because Billy left you a bar at discount?"

"You know how bored I am."

"That's a cop out. You're betting there's a connection, aren't you—a connection to Billy's murder. For God's sake, you're a lawyer not a detective."

So I switched tacks. "It's a chance to move south—get out of the city, bring some change to our lives. It could be fun. You've said so yourself."

"Don't fight dirty. I've said it—yes. But this isn't exactly what we had in mind."

"The result's the same, isn't it?"

She thought about that. "But why didn't Billy ask you if—?"

I reached for her hand. "I don't know. His way of surprising me, maybe."

"Is that what you believe? Truly?"

"Sure."

Her smile was thin. "There may be nothing else, you know—no answers to any of it. So if we do this it has to be for us, Cage. For *us*."

The truth, Royce. Speak the truth. "I know," I said. "And it is."

Mostly, it is.

"Uh huh. Right." Her eyes softened. "Okay, so now there's something I want to talk to *you* about."

"And that would be something about Luke I suppose?"

"No, Cage. It's about the other night. You haven't come near me since. Snuggles, yes, but no intimacy—not even a hint at it."

I glanced around quickly at the nearby tables, certain that we were about to become the center of attention. "Jamie, not here, okay?"

"No, *not* okay. Here is fine. Here is *good.* Candlelight and everything. Now pay attention because I'm about to tell you in vivid detail what I have planned for us tonight. But first, do me one favor, okay? Take me back down from whatever pedestal you've put me on. I was not a virgin when we met. Sorry. And, yes, I had a cousin who tried to rape me. I have zero guilt over it. None. No, I didn't help bring it on. No, I'm not ashamed that it happened. So don't you be, huh? None of it meant anything. It's *you* I love. You. The only man who will ever touch me for the rest of my life. Got it?"

I broke eye contact and took a deep pull on my drink, stalling for time, scrambling for the right words. "Jamie, I never thought that you—"

"Yes, you did. Somewhere inside of you the little cherub with the wings and the one with the horns had a little battle, didn't they. Maybe just for a second, but it was there. It's the natural response—almost an involuntary reaction. Sometimes it builds to the point where people divorce over it. It makes you mad—makes you feel inadequate. Makes you feel like—"

"Like smashing in his face."

Jamie smiled. "Do you know how big a compliment that is? And how insecure that makes you look? And why do you suppose that is? Why do you suppose this is all coming out now? Well, duh. I'm not sure how much grief one man can take in such a short space of time. I wasn't even sure at first why I told you what I did. Maybe I thought I'd just throw my shit into the ring while the emotional fight was beating up on both of us. What the hell, right?" She shook her head slowly. "Nope. Not it. Here's what I *really* think. I was hiding something from you just like you were from me. You shut me out. It hurt. It made *me* feel inadequate because I couldn't help you. I think subconsciously maybe I wanted to hurt you back. I knew how you'd react. So, whoopie for me, I got what I wanted. And it makes me feel like a fool—like a bitchy little high school girl. I'm sorry, babe. I will never *ever* let that happen again."

I felt like an idiot. "I was just so goddamed self-absorbed in my own feelings that I added it to my 'be pissed' list without putting a rational thought to what you'd told me."

"We both were." Under the table Jamie began rubbing her bare foot against my leg. "So, what do you think?" Her eyes sparkled. Her nose crinkled with her smile.

"That I'm all ears."

She leaned in close to me. "You're more that that, stud. Way more. So here's the deal . . . ."

As she finished describing in pornographic detail the planned activities for the hours ahead, the waiter stopped by to take our dinner order. Jamie opened her menu, then peered at me over the top. "Whatcha havin', sweetie?"

"The Minute Steak," I said to the waiter. "To go."

THE WEEKS THAT followed were filled with the details of our coming move.

Luke handled everything with Vinnie. He assured us the deal would be without complication where the silent partner was concerned. I had my own private thoughts on that issue. A little complication that might drive whoever it was into the open would be fine with me.

Jamie maintained her doubts about Luke, and about my motive for the move but in the end allowed her excitement to become the mitigating element in trusting our decision. That and the fact that absolutely nothing out of the ordinary—another mugging or burglary—had occurred since our return.

We slept fitfully the night before sharing the news of our impending departure with our respective business associates.

Despite the thought of exiting a practice I'd grown to detest, I'd be leaving a good number of friends and colleagues in the partnership along with the few clients I actually cared about and felt a mild pang or two along the way to the final decision.

Jamie's leaving was a lot harder. It meant severing emotional ties. More than once she'd failed at keeping it all inside and I'd held her while she cried. But troubled teens live everywhere, she finally reasoned, and re-establishing a practice in our new home town if she decided to wouldn't be at all difficult.

As we left the apartment on that day, everything seemed right.

I walked Jamie to her building then continued on to my office where I spent the morning meeting with the senior partners then shaking hands and handing over files.

At noon I went to the club to work out. It was to be the day I'd gotten Luke Carey's call while standing in a cold drizzle on a curb across from the New York Athletic Club—a day that would end in one revelation, and lead us blindly toward another.

To the eventual discovery of my brother's killers, and our own little piece of Hell on earth.

"Hey, buddy! Hey, you sleepin' back there? Or are you in one of them what-da-ya-call-its—one a them catamatonic fit things."

The cabbie's harsh voice drove me from my deep reverie. "No, I'm fine. Ah, we're here. Great."

"Yeah. We're here for a whole two minutes, seems like. Good you're alive on account 'a you owe me ten-eighty and I got another fare out there hangin' on the handle waitin' for you to pay up and get the hell out."

"Sorry. I must have dozed off."

"With your eyes open, staring out the window? I knew it. Catamatonic fit."

"You're probably right."

"Got a nephew in med school. I pick up a few things here and there."

I paid the fare and gave him a good tip and dashed off in the rain.

A T EIGHT THAT evening, I went into the study of our apartment and returned Luke's call as we'd agreed.

Jamie joined me so I punched the call to the speaker phone.

"Hear us okay?" I asked when Luke was on the line.

"Like talkin' in the bottom of a trash can," he said. Then came the sound of his Zippo snapping shut, followed by a long exhale. LuAnn refused to let him smoke in the house so I knew he had to be out on the deck using the old style portable phone, one of the ones with a two foot telescoping antenna. Luke was a model of frugality.

I pictured the setting sun and felt a twinge of envy, then reminded myself that we'd be there soon. "So what's up?" I said.

"You remember Enis Shine?"

I saw a flash of the Franklin County Sheriff's face in Hough's office. "Yeah, sure."

"He says they've found Billy's killer."

The words carried an impact like a punch. I shot out of my desk chair. "Where? How?" I exclaimed. "They get a confession? Is the case—?"

"Slow down," Luke said. "There's a bit of a complication."

"Don't tell me some local cop forgot to read him his goddamned rights!"

"No, no, it's nothin' like that," Luke said evenly. "Unfortunately, it's worse. Let me explain . . . ."

***

THE KILLER'S NAME was Bo Crowley. He'd been found dead in a run-down mobile home on an isolated dirt road near the village of White City, Florida.

Crowley had missed his rent payment; when his landlord couldn't raise him by phone she'd gone looking. What she found sent her racing to Gulf County Sheriff Ray Starkes in a state of near hysteria.

When she'd calmed enough for Ray to get a grip on what she was saying, he called in one of his deputies and together they followed Hattie Strickland to Bo Crowley's trailer where Ray was to discover that old Hattie hadn't exaggerated one bit about what she'd seen.

As they got out of the cruiser the smell nearly knocked them over. The trailer's front door stood open, testament to the way Hattie had run from her earlier, terrifying visit. This time she stayed in her car.

Ray was first to go in, lasting only a few seconds before stumbling back out to toss his bacon and egg breakfast on the dirt at the foot of the metal steps.

The deputy was next to try. Although his stay inside was long enough for him to mentally document the situation, the result was the same: He threw up all over his uniform.

The next assault on the trailer found the pair better prepared, wearing surgical gloves and the masks they'd brought along designed to cover the stench of rotted flesh.

Inside, the single-wide was teeming with flies. The television set was on—must have been from the time of death. From the looks of things that was a goodly number of days ago.

The decomposing body was slumped over on an old vinyl sofa, naked except for a pair of once-white boxer shorts. An empty bottle of Jack Daniels stood on a cheap coffee table. Beer cans were strewn around the living room and on the kitchen counters sharing space with crusted dishes, discarded fast-food containers and an army of cockroaches that scurried around like a splintered shadow.

On the coffee table next to the whiskey bottle was a syringe and what looked to Ray like drug paraphernalia, the kind used in the instructional films he'd seen about heroin use and how to spot it. There was no trick to figuring this one, he quickly decided.

The deputy went back out to the patrol car to get the cheap digital camera he used to photograph traffic accidents, then took pictures and made notes on what they'd found.

Ray used the opportunity to vacate the premises, get some fresh air and look around the rest of the area outside.

Out back he found an old Chevy up on blocks, its engine suspended over the hoodless motor compartment at the end of a block and tackle rigged to a limb of a large shade tree. Beyond that was an open wooden shed with a rusted tin roof.

Sitting in the shed were a pair of airboats. One sat on the dirt partly disassembled; the other rested on a boat trailer that was attached to the hitch on a faded red pick-up and looked to be in reasonable repair. He made his way down the length of the truck-bed, back to the boat trailer where he put a foot on a tire and hoisted himself aboard.

He stood in place for a minute, sweeping his eyes from bow to stern then reached up to open a canvas bag held to the underside of the pilot's seat by shock cord and had a look at what was inside. What he found was an empty flask and an assortment of tools and such but nothing of particular interest.

Next, he went aft where he opened a storage locker. When he saw what it contained he found himself frozen in place. The stainless steel revolver that lay on the bottom of the locker next to the cut lengths of rope and the roll of Duct Tape told Ray Starkes all he needed to know: The Royce case. He'd found the killer. All the details had been in the bulletin. He could hardly contain his excitement and damn near wet himelf.

Ray made a bee-line for the radio in the cruiser, called in and had himself patched over to Enis Shine's office in Franklin County where he excitedly shared the news of his discovery, laboring over the details of the scene. He attributed the cause of death to what in his trained opinion was an obvious overdose of drugs and booze.

Enis made it to White City in less than thirty-five minutes. On the way he called over to Panama City Beach to fill Wes Harland in on the facts as he knew them.

Wes met Ray and Enis at the site an hour later.

Before Hattie Strickland left, she'd made a claim for the reward—all five thousand of it. It was hers, she said, plain and simple.

"THERE'S NO DOUBT that he's the one who shot Billy?" I asked when it seemed Luke had stopped to light another cigarette.

"Took 'em a while to positively I.D. the body the state it was in, but it was Bo Crowley all right. There's plenty of hard evidence to make him the killer: Ballistics and the prints on the gun checked out and the rope's identical to what was found at the scene in Tate's Hell. There were hair and tissue samples embedded in crevasses in the bow. I imagine they'll get a DNA match to Billy when the report comes back. But trust me, Bo's it. They got him—dead—but they got him."

I felt gutted, my chance to confront Billy's killer gone, nothing explained. Then a bulb lit up in my head. "Something doesn't feel right, Luke. Why *is* that?"

"Because that legal head of yours tells you it's way too simple and way too obvious. Whoever whacked Crowley wanted to be sure that even the dumbest of the dumb would conclude that he died of an overdose, and that the case would be buttoned up pronto and without fanfare. Hell to that, partner. This is nothin' more than one murder coverin' up another and we both know it.

"But Starkes is adamant on the overdose. Enis probably knows better, but he gets to write it off as a murder case in his jurisdiction that got itself solved. Not bad press come re-election time. He promised to dig around a little but I doubt it'll be for too long. That leaves you, me, Wes—and maybe FDLE if they're interested in followin' up."

"Then that'll have to be enough," I said.

Jamie cast her eyes at the wall, . . . moved away from me.

"No chance Crowley was the man Billy had the fight with?" I asked.

"Zero," Luke said. "Description's way off."

"So Crowley signed his own death warrant when he pulled the trigger on Billy."

"Seems so to me. Which clearly means that what we're dealin' with here, Cage, are people who don't leave a trail."

I looked at Jamie who now stood by the door. "Don't worry. Everything will be fine," I said.

"Sure it will, Cage. If you say so." She turned and left the room.

I switched off the speaker phone and picked up the handset. "Not what she wants to hear," I said to Luke.

"Who does?" Luke said. "But I get the drift of it. So maybe you can sleep on the sofa 'til she cools off. Anyway, the investigation confirmed that Billy and Bo knew each other . . . ."

They'd spent time working the same marina—Billy as captain for an absentee charter boat owner, Crowley as a now-and-then deck-hand for hire.

As for motive, money for drugs won the day.

The boat Billy had skippered had been moored at St. Andrews Marina on the Panama City side of the bay, had disappeared quietly before his body had been discovered, and had not returned. Dock records that would have provided information about its registry had somehow been tossed. Or taken.

With Crowley's death ruled an accidental overdose police interest in pursuing the matter quickly waned.

There was little hope remaining that a contradictory reason for Billy's death would turn up whether we dug into the matter, or not.

"That's about it, partner—it's all I got for now," Luke said. "I'll see y'all in a few days. Safe trip. And, Cage . . .?"

"Yeah?"

"Maybe with Crowley dead and no other leads and nobody else sittin' on the doorstep waitin' to be arrested, this'll give that gal 'a yours a nudge of confidence that ya'll 'er makin' the move to Florida for all the right reasons—for the good 'a the two of you, not so you can go off chasin' a phantom killer."

"Maybe you're right," I said.

Then again, I thought to myself as we clicked off, maybe we'll flush out that silent partner.

TWO

The only thing necessary for the triumph of evil, is for

good men to do nothing.

—*Edmund Burke*

CHAPTER 9

EIGHT MONTHS LATER

JAMIE PULLED A comb through hair still wet from her shower as she stood looking out across the water. Thin rivulets of liquid crystal ran down her naked back, glistening against the sheen of her darkly tanned skin.

I got up from the bed, moved behind her and drew her against me.

"We're incredible together," she said, leaning her head back against my shoulder.

"So I've noticed."

I drew her out onto the small privacy deck off the third floor master bedroom of the remodeled building that houses *The Ship's Hatch Café* on the ground floor and our residence on the two floors above.

Before us lay the Gulf of Mexico, shimmering like polished silver melted by the intense August heat.

The sun had fallen below the horizon and threw off cascades of color that painted wisps of evening clouds in a way no artist ever could.

Jamie turned into my arms. "Billy knew it was right for us, didn't he," she said.

"Not the way any of us would have written it, but yeah, he sure did. Some debts are tough to repay. Maybe impossible."

She pressed a long slender finger against my lips. "It's not a debt, Cage. It was Billy's wish. Don't cheapen it with misplaced guilt."

"I'm working on it boss."

"That's a good boy," she said, standing on tiptoe, kissing my forehead as though doing so might bring comfort directly to my brain. "Now hit the shower. Our wards await and it sounds a little rowdy down there."

We'd taken ownership of *The Ship's Hatch Café* in February—actually more of an adoption process than the closing of a real estate transaction.

"To me the business is kind of like a half-way house, or maybe a nursin' home except not everybody's an old fart," Vinnie had said as we'd signed the final documents that closed the deal. "It's like you're responsible for the people, you know? You gotta make 'em feel like they belong. Like somebody gives a shit. They come in for all kinda reasons—maybe just for a few beers, or 'cause they're hungry. Maybe they're tourists you'll never see again. Or maybe it's on account of the old lady or the old man kicked 'em out, or they lost a job. Maybe everything in their lives is in the friggin' dumper. Point is, you never know. So take care of 'em, huh? Fix the place up a little like your brother was gonna do. I liked him, Cage— liked him plenty. And he liked the people. Do it right, like he woulda, okay?"

We assimilated easily into our new surroundings, certain that this was where we belonged. While the renovations were being completed under Jamie's watchful eye, I made a handful of trips back to New York to wrap up some pending cases, then became licensed to practice in the State of Florida. I wasn't sure how much time I'd devote to it, but didn't want to abandon law completely.

Jamie assumed the day-to-day duties of running the place and in short order the books showed a nicely growing profit margin—not the stuff of empire-building but plenty for our needs.

As the months passed, Luke and I struck up a casual relationship that became a real friendship that led to forging an alliance as law partners.

It was the type of practice I'd really wanted all along—the everyday vintage, helping people cope with real-world problems that life had a habit of handing out or they'd handed themselves in a time of trouble, weakness, or too often, blind stupidity.

IT TOOK ME ten minutes to shower and dress. I came down the back stairs of our residence and went through the door that opens onto the side of the main bar. Jamie was drawing a draft beer from a row of taps with decorative handles that stood at attention like miniature soldiers. She looked damn near just as she had when I'd first seen her in a pub on Newbury Street in Boston years earlier.

She saw me and came to the end of the bar. "You're staring," she said "What's the matter? I forget my bra or something?"

"Just surveying the property."

"One great orgasm, and you're my lord and master?"

"One? I distinctly remember—"

"Yeah? Well, maybe I faked the other two." Her expression changed. "Anyway, Luke's looking for you. Be warned. He's moody."

I found him sitting down on the beach smoking a cigarette.

"Evening," I said.

His gaze was fixed on a spot of blood-red light that marked the meeting of sky and water, the last speck of descending color that seemed to pull day into night. He dug a hole in the sand and dropped in the glowing cigarette butt, then covered it up, smoothing the sand back in place with great study. "Wesley says FDLE closed the file on Billy today. Their interest in your brother's murder has timed out." He tapped another cigarette out of the pack he kept in his shirt pocket and lit it with the Zippo. "Officially, it's over."

"Shit," I said.

"The damn fishin' docks hold the key. I'm certain of it," Luke said.

It was a repetitive theme.

"We just haven't found it yet, right?"

"That, and Billy's silent partner."

The other thread I'd been holding on to.

"Buyout money was sent up there months ago. I thought we'd 'a heard somethin' for sure. But still not a friggin' word on the subject. Not yet, anyway."

"You mean *laundered* money for his anonymous partner in crime." I said. "What did you expect we'd get? A fucking thank you note?"

"Don't get hot on me, now. It's just somethin' to consider."

On the surface the idea that Billy was involved in some sort of illegal activity was hard for me to accept. But deep down an undercurrent worked like water on rock, slowly eroding the wall of defense I'd constructed around my brother's memory.

The first crack appeared when I discovered that his trust account—valued at three-quarters of a million dollars at the time of his inheritance—was less than four hundred thousand when he died. And he'd only put a hundred thousand down on the bar.

I got up and brushed the sand off the back of my shorts, flashing as I did on the memory of a fall afternoon when I'd sat next to Billy's grave pitching stones. "Thanks for coming by."

"Fine. Say hi to Jamie." He started up the beach toward his house.

I called after him. "Look, I'm sorry. It's just that . . . ."

He turned and walked backward for a few paces. "It's a lot 'a things, Cage, idn't it? A lot 'a things."

I stewed for five minutes before going back up to *The Hatch* where I plunked down on a barstool.

"Long face," Jamie said.

"They're closing the book on Billy's murder. It had to end sometime, I suppose." I sailed a cork coaster angrily at the mirror behind the bar. "Luke says he's hanging tough. As if it'll make any difference. Fuck it. At least the bar came out well so it's not a total loss, huh?"

"Yeah, it did. Billy would have liked it. Now stop beating yourself up and tell me something. Why does he do it? What's in it for him?"

Her question struck me oddly. "Why does who do what?"

"Luke. Why does he keep after it? It's not like he and Billy were lifelong friends any more than the two of *you* are."

"Why does there have to be something in it for him?"

"Okay, so maybe I'm wrong." She dunked an empty mug into the bar sink with more enthusiasm than was necessary. Soap splashed up from the tub and onto her cheek. She flicked it away. "But ask yourself this: If things were reversed, would you do the same for him?"

I didn't like the question. "I really haven't considered it."

"Maybe you should."

At eleven I went for a run on the beach, something I often do for the sheer physical pleasure of working up a sweat in the soothing coolness of the evening air.

Not the mission that night. Jamie's question was bugging the hell out of me. Not because she'd been so pointed in asking it but because I *had* given it consideration.

A lot of it.

I'd looked past the bends and twists in Luke's brand of law: not everything *by* the book, he liked to say, because not everything is *in* the book. Fine. I could live with that, use it where things got a little sticky and needed a little grease or a bit of pressure—DUIs, divorces, the majority of our little beachside practice.

But this was murder. Case now closed. Over the months I'd dealt with the possibility that I'd have to accept it, thinking at times maybe it would be better to let it go and move on. Why not? Jamie and I were doing just fine.

But if I chose to keep digging and found that my brother had dirt on his hands, that was my business, not Luke's.

Alright, then, why *should* he want to push ahead?

And why should I tag blindly along?

Jamie's point. Not unreasonable.

I passed the Careys' house ten minutes up the beach. It was dark. Luke had gone to bed, I thought. No questions tonight. A bit of a relief.

Then as I turned back toward *The Hatch*, my eye caught the glow of a cigarette up on the deck and in it, the outline of Luke's large frame.

"C'mon up," he called.

I climbed the stairs and stood next to him at the rail.

"It's Jamie," I said after thirty seconds passed in silence. "She's not happy about this whole business. I think she's concerned that I'll turn into a vigilante or something if I don't give it up."

He gazed over water so calm and dark it might have been pavement. "You know the sayin' about not askin' for something you don't really want, don't you? Well, the answer in this case could be waitin' at the next bus stop. This whole blessed bidness has takin' on a life of its own. It's got her bothered on account of it's workin' on your head and bendin' you into a shape she's not used to."

"Actually, I think she's unhappy with both of us."

He chuckled. "That's a gentlemanly way of sayin' what I've read in her eyes for some time now, Cage."

"She's questioning why we're still pushing for answers."

"Not *we*, my friend, *me*," Luke said. "The reason you're still after it's understandable. But where I'm concerned, things get a little fuzzy, right?"

"You're my friend. For me, that's reason enough."

"Ever asked yourself if it would be if *you* were sittin' where I am?"

I searched his face in the uncertain light. "Behold The Amazing Mind Reading Luke Carey. That's the same question Jamie asked."

"So answer it. It won't hurt."

"Truth is, I don't *have* an answer."

He pulled on his cigarette and studied me carefully. "I appreciate your honesty. Most wouldn't even consider the thought. Man's a pretty solitary animal when you get down to it. All comfy in his own shoes."

"*Is* it because we're friends?"

He flipped the butt of his cigarette down onto the sand. "Fair enough. No, it's a lot more than that," he said in a low voice. "It wasn't the long hours that cost me my first marriage, Cage. It was her findin' out what I'm about to tell you."

L UKE'S SISTER HAD been an artist, a scholarship student studying at Berkeley at a time when America's involvement in the Vietnam War was nearing its end.

When she'd decided to make peace not paintings and protest the conflict, she moved into a Victorian house with seven small bedrooms and three communal baths in the Haight-Ashbury district of San Francisco.

The hallways were dingy and dark, the kitchen filthy. The shared living area was little more than a trash heap with sparse furnishings, used mostly for smoking dope or to jeer at the reports on the failed *conflict* and curse the political speeches that spewed forth from a rented black and white Zenith console.

The fifteen or so people who lived there were flower children and acidheads whose faces changed weekly—strangers who came and went, handing off their part of the informal lease arrangement to each other like a baton in a drug- stupored relay race.

Luke and his sister were at odds: she'd been protesting the same war he'd been fighting for the past year as a young Special Forces recruit. Weeks before the helicopters prepared to evacuate the remaining troops from Saigon, he'd been reassigned Stateside.

On leave, Luke traveled to see his sister in San Francisco, hoping to surprise her by his visit—to somehow make peace between the two of them.

He found the house on a steep side street. As he entered the partially opened front door, he heard the distress of muffled voices buried in loud music coming from the top of a long staircase. On instinct he charged up the stairs and burst into the locked bedroom.

What he saw singed his combat-blistered sanity and set him afire with outrage.

Molly's two roommates lay together on the bare wood floor in a corner, bound and naked, candlelight reflecting off two sets of zoned-out eyes. His sister sat on the bed, hands tied in front of her, a rawhide lace twisted around her upper arm, the long-haired boy next to her working a needle into her vein.

The doper whipped his head around. His dirty hair was beaded at the ends and lashed across his hollow face like a warning rattle. Quick as a snake he shot out an arm, grabbed a knife off the night stand and whipped it at Luke. "Fucking baby killer!" he screamed.

The blade tore through the leg of Luke's uniform pants and buried in his thigh.

Ignoring the immense pain, Luke flung himself at the freak, swept him up and threw him with violent force head-long into the wall. The plaster gave under the impact, and broke away.

Luke gathered a handful of greasy hair and pounded the boy's head against the oak flooring until the hollow *thunk* that marked each meeting of bone and wood softened and the floor became carpeted in blood.

"I DRAGGED HIM TO the landing and tossed him down the stairs," Luke said to me as he lit another cigarette. "'Bout half-way to the bottom his neck snapped like a twig.

"Molly's brain was mostly fried on LSD, pot and heroin. She never painted another brush stroke. Married and divorced three total losers between stints in rehab. Finally she just up and died. Fifteen years ago, it was."

Luke's gaze returned to the Gulf. "Anyhow, it never went to trial. I was a soldier who'd walked in on a den of thieves bent on stealin' America's honor. They'd been raped. The three of them. I'd had a knife stuck into the meat of my thigh. Justifiable homicide. That's how the D.A. saw it. It was all swept up and thrown in the basket. My only regret is that I couldn't 'a killed him twice." Luke's eyes glistened as he turned toward me. "You okay with that, partner?"

I tried to answer but my throat squeezed shut and I swallowed the words like fragments of broken crockery. Finally I said, "I'm sorry for what happened to your sister. And that I needed to ask for a reason beyond friendship."

"Don't be. But know this: Friends can sometimes do each other more harm than good tryin' to help out. Seems Jamie understands that. You might want to think about it, too."

Luke crushed out his cigarette on the deck rail, then turned away and went into the house without another word.

CHAPTER 10

T HE WEEKS PASSED. October arrived, according to Luke, the beginning of a stretch of eight perfect months of weather.

For me it marked something else, the first anniversary of my brother's death.

Luke and I sat in the conference room between our adjoining offices revising a draft of an offer for pre-trial settlement on a DUI with injuries when the intercom buzzed.

LuAnn's voice seemed to sift through the outdated box on a tightly drawn string. "Oh my God. I think you need to take this call."

"Who is it?" Luke asked, depressing a button in order to be heard, tossing his pen on the documents in front of him.

"Samantha Graham. SG Investments."

I leaned in, a tap suddenly opening and sending ice water running into my stomach. "Billy's silent partner?" I said, not as a question, but as confirmation of what I'd heard but was too dumbfounded to process.

"That," LuAnn said, "and . . . his girlfriend."

"Christ-'a-Mighty," Luke said under his breath as he punched up Line 1 and put it on the speaker phone. "Ms. Graham?"

"Mr. Carey?" The voice on the other end of the line was soft-spoken but firm. "It's been a year, I know. I should have made contact before this, but— Well, I wasn't sure exactly what to say. Or what good it might have done. Now none of that matters."

"First things first, darlin'. Where is it you're callin' from?" Luke asked.

"The airport. Here in Panama City. This may not be the smartest thing I've ever done, but I'd like to come to your office if that's all right?"

Luke and I locked eyes. "Miss Graham," he said, "it's more than alright."

"Thank you. And . . . Billy's brother, Cage? I saw his name on the documents for the Hatch. Do you suppose you could call him and have him meet with us—assuming that he's in town, I mean."

"He's not only in town, Miss Graham. He's sitting right across from me."

L UANN BUZZED US a half hour later. Our guest had arrived. I'd been pacing the room as though awaiting the jury's verdict in the most important case of my life. Now, as the door opened, I froze in place. Word was about to come in.

Samantha Graham—Sam—was in her late twenties, a blonde with her hair cut in a short style. The large diamond studs in her ears winked brightly as they refracted the sunlight that streamed in through the windows. The simple yet expensive cut of her white blouse and fitted skirt, added to the way she carried herself, spoke of a privileged if not wealthy upbringing. Her athletic, well-muscled body radiated confidence.

Her blue eyes darted from Luke to me then settled intently on my face. "My God," she said, then for a long moment didn't speak. "I'm sorry. It's just that— I can't believe how much you look like Billy. It's like seeing—" She shook her head as if chasing away a thought. "It's just . . . very hard for me."

We settled around the conference table.

"Mr. Carey, I'm sorry for all the secrecy. But it's the way Billy wanted it—the only way he'd do it."

"The silent partnership?" I asked.

"Yes. He didn't want me to front the balance after the down payment. He fought against it. But he had his money tied up in . . . in another business, and we were doing the bar thing for both of us. Then when he died, I didn't want anything to do with it. But when I learned that he'd left The Hatch to you—that you were buying it—I couldn't resist meeting you no matter what trouble coming here might bring me."

"Trouble?" Luke said.

Sam closed her eyes and took a deep breath. When she opened them again, it was with an expression of resolve. "Billy called me from jail after he was arrested because of that fight. He said I wasn't to worry because he had a good attorney and that things would be fine."

"Was that the last time you talked to him?" I asked. *Was that the last time you spoke to him before he had half his face blown away?*

"No. It was Friday morning, the day you were to arrive. He showed up at our condo. I didn't know he'd been released." She looked down at her hands. "All this time and I haven't told anyone what I'm about to tell you. Not even the police. *Especially* not the police. I'm having trouble knowing where and how to begin."

"Then you know what Billy wanted to see me about. What he wanted to tell me."

She looked at me for a long moment, her eyes threatening tears, but held her composure. "Yes. I do. I loved your brother more than anything in this world, Mr. Royce. You must believe me. But you might not like what I have to say."

Blood pounded in my ears. "Please. Call me Cage," I said. "And I doubt there's anything you might say about Billy that would surprise me. He was my brother and my best friend. No one knew him like I did."

"You might be wrong about that. I know *I* was."

"It's okay. Go ahead and say what's on your mind," I said, far more coldly than I had intended.

"Be patient with me. Please. I've thought about this for a long time—how I might get you to understand what happened and why. I need to do this my way, okay?"

I started to respond, but Luke blocked anything else I might have said. "That's fine, Sam. We're here to listen."

"Thank you." She settled back into the chair. "I'll start . . . at the beginning."

SAM MET BILLY in March, she said, seven months before he was murdered.

She'd been on vacation in Destin, a Gulf Coast resort community west of Panama City Beach.

She and her friends planned to do as much as possible in the week they had. That included deep-sea fishing. Sam loved boats. Her family had a summer home near Traverse City on Lake Michigan where over the years they'd kept a series of large fishing yachts.

On the third day of their vacation they headed to Destin Harbor where they walked the docks in the early dawn, considering the available charter boats with no real idea of which one to hire.

Then, Sam spotted Billy.

"He was in the cockpit of this big sportfisher," she said. "I'd never seen a more gorgeous man in my life." A blush spread across her cheeks. "I was gone. Something inside sort of . . . popped. I can't really explain it. It just . . happened."

They hired the boat for the day. Billy was working crew and took care of the tackle and bait and helped the three ladies reel in their fish. He was funny and kind. A gentleman. They talked easily. Sam learned that Billy had his captain's license and hoped in time to a buy boat of his own.

That evening, they had dinner.

By the next morning, they were lovers.

When it came time to return to Michigan with her friends, she stayed. There wasn't much to go back for in any hurry, and now she had a good reason not to. She phoned her parents who said they understood and were happy for her, as long as she knew what she was doing. She assured them that she did and that she'd be home for a visit in a few weeks. She even talked her mom into packing up some clothes and sending them along.

Sam and Billy stayed in a little beach house he was renting by the week. When the owners called to say they would be coming down from Indiana at the end of the month, he and Sam began looking into other accommodations, talking in terms of a more serious commitment. They'd been hit hard by the heat and depth of a relationship that developed in a short span of time. Neither questioned it. They were impulsive by nature and believed that if it felt right, then it had to *be* right.

Sam called her parents to say she planned to bring her new boyfriend home for Christmas.

"On the morning Billy told the captain he was working for that he'd be leaving," she said to us, "the captain was disappointed. But we weren't having great luck finding a place to rent on such short notice, and Billy really wanted to try and find his own charter to skipper.

"When I went down to the dock to meet the boat the following evening, Billy and the captain were having a serious discussion—but friendly. I asked him what—"

"Back up a minute," I said. "Earlier you said that Billy showed up at 'our condo'." This wasn't the rented beach house, then. You meant, a condo that was yours and Billy's?"

She slipped her shoes off and drew her feet onto the chair, tucking them under her short, blue skirt. "Yes, that's right."

"So, why was he staying at the Careys' and not with you after he was released on bail?"

She sat in silence, considering a response. "I'd rather explain that later," she said. "There are other things you need to hear first for that to make sense. For any of this to."

I sat quietly under Luke's warning glare as she continued.

"The captain called around for Billy to see what boats might be available. . . . "

When nothing turned up in Destin, he talked to a friend of his in Panama City Beach—an older captain and boat owner whose health was poor and who'd mentioned not long ago that he'd need to sell out if things didn't improve. They hadn't. He'd be happy to consider an offer.

It was a fifty-two foot Hatteras, only five years old. Sam knew the basic boat: Her family had at one time owned the forerunner–a fifty-foot convertible. She also knew they were quite expensive.

I glanced at Luke and ventured another question. "Do you know how he planned to pay for it?"

"He said that sometimes people put a commercial boat like that into a syndicate. Kind of a limited partnership thing. That's what the current owner had done and he'd offered to help Billy do that too, if he wanted."

"Did he mention how much he'd need up front? Or where he'd come up with it?"

"No. He didn't. And I didn't pry," she said. "He knew that I had money—that my family did—but flat out refused to have me help him. As it turned out later, my putting money into the bar became a battle. He never would have allowed me to do it, he said, if the boat hadn't been in the picture."

"So he bought the Hatteras," I said.

"The next week. We were really excited. Billy was so proud. We both were. But he didn't want anyone else to know about it—not until it was paid off and totally ours."

Why all the secrecy, little brother? "Didn't you find that a little . . . odd?" I asked.

"As I said, it wasn't like me to push." She looked at me, her eyes now defensive. "Anyway, the boat was moored at the Treasure Island Marina in Panama City Beach. Most days I'd crew for him. But when a group came along that Billy felt might become a little too raucous, he'd hire on day help."

"Anyone in particular you might recall?" Luke asked.

"Like . . . Bo Crowley for instance?" she said. "I've been away, but I've kept in close touch with—you know, with . . . friends. Anyway, Crowley came later."

Luke and I exchanged glances. "Are you protecting someone besides yourself, Sam?" I asked.

The answer was in her silence.

"I think we should discuss something before we go any further," I said. "It has to do with— It has to do with whatever you might know about Billy's murder."

She started to protest.

I stopped her. "Sam, please. This is for your benefit. We want to do all we can to help. To protect you if necessary. I'm going to ask you some questions, but don't jump to any conclusions. And don't answer if you don't want to, okay?"

She nodded her understanding.

"Is Luke being a lawyer part of the reason you called? Not just because you saw my name on the papers for the transfer of The Hatch?"

She chewed nervously on her bottom lip. "I guess so—that I've *thought* about calling him."

"And you think you might be in trouble with the authorities because of Billy's death?"

"I . . . I'm not really sure. It's confusing."

"Would you feel better with formal legal counsel?"

"I can't— Maybe. I can't think clearly right now."

"I know this is hard," I said, "so let me clarify. If you were to retain either one or both of us as legal counsel to represent you, or to offer advice, anything you say to us regarding what might have already happened doesn't go outside this office. Any information—anything we talk about—is considered to be privileged. Is there anything you want to say that might call for that kind of protection?"

She thought about it. "I guess I can see where that might be best. I mean, I didn't have anything to do with his *death* or anything. But I— There's just no way I can go to the police with what I know. And I'm afraid that if they find out I'm here they'll want to talk to me. And that might put me in real danger. But I can't just disappear again, either. I did that for a whole year, and look at me. I came back anyway, and honestly? . . . I'm a wreck. And one of the things I have to take care of isn't just going to . . . go away." She took a couple of deep breaths then began to shake. "God . . . what did we get into?"

"Whatever it was it got my brother killed."

Sam stood up quickly. "Maybe it would be better if I just—"

"No!" I snapped. "I mean . . . no, please, Sam . . . stay. I'm sorry. It's just that I've waited a long time to hear this."

"Then I suspect you can wait a bit more," Luke said. "Sam, you want to think about it?"

"Please." She turned to me. "You're different than Billy. He was so gentle. So understanding. You look amazingly the same but it ends there, doesn't it."

I felt myself flush. "No, Sam, it doesn't. We were different, yes. But I'm no less concerned about your welfare then he was.

I'll help in any way I can. It'll be alright," I said. "I promise it will."

She held my eyes, then began to cry softly. "That's just what Billy said."

"WHY SO QUIET?" Jamie asked as we lay in bed that night.

"I figured that if we got lucky it would come from the cops—not like this, not from Sam. Not from Billy's *girlfriend*, for Christ's sake. I'd just as soon scrap the whole thing. I nearly scared her off as it is. Maybe she should just . . . go home."

She kissed me lightly on the forehead. "Gold star for the thought. But it's not possible. Not now. Not for either of you."

"But you wish it were?"

"I love you, no matter what I might think." She rolled over, her back to me.

Ask only those questions whose answers will support your case, not damage it.

Had I missed that class back in my first year of law school?

CHAPTER 11

THE NEXT MORNING at breakfast Sam looked and sounded more relaxed.

Jamie had insisted that she stay with us at *The Hatch,* rather than at a motel.

When she accepted the invitation without protest, I was secretly relieved: I wanted her to feel safe, yes. I also wanted to avert the possibility that after my poor performance at the office she'd be tempted to take off without my knowing it.

It was Saturday. Small groupings of lounges and umbrellas appeared at intervals along the beach, colorful oases in the stretch of blinding white sand. A steady breeze blew onshore. The air was salt-water fresh.

We changed to swim suits and brought low-slung chairs down to the beach, placing them in a small arc that faced the water.

"I didn't mean to be such a snot yesterday," Sam said, squinting against the sun as she looked at me. "I was just scared and uncertain. And tired. I thought it all over last night. I've decided that it's best if I talk about the rest of it with you. Billy was your brother. It should be up to you how much of it you want Luke to know. If anything. Only . . . I need you to promise me one thing first—what I said yesterday about not getting the police involved?"

"You've got my word. But do you really think they'd be that interested in you?"

She was slow to answer. "It's more than just the police I'm worried about. It's the reason I left in such a hurry a year ago and why Billy kept me so removed from everything."

I counted to five—literally. "I'm listening," I said.

She measured me carefully. "Billy was killed because— He was killed because he was involved with running drugs."

Her words were like a telegraphed left hook, one I'd seen coming for a long time but figured that when it was finally thrown, I'd find a way to slip it. I blew out a long breath. "Shit. So there it is. But why in hell would he get himself messed up in—?"

"Y'all seem mighty engrossed."

I looked up. Luke towered over us. He'd walked the beach to *The Hatch* for lunch. A Saturday tradition. He lowered his bulk onto the sand.

I offered to get him a chair.

"No thanks. I can get in 'em, but me tryin' to get back out is not a pretty sight." He smiled at Sam. "So how goes the mornin'?"

"Much . . . better," she said to Luke, then looked at me.

In the silence that descended on our little group like a sudden fog, I heard the waves tumble on the sand, a bird calling, the sound of my own breathing and the grinding of teeth.

"Okay, so what the hell. Billy was involved with running drugs, Luke. Sam was about to tell us all about it."

"That so?"

"I think we both knew goddamned well it would turn out to be the case," I said. "So while I appreciate it all the same, drop the fucking look of wonderment, huh?"

"Oh boy," Sam said under her breath.

"It's okay," I said. "Go ahead. Luke should hear this too, although I'll bet we can pretty much guess what happened. The count came up short, maybe? Or he took a cut off the top? A bit more each time until—"

"Stop it!" Sam yelled, getting to her feet, turning heads from thirty yards away. She looked around, blushing from anger not embarrassment, then glared at me, tears streaming down her reddened cheeks, her fists clenched. "You said you knew him better than anyone. Billy was a *thief*? Is *that* what you think? He was the best man I ever met. He messed up, that's all. It happens to good people every day. If you loved him—if you *understood* him—how could you believe such a thing?"

Sam turned and ran toward the water.

How? Because it made it more acceptable to me. That's how.

Jamie had tried to warn me, tried to get me to talk with her about my fiercely guarded feelings, about the anger and resentment I had built and directed towards my brother when in fact the truth of its root was the personal assessment I had made of my own perceived failings, as wrong and selfish as that was.

I went to Sam who stood at the water's edge.

She looked away.

"Please," I said. "Yes, he was my brother. And I tried to understand what he was all about. I'm dealing with this the best I can. Same as you. I just don't know what to do—what to expect."

Sam turned into my arms, her body wracked by a deep, silent cry. "I forgive you," she said at length. "And I hurt for your loss. For both of us. My God, I thought I'd cried all the tears I had." She pushed back. "But I'm finished now. I had to come back for the reasons I told you. But I had to come back for you, too. I owed it to Billy. He loved you—looked up to you. He couldn't wait for us to meet. He wanted to show me off, he said. Wanted you to see that he'd done pretty damn well in life after all. I'm not sure what he meant by that but he was laughing when he said it. A happy laugh. He thought that Jamie and I would be like sisters." Sam glanced toward the beach. "I can see why he felt that way." She turned her eyes up to mine. "You're a lucky guy, buster. Don't screw up." She wiped her eyes and gave me a peck on the cheek, then walked back to join Luke and Jamie where they sat in the sand.

I took a swim—a long one—the salt water of the Gulf burning my eyes. When I returned to towel off I found a note from Jamie stuck in the webbing of one of the chairs saying that Luke was half-starved and they'd gone up for lunch.

I joined them on the deck, ordered a ham sandwich and a beer and then listened with a softened attitude and a measure of humility as, without prompting, Sam continued to turn over pieces of the puzzle of her brief time with Billy and fit them together.

It had all started, she explained, when Billy decided to buy the Hatteras.

He went to Panama City Beach to meet with the owner and discuss the price and the terms. He took the boat out on a shakedown cruise, spent the night on board then called Sam in the morning and told her the deal was done. Pending financing. He'd decided not to go to a bank for a loan. He was making a decent down payment and the current owner had sold him on the benefits of the syndicate he was in.

A meeting was arranged in Miami for the following day.

Ironically, the syndication company was partially based at the same marina where Billy had worked after college. Back then it had been owned by the parents of a friend he'd met at Boston University. When they'd sold out, Billy left and hadn't seen or talked to his friend in years. When he found out that his friend had stayed on and now worked for the company, it gave Billy additional confidence.

"By the time Billy got back," Sam said, "I'd leased a condo. Turns out it was near Luke's house although obviously I didn't know that at the time. Anyway, his friend, Jorge something-or-other—'Georgie' Billy called him—had been out of the country so Billy hadn't actually seen him. But the people he'd met with had no problem with assigning the syndication agreement to Billy. They were involved with several boats up and down the east coast of Florida and in Alabama and the Carolinas I think Billy said, but nothing along the Florida Panhandle other than the boat Billy was buying.

"Billy said that he would remain essentially independent, own the majority interest in the boat and run the fishing charters pretty much as he saw fit. A set percentage of the net revenues would be paid out to the syndicate, and from time to time the company would book the boat directly from Miami for VIPs. For those bookings he'd be paid well above his normal rate because the company charged a much higher tariff for those charters. It was another reason they were so interested in picking up the deal on Billy's Hatteras. She was a class boat.

"For the first couple months," Sam went on, "everything went really well. We moved into the condo and I continued to work the boat with Billy, but less frequently than before. I'd started to make some friends and began playing tennis and going to the gym. Doing lunch. Shopping. You know, girl stuff.

"Then things began to change—not between Billy and me. God, we were *way* out there in love. I couldn't have been any happier. It was the boat, the deal with the syndicate that began to sour.

"Billy'd been operating out of the Treasure Island Marina where he'd taken on the balance of the current lease for dock space from the boat's former owner. It was expensive, but it was also the best area on the Beach for charters and would be okay until we were able to move the boat out to Destin Harbor. We loved Destin, and the tourist business was booming. Dock rates were really high, but so were the charter rates. Billy did the math and figured the two would more than offset each other.

"But a move would represent a material change in his agreement with the people in Miami and he'd need their approval.

He didn't think it would be a problem. Well, he was wrong and not very happy about it. In fact, they wanted him to move the boat over to the St. Andrews Marina in Panama City instead."

"I can see where that wouldn't sit too well with him," Luke said. "More for commercial fishing. I don't imagine the charter bidness there is near as good. But it sure explains how he came to be there just before . . . everything happened. 'Course he told *me* he was there workin' for somebody else, and that he'd quit—didn't have a job. And he never mentioned anything about you, Sam, or that you had a silent partnership interest in The Hatch."

"He was protecting me from the syndicate," Sam said to Luke. "From the whole business. Anyway, he'd argued against the move to St. Andrews. But it was a new relationship and his partners felt that it would work better for the referral charters. Something about proximity to the airport and being on that side of the bridge.

"He didn't push it. You know how he was. He said that once the relationship was further down the road he'd find a way to change their minds. But I was beginning to think there was something else—something that had started to affect his attitude. When I asked him about it he said it was my imagination. If it wasn't working to his liking after six months, he could move the boat over to Destin.

"But I didn't buy it. It didn't feel right and I began to worry. Billy said he'd rather I didn't come down to the dock on my own. So unless it was a time when I could go out with him I stayed away." Her eyes softened. "Once in awhile he'd take a day or two off and we'd go out on the water. Just the two of us—cruise the coast, put in somewhere overnight. We went to Destin three times. On the last trip we had dinner at the same restaurant overlooking the boats where I'd been the night before I met him. I even made us wait for the same table. There we were, just the two of us, the boat sitting at her moorings below in the harbor.

We had so many good times ahead. It's what I hold on to the most. The way I remember us."

She became very still.

"Sam?" Luke said so softly that at first I wasn't certain he'd spoken. "Do you know what became of the boat?"

Sam closed her eyes, seeing something that was lost to the rest of us. "It's here," she said. "She's one of the things that brought me back."

A year with nothing—not a clue.

Then Sam.

Now Billy's boat.

"Here meaning . . . ?" I asked.

"In storage," she said.

In the end, that's where it should have stayed.

Then none of what was to come would ever have happened.

Maybe not the worst of it, anyway.

CHAPTER 12

"THE DAY HE disappeared, I heard the back door of our condo open," Sam continued after our waiter brought another round of drinks to the table and cleared the lunch dishes. "I came down to the kitchen. Billy was leaning over the sink splashing his face with water. He was out of breath and sweating. I was surprised to see him and told him that I couldn't understand why he hadn't called me to tell me he was getting out of jail so I could've picked him up . . . ."

"I couldn't," Billy said to Sam as he snatched a dish towel off the counter and dried the water from his eyes. "I stayed with my lawyer last night. I didn't want to risk coming here and getting you involved."

"What are you *talking* about? Involved in what?" Sam asked, alarmed by both his words and his demeanor.

"It'll all work out."

She loved him, and doubt wasn't supposed to be part of the definition. But that's exactly what she was feeling. It had been building for some time. "Billy, please, whatever's been going on, I need to know. We've got to trust each other. Don't treat me like a child."

Billy wiped a hand over his face. "Okay, okay. I'm having some trouble with the syndicate. They want to extend the deal. I told them I was finished. They don't want to accept that. They sent someone from Miami to help change my mind. I sent him back with a definite, no. The boat's ours and I'm going to see that we keep it. I've talked to my brother. He's coming down tomorrow. Between the two of us we'll figure out a way to handle it."

"They can't just . . . take it back, can they?"

"No. I won't let them. But it might get unpleasant and I want you away from it."

"*Away*? As in, without you? Not a chance!"

Billy's hands came to rest on her bare shoulders. The message in his eyes was clear.

She knew there was bigger trouble. "You're scaring the hell out of me."

He smoothed her hair. "Brian's taking the boat to a yard in Fort Walton Beach tomorrow morning. I'm having it hauled. Then I'm storing it. He's on his way to Destin with her right now. I want you to pack whatever you need and meet him at the harbor this afternoon. I'll join you tonight. I'll take care of closing this place up then get my stuff from Luke's."

Sam was shaken by the tone of Billy's voice—by the speed at which things were happening. "Just don't leave me too long without you."

Billy pulled her close and kissed her. "Only for a few hours," he said. "And then we'll have the rest of our lives together."

"I packed my things in a hurry and we left the condo. Billy had me drive around until he was sure my car wasn't being followed. Then he had me stop. He got out and told me again that I'd be okay with Brian, and that— He said he'd see me later that night. Then he started jogging back toward the condo. I watched until he turned the corner and disappeared and then I headed for Destin Harbor. I never— I never saw him again."

"Who's Brian, honey?" I asked.

"Sorry. Brian Martin. Billy's best friend. He crewed for him on a full-time basis. When we hadn't heard anything from Billy by eleven o'clock, Brian said we couldn't wait any longer. I asked him what was going on but he wouldn't give me a straight answer. All he would say was that I had to trust him.

"We locked up the boat and got motel rooms. In the morning, I dropped him in the middle of town. He walked to the harbor and took the boat from Destin to the yard in Fort Walton Beach. I drove my car to the boat yard there and picked him up. Then we went back to the motel. He said that everything had gone just fine.

"For two days we watched TV and checked the answering machine at the condo every hour. Then on Monday morning, Brian knocked on my door with the newspaper. It was like . . . like I was in another galaxy," she said of her reaction to the article. "I read it, and read it, and read it but I couldn't believe it. Eventually, it all took hold. I wanted to die.

"I hounded Brian until he told me about the drug running. I'd suspected something like that all along, I suppose, but I'd put it out of my mind because I didn't want to confront Billy with it. Then Brian told me the reason Billy wanted out. It was because he loved me and wanted to marry me and one day be a father. He'd been foolish to get involved with the whole business in the first place, and he knew it. He wanted so badly to set everything right for us."

In the beginning, Brian told Sam, the simple truth was that Billy wanted the boat badly enough to rationalize everything and run drugs for the syndicate. So what if a few adults had some harmless fun with a little recreational dope.

Justification born in a moment of greed—an instant of moral lapse.

The first four charters assigned by the syndicate came off without a hitch. Brian had been on all of them. Each one was carefully set up to look like any other day-long fishing excursion.

But Billy's last charter turned out differently. Brian hadn't been on that one, he'd told Sam, because Miami advised that it involved a new supplier. No additional crew was allowed. Billy didn't like the sound of it. He reminded them that it was to be his last run; what a new supplier did or didn't want wasn't his concern.

At eleven that night, after the boat was docked, Brian got a call from Billy who said he had a serious problem.

Brian met him at a bar near the marina. Billy told him that two of the men on the charter were guys he'd never seen before. But the third man, he knew well. It was his old friend, Georgie. He was pretty high up in the organization and his being there made no sense. The exposure was too great—completely out of character. Part of the deal was that the runner accepted all the risk. That's why the payoff was so big.

They'd gone out about seven miles and begun trolling. As darkness set in, they pulled in the lines and Billy made course for the rendezvous point.

Billy and Georgie got into a conversation about Billy's ending his association. He'd performed as promised and was now entitled to ownership of the boat.

But Georgie told him there'd been some sort of misunderstanding—that he was far from finished and the only time he was going to get out was when *he* said.

Billy tried to reason with him. He told him that he could be trusted never to say anything to anyone.

But Georgie said it was too late, that Billy was in all the way. There was nothing more to discuss; he should forget about leaving and enjoy the money.

Bullshit, Billy told him. He was out. Period.

"I'm sorry that I can't give you more than that. But that's all Brian told me," Sam said to me, then turned to Luke. "And I'm sorry about breaking into the storeroom at your house. I just wanted to have whatever there might be of Billy's as a keepsake."

Luke was stunned for a split second. No one else caught it, but it was there in his eyes.

"Billy'd told Brian where his duffle was. Boat stuff, mostly
. . .the rigging knife I'd given him along with a few other things.
Not much, really. Not to anyone else. Brian was with me, of
course. Otherwise I'd never have gotten in there because of the
lock. I'd gotten your address from the phone book, Luke. We
stopped on our way out of town. Brian was flying out of Atlanta
and I was driving back to Michigan. I'd called my parents and
told them I'd broken up with my boyfriend and just . . . needed
to come home.

"We could hear you moving around upstairs and thought
about knocking on your door. Only we couldn't decide whether
or not we should risk talking to you just then. So we just took the
chance and busted the lock and got Billy's things."

L UKE CAME BACK to *The Hatch* later that evening.
The night turned out to be fairly rowdy and he hung around
to pitch in with the clean-up. "Christ 'a Mighty," he said as we
cleared the last of the tables, "they'd 'a come upstairs, they'd 'a
been history. Small wonders."

"I don't even want to think about it," I said. "At least now we
know where the boat disappeared to. But wouldn't the syndicate
come looking for it to recover their investment?"

"And risk exposure for what to them was no more than
pocket change? They might look, but they wouldn't touch,"
Luke said.

We killed the main lights and went out on the deck. A thin
layer of clouds covered the moon with a milky haze.

Luke leaned against the rail and lit a cigarette. The flame
of the old Zippo cast an eerie circle of light around his face,
deepening the lines and sharpening the angles. "Let's have your
thoughts," he said with his first exhale.

"For one, the drugs," I said. "If you've got several boats
in the chain why the big concern about Billy wanting out?

In fact, I'm not settled with how he became involved to begin with."

"Okay. Now, two. What'd you make of Sam's breakin' into the store room?"

"I don't buy Brian taking that kind of chance for sentimental reasons—not when he was so concerned with physical danger."

"Then it was Brian who was lookin' for somethin' in Billy's gear. The boys upstairs were doin' the same."

"We've got to talk to him," I said. "To Brian."

Luke crushed his cigarette butt on the rail, then brushed the ashes away. "We'll have to wait it out, see if she's willin' to involve him again," he said, then walked down the stairs and faded into the darkness, a wave of a hand as large as a flapjack his parting gesture.

CHAPTER 13

I SPENT A RESTLESS night wrestling the sheets. At six-thirty I gave up and slipped out of bed and into a pair of shorts and a sweatshirt, then went down to the kitchen and fired up the coffee maker.

I poured an oversized mug, retrieved the *Sunday Herald* from the steps of the side entrance and headed for the deck.

The morning was sharp and clean, the air purifying.

Jamie joined me a few minutes later.

"Didn't mean to wake you," I said.

"That's okay. I tossed around most of the night. Couldn't sleep. You either, I noticed."

The sun was rising in the sky, casting the deck in the deep dark shadow of the building.

"Something to do with what you and Luke were talking about down here after I went to bed?" she asked.

"Something I can't square up. Billy told Sam that someone from Miami had come to visit him, right? Wanted to reason with him about staying in the deal. Instead of just turning them down, Billy beat the hell of him."

Jamie thought for a minute. "So after that, they figured Billy would go against them."

I shook my head. "That's the problem. It doesn't work."

"Why not?"

"Because, between his arrest and his disappearance on Friday he had a chance to throw them in. He was in jail, remember? He could have easily spilled it all to Wes, then let the DEA move in—worked a plea bargain with no sweat. But he didn't. And that would have indicated to the syndicate that their grip on him was tighter than ever. The proof was in his silence. Whatever they were holding over his head passed a serious test. He wasn't about to say anything to anybody."

"And if that's the case, you're right. His murder makes no sense."

"Exactly. Why bring the cops in to snoop around a murder case—two, counting Crowley—and risk having them stumble onto something you'd rather they didn't?" I took a long sip of bitter coffee. "We've got to convince Sam to put us in touch with Brian," I said. "Meanwhile, there are a couple of things we might consider doing ourselves."

Jamie looked uneasy. "Such as . . . ?"

"Such as having a little off the record chat with Wes and then taking a drive out to Fort Walton Beach to see a man about a boat."

L UKE PICKED ME up at two. He'd called Wes who'd said, sure, come over anytime, he was spending the day just hanging out with Tisha and the kids.

We found him in the pool floating on an inflatable raft, dogged by three offspring whose mission in life at the moment was to dislodge Dad from his perch and claim it as their own. When he saw us come through the gate, Wes obliged their efforts, shunned the ladder and hoisted his bulk out of the pool and onto the deck with the ease of a gymnast.

He passed a towel over his body, then tossed it at his wife who was stretched out on a lounge. "Keep your top on, woman," he said loudly enough for us to hear. "We got company."

"D AMNIT TO HELL, Luke. You can't come waltzing in here, throw a turd like that on the floor and expect me to ignore it!"

We'd gone into Wes's study.

"And don't go shovelin' all that lawyer-client bullshit at me. Christ, that's all I ever hear these days. How the hell am I supposed to do my job–answer me that."

"For a start, by calmin' down," Luke said.

"Don't you go tellin' me—in my own *house*, yet—how I'm supposed to act." Wes paced the room, his anger slowly bleeding away. "Shit. Look at me. I'm drippin' all over the damn rug. Tisha's gonna have my ass. Wait 'til I get out of this wet suit." He stepped toward the door. "Damn. Some days . . . ."

"You're doing nicely so far," I said to Luke.

Wes returned a minute later and sat down behind his desk. "I gotta tell you, Luke, '*we think we're on to why Billy got killed, but we can't let you in on everything just yet*' is not—I repeat, *not* a great opening line."

"That what I said?"

"Close enough. So what *can* you tell me?"

Without mentioning Sam or Brian by name I told the story to Wes, for the time being leaving out certain items.

"You don't seem surprised. At least, not about the drugs," I said when I'd finished.

"Disappointed, yes. Surprised, no. You must have one hell of a source."

"You could say that," Luke replied.

Wes narrowed his eyes. "Reliable?"

"Please."

Wes realized the foolishness of the question. "It's just that this doesn't sound like small-time stuff and I don't want you two runnin' down a blind alley not knowin' what's at the other end. What are the chances of picking up more information, getting some corroboration?"

"Reasonable," I said. "We'll know soon."

Wes sat back. "Interesting that whoever your source is surfaced after a whole year. Or that they're alive at all if you want the truth."

"Sorta answers your question about the need for all the secrecy, doesn't it?" Luke said.

Wes came around the desk and sat on the front edge. "Tell me more about this boat."

"Maybe Billy thought he'd use it as a bargaining chip," I said. "Their investment against his freedom."

"What they had in it wouldn't have meant shit to them," Wes said, lending independent confirmation to Luke's take on the issue. "Most likely he was just determined to keep the damn thing." He glared at Luke. "Of course, it *would* be nice if we knew where it was." He sat down again and rested his large forearms on the desktop.

I glanced at my partner.

Why not? his nod said.

"It's in storage," I said. "The people making the payments have used an escrow account. No way to trace it back."

"That's good," Wes said. "Scared, but still thinking. Keep it that way." He narrowed his eyes at both of us. "And thank you for your fucking confidence, gentlemen."

"We're walking a rope, here," Luke said. "The question is, how much can you handle and not feel like you gotta invoke the badge?"

Wes waved him off. "My problem. Don't sweat it. Now, it's possible that this syndicate y'all are talking about doesn't have a clue as to where the boat is, but we'd have to be dumb-asses to make that assumption. I'd guess the two of you plan to have a look yourselves. I don't recommend it but I don't suppose that makes a shit's worth of difference. And one other thing: These two old salts, the skip Billy worked for in Destin and the one that owned the boat before Billy. Any idea who or where they are?"

Sam knew them by sight and as Captain Bob, and Captain Toby. I gave the names to Wesley.

"We might be able to get a line on 'em," Wes said as he jotted the names on a pad on his desk. "But if they were involved with this thing—and it would appear that at least one of them was—and they're alive, you wouldn't have a prayer of linking them to anyone in the syndicate let alone a fleet of charter boats."

"So if the syndicate higher-ups insulated themselves from the day-to-day operation, why would Billy's pal Georgie show up and risk getting caught in a bust? Unless of course he planned to kill Billy that night," I said.

"Good question. People in the trade don't go around cappin' their runners for the sport of it. Not if they want to keep a low profile," Wes said. "Fact is, the longer a runner stays around the of a less reason anyone has to suspect anything. A suddenly dead skipper out at sea doesn't do anybody any good. And in Billy's case, he was only trying to *get* out, not *rat* them out."

"So why *is* Billy dead?" I said.

Wes folded his arms over his chest. "What I should say right here and now is that the best way to determine that is to play it by the book and blow it all open and see what pigeons fall out of what trees. Conventional wisdom, right? But off the record, there isn't enough to move on—not without risking somebody else getting dead. So I'll compromise. To a point." He walked over to the picture window and looked out at the swimming pool. " Reason? Those kids out there. I catch some scumbag tryin' to peddle shit to my babies I'll rip their arms off with my bare hands—*fuck* the badge."

He cut his eyes in my direction.

"No disrespect to your brother's memory. But I can't make excuses for him. The man didn't consider the end-product of what he was doing. So you'd best be straight with me. Because I swear, if I see one more kid go the way of the needle and I find out who that somebody is . . . ?"

"No one in our camp is in the drug trade, Wes. Trust us on that. We'll be straight as long as it doesn't break a confidence or put someone else in danger."

"We're al*ready* in danger. The whole fucked up country is."

He saw us to the door. "I'm here if y'all need me. I'm counting on you to let me know when you do. Just don't be figuring that shit out too late."

CHAPTER 14

EARLY THE FOLLOWING morning Sam came up the stairs from the beach sweat-soaked and breathing hard from a run, her expression one part annoyance, one part concern.

Jamie set aside the purchase orders we'd been reviewing. "You okay?" she asked as Sam joined us at the table.

"Sorta spooked," Sam said, "if you want the truth."

"What happened?"

Sam leaned back in her chair. "I'm really not sure. My Ipod craps out, right? When it does, I realize someone's running behind me. I glance over my shoulder and he's right on my heels—like maybe three feet away. I pick it up, and he— He keeps pace with me, and then he . . . he starts *singing* to me." She took off her sunglasses. "Do you guys know the song, *Lady in Red?*"

Jamie smiled. "Your halter top," she said, noting its color. "How original. A pick-up song instead of a pick-up line."

"It wasn't like that. It felt . . . creepy."

"What did he look like?" I asked.

"Young, I think. He had on a baseball cap and shades. Anyway, he stays just behind me for a few more yards. I'm getting really nervous. Then he stops singing and says something to me. But I don't know what because I don't speak Spanish. Then he falls back and drifts off in the other direction."

"Probably nothing," Jamie said. "He thought you were cute, that's all."

"Great. Just what I need. Some annoying dweeb singing me a love song."

That evening, I worked inside while Jamie tended bar on the deck.

Sam came down at six and took a stool. I poured her a white wine. She nursed it for a good ten minutes in silence while I went about my business.

"It's tomorrow," she said as I uncorked a new bottle and topped off her glass.

"Yeah. I know."

"One . . . whole . . . entire . . . year. I knew his heart, Cage. What I said to you on the beach was the God's honest truth. Billy was a good guy who made a dumb mistake. That's all it was."

"Sam?" The quiet voice came from a lanky man about Sam's age who'd moved in to her left. His hair was drawn back in a ponytail. A gold stud dotted the lobe of his left ear.

At first Sam was startled and I tensed. Then she jumped off the barstool. "*Brian?*"

He opened his arms. "In the flesh," he said.

"Oh my God!" Sam flung herself at him. "What—? What are you *doing* here? You *promised* you wouldn't." She stepped back and held him at arm's length. "You look so . . . *different!*"

"That would be the idea." He eyed me with a look of familiarity as he extended a hand across the bar. "Brian Martin," he said. "Sam called me last night to tell me she was here. I drove down from Atlanta. I hope you don't mind my coming. I can only imagine what you must think of me."

The fact that he'd shown up told me all I really needed to know.

"I didn't realize that the resemblance would be so strong," he said as we shook hands.

Sam kissed Brian's cheek. "I'm going out to tell Jamie you're here."

Brian watched her go. "I've wanted to come back for months. Truth is I never wanted to leave. It's not my style to run from a problem. I'd like to help set things right if I can."

"I'd say you did everything Billy asked, including taking care of Sam."

"I'd have been a better friend if I'd pushed him into looking for help from the law."

"Might have made things worse," I said.

"That's what I kept telling myself. And after— Well, after what happened to Billy it didn't seem to matter anymore. But it sure as hell does. It took Sam's courage in coming here to make me see it. I don't mind telling you that I'm more than a little embarrassed by that."

I reached into the cooler and grabbed a pair of long-neck beers and snapped the tops off in the opener. "Don't be," I said, handing him an amber bottle that glistened with sweat. "Come on, there's another special lady I'd like you to meet."

It was Monday, and the deck crowd was light. The sun was long below the horizon, pushing it's warmth toward remote parts of the globe I'd never seen and probably never would.

The evening had taken on an October frostiness.

Jamie was behind the bar in conversation with Sam when I brought Brian out to meet her. She lifted the hinged access in the bar top part way and ducked under it and shook hands with Brian. "It's great of you to come."

I signaled a waiter who pointed us to a table by the rail.

"Must be how it feels the first day out of prison," Brian said as he gazed at the Gulf. "It's been a long year but being back here makes it seem like it all happened yesterday."

"Anything you can add to what Sam has told us?" I asked as chips and salsa were set before us and drink orders were taken.

Brian appeared to be sorting through his thoughts like a person shuffling through old photographs as we sat under the blanket of warmth cast by the gas heater above us. He looked at Sam. "Maybe we both have something to add."

Brian and Sam had gone to the Careys' house, Brian said, broken into the storage area then driven directly to Atlanta where Sam left him at Hartsfield-Jackson International and began the long drive home to Michigan.

Once there, Sam said, she moved back in with her roommate, saying only that she and Billy had broken up.

Her family was supportive but had trouble dealing with her constant state of depression.

With the anniversary of Billy's death nearing, Sam became despondent. The friends she'd been with when she'd first met Billy coaxed her into a trip to the Bahamas.

Three weeks of sun and sea helped. She returned to Michigan more mentally together, hoping she'd find the guts to come back to the Beach. There were two things in need of resolve. One was the boat; the other was the safety deposit box she'd opened at a local bank. In it she'd left a large sum of cash and a substantial amount of jewelry, most given to her by her mother. But one piece was a gift from Billy—a ring—and *that* she cherished most.

Brian never left Atlanta, he explained. Instead of going to his sister's in Texas as planned, he found a job at a marina on Lake Lanier north of the city where he'd spent the year dealing with apprehension and self-doubt. He'd kept in touch with Sam and had often thought about calling Luke. But something worked on his mind and held him back.

His eyes shifted to the table as he made the comment, the involuntary act of a key witness holding back on something of importance. I resisted the urge to follow up and instead asked about the boat.

"It was becoming a problem," he said, "my calling to extend the storage from a couple of months to a year. I could tell that the boat yard was starting to wonder what was going on. So when the yard foreman finally asked me directly just who would be coming for the boat, I sort of got spooked and said that the Hatteras should be made ready for launch the third week in October."

He'd regretted his impulsive, defensive act as soon as he'd hung up, and immediately called Sam to tell her what he'd done.

She told him not to worry, that she'd figure something out. She thought Luke was their best bet in helping deal with the problem. And she'd seen my name on the paperwork for the sale of *The Hatch*. My help added to Luke's, she hoped, would be all she'd need. Brian wouldn't have to be involved any further. He'd done enough to help her already. So Sam told her friends that the guy she'd broken up with the year before wanted her back.

Her friends advised against it. Cute or not, this guy was a total jerk among other things for putting her through such misery.

No, she said, he wasn't a jerk. He was the most incredible man she'd ever met.

You're making a big mistake, they told her.

Maybe so, Sam thought. But for a different reason. *With Billy gone, what more was there left to lose?*

CHAPTER 15

THE NEXT MORNING Brian and I walked the beach to Luke's. To the southwest, thunder rolled. A sharp wind whipped the surface of the Gulf into four-foot waves that pounded the shore and filled the air with a cloak of salty mist.

I tapped on the sliding glass door, slid it open and led Brian in. The heat of the fire was welcome after a fifteen minute walk that turned out to be a few degrees shy of invigorating.

Luke was in the kitchen, his large frame partially visible in the gap between the overhead cabinets and the countertop. "Cage, I swear if I didn't know better I'd figure you for Minnesota or Canada, see you walkin' the sand on a mornin' like this." He came around the corner and extended a big paw toward Brian.

Their hands clasped with a meaty slap.

"Listen, I'm sorry about—"

"What? The storage room?" Luke said. "Hell, don't give it another thought. The rules of engagement shift with the situation. Like we think it did for Bo Crowley. You knew him?"

We sat in front of the fire.

"He worked for Billy a few times. Twice with me, but never on the runs."

"Would Billy have known him well enough to talk to him on the street or let him in if he came knocking on the door?" I asked.

"Sure."

"Whose idea to go for the gear in the storage room?" Luke asked.

"Mine. I was hoping Billy might have left a message or a lead of some kind. Sam wanted his things, so I played off that. We were taking a real chance, although she didn't know it. If they'd been watching we'd have been screwed."

I glanced at Luke, then back at Brian. "They were right above you ransacking the house."

Brian looked at me as if I were a judge who'd just pronounced the death sentence. "Jesus Christ. It makes me sick to even think about what could have happened."

"So what haven't you told Sam about that last cruise?" I asked.

Brian looked at me with some surprise. "She'd have gone over the edge if I'd told her all of it—what Billy described to me that night at the bar . . . ."

The drop came off in the usual fashion. Billy proceeded to the rendezvous point. Another boat drew alongside and the two were lashed together for the exchange—money for drugs.

Billy sat in the captain's chair of the Hatteras. Georgie stood behind him. They'd been arguing about Billy's deal with the syndicate.

"This is it. Last run. I'm out," Billy said.

Georgie laid a hand on Billy's shoulder, then bent close to his ear. "Try it, and we kill your woman."

Billy grabbed Georgie by the neck and slammed him against the dash.

Georgie sneered. "It wouldn't be right away, either," he croaked. "In time, Billy. And ugly. Really fucking ugly. If you can live with that? . . . fine. But it *will* happen. You'll have the rest of your life to remember it."

Billy shoved him away. "Go near her, and you're dead."

Georgie shouted to the men below. One came immediately topside armed with a hand gun and trained it on Billy.

Georgie rubbed at his throat. "You are stupid, my friend. You don't have any say in this thing." He went below leaving Billy up top with the gunman.

When the transaction had been completed and the lines were about to be freed, Georgie called up to Billy from where he stood straddling the gunnels of both boats.

Billy went to the rail.

"No hard feelings, man, okay? Everything's cool." He swung himself over onto the other boat. "Just so you know we're still friends, I got you a present."

Georgie disappeared into the salon, returning a minute later with a striking young woman who stepped away from him and looked up at Billy with a big smile. She reached around and unhooked the top of her bikini, letting it slip from her hand and onto the deck. "I wan' you, Beelie. I wan' to *pleeze* you."

Billy watched as she stepped out of her suit bottom and climbed up onto the gunnels where she began a rhythmic sway of her hips in the muted glow of the cockpit lights.

Then in a single swift move, Georgie stepped behind her, encircled her waist with his arm and drove a knife up under her rib cage, working it back and forth.

Her eyes flew open and fixed on Billy in shock; a slick, dark flow appeared, streaming from her nose and mouth as she wretched and gagged.

Georgie yanked the girl backward and flung her to the deck of the cockpit.

She lay there on her back, blood pooling around her head and soaking the fan of black hair that spread in a dark halo around her face. Her mouth worked like a dying fish. At last, she was still. Her dead eyes stared blankly at Billy.

Georgie called up to him. "Hey! Amigo!"

Billy's eyes were drawn to Georgie. His stomach began to convulse.

"You think about that, okay? What happened to this sweet young thing? Maybe you don't have such a hard choice after all, man. Adios."

The lines were cast off. The other boat started backing slowly away. Georgie's laughter filled the night air as Billy looked at the dead girl lying naked in the cockpit.

"If they'd been alone," Brian said in cold, heavy words, "Billy said he would have killed Georgie right then and there."

"Christ 'a Mighty," Luke said. "And I had a chance at one of them and missed."

Brian reached for his back pocket, retrieved a folded piece of paper and handed it to me as he said to Luke, "Maybe you'll have another opportunity."

"What's this?" I asked.

"I found it in the gear bag Billy left in the storage room. Most of it's routine maintenance and check-list stuff. But one of the items has been driving me nuts. It doesn't make sense."

My eye was drawn to the fifth entry down, my mind racing backward in time, pictures firing in rapid sequence in my head. The old neighborhood; our house. "I'll be damned," I said. "We were kids. Billy knew I'd never forget."

The item read: CHECK T-MAGS BEFORE NEXT CHARTER.

"What does it mean?" Brian asked.

I refolded the note. "It means that we need to get aboard that boat."

CHAPTER 16

LUKE AND I met at the Panama City Beach Police Department early the following afternoon, the result of a verbal summons delivered by phone.

Chief Wesley Harland sat doing paper work, filling in the form in front of him as though he were doing his best to inscribe the words on the surface of the desk beneath it using the pressure he exerted on his ballpoint pen. "This," he said, tapping a finger on an open folder, "this is why we don't have enough time to catch the real criminals. Paperwork. It gets worse all the time." He leaned back in his chair. "So then, let me share a bit of information that might—"

"Billy was witness to the slaughter of a young girl," I said. "It was meant as a warning. An insurance policy to guarantee that he stayed in."

Wes looked up, his eyes hooded. "Good afternoon to you, too. Thanks for stopping by." He bounced his pen angrily off his desk top then batted it across the room with an open hand "I won't ask how you found this out, but I can guess. No matter. These pricks got no conscience. You think for even one minute that you're in their league and some bad shit's gonna come down . You dig? And it won't be just *your* ass suckin' wind." His expression and tone of voice made it clear that his intent was to burn the message deep into my skull.

"Point made," I said.

"I sincerely hope so."

"We've got the lives of two people Billy loved and trusted hanging in the balance. We won't be stupid."

"See that you're not. Okay. So here's the deal. I talked with a buddy of mine from the DEA in Miami. A lot of manpower is being thrown against the bulk shipments of tar and coke coming in from Mexico and Asia. Result: supplies of cocaine and heroin are being squeezed at the same time that demand is way up. Price and profit follows." He opened a folder and extracted a sheet of yellow, lined paper. "Example: A kilo of Colombian heroin wholesales for around a hundred grand. That translates to almost three-quarters of a million dollars once it's cut. Some of the smaller cartels have gone back to using mules. They're mostly drug flunkies that put it in their shoes or up their assholes or down their gullets for a few dollars or a fix and get busted on a regular basis coming into the country. Profit per carrier is small on what does get through."

"So, while the Feds are closing the borders and looking for the small-time carriers," I said, "Billy's guys bring it in via this fleet of theirs and rack up a shit-load of money per run?"

"Bingo. What we don't know is if they're middlemen, or the whole fucking bank. If they are then the money doubles. At least," Wes said.

"And your guy thinks this stuff's Colombian," Luke said.

"Geographically, the most obvious. But there's something else that says so, too. Most of the Colombian product is sent to the Northeast: New York City, Newark, Philadelphia. And to Boston. See any connection?"

"You mean like, to Georgie and my brother?"

We looked at each other for a beat. "Yeah, like that. And we might assume to some real muscle given the big city playground. Which tells me maybe y'all should back away from it and let the Feds do what they can on a broader scope."

"Maybe so," I said. "But it's not just our call. We'll talk to our charges. That's a promise. But if they still want to try and open these guys up, we've got to move quickly."

Wes shook his head. "Moving fast is not the most advisable way to start," he cautioned. "It could be suicidal."

"I don't argue that," Luke said. "Only, it's already been set in motion. Billy's boat is due to hit the water again in a few days and somebody's expected to be there when she does."

W̲E GATHERED IN the small confines of the office back at *The Hatch*.

"I doubt that either of you are targets. Not after a year," I said. "You need to think about this carefully."

Sam glanced at Brian. Both looked pale after I'd laid out what we'd discussed with Wes Harland. "But we can't really be sure that we're *not* targets, either," she said.

"No, we can't. But if we go poking around you most certainly will be."

"You don't know what it's like looking over your shoulder every minute. What it's like to be literally scared of your own shadow," Sam said. "*I* do. For all we know they're just waiting to kill me like they did that girl to send a message to someone else."

Luke turned heated eyes on Brian.

Jamie had eased into the office.

"*No*, Luke," Sam said. "I knew damn well there was more. I asked for it. It's not Brian's fault. It's horrible but I finally know what Billy was hiding from me, and why. So now I'm petrified. At this point all that does is make me more determined. They know who I am and who Brian is. We're not safe anywhere."

"Sam, what are you talking ab. . . ?"

It's all Jamie managed before I caught her eye and warned her off.

"We want it to be over," Sam said. "And we need your help."

My thoughts drifted back to the first sunset I'd witnessed from the Careys' deck—to Luke's words about a fucked up world.

I thought about the years spent in New York City; about seemingly important cases and a hundred other meaningless moments that over time become the collected trophies of life.

Wes Harland—the cop, the pro, the voice of reason—had tried to change our minds, but not convincingly. He felt the passion and didn't want the syndicate operating in his waters. Or in any waters, if he could help it.

Sam and Brian were tired of hiding, fearful of what might be around the next corner. And, I suspected, felt they owed it somehow to Billy to even the score.

If I walked away from it, away from my brother, away from the woman he loved, away from his best friend, away from what burned inside me then part of me would be lost forever.

And I didn't much care for the prospect of what would remain.

THREE

Of all men's miseries the bitterest is this, to know so much and to have control over nothing.

—*Herodotus*

CHAPTER 17

IWENT UP TO the third floor and opened the slider, letting the night-breeze drift through our bedroom as if it might help dissipate the anger that filled the air.

Jamie wasn't thrilled that I'd used a visual ax to chop short the question she'd started to ask and had marched out of the office with ice in her eyes. Now she sat at her makeup table combing out her hair, the tension showing on her freshly-scrubbed face.

"What *message* was Sam talking about?"

"Something to convince Billy that he should back off on his decision to quit the syndicate. Something you don't need to hear about."

She scowled at me in the mirror. "Where would you like it, buddy? The nose, or square in the stomach. We don't do that to each other."

"I'm sorry. You're right. We don't." I placed my hands on her shoulders. "So here it is. The syndicate murdered a young lady in front of Billy to make a point."

She stopped her brush in mid-stroke. Her mouth worked for a time but no words came out. "My god, Cage, you can't go through with this."

"It's precisely why we *have* to. You heard what they said down in the office. This isn't living for them."

"But they're *alive*. So are you. And I'd like to keep it that way."

"That's a little dramatic."

"Like hell it is! They *kill* people. Pardon me for being rational here."

"Aren't you the one who told me that this is as much about Sam as it is me? That neither one of us could walk away from it?"

She whipped around. "Don't you *dare* throw that back at me now. I had no idea about this . . . this killing. It changes everything."

"How, for Christ's sake? Sam and Brian are left with no guarantees about living, and Billy's still dead."

"What about *our* future? Where do *we* fit in all this, Cage?"

"This *is* about us—and yeah, okay, about me. By definition, that *means* us."

"Great. Just fucking great." She threw her brush on the table, stormed into the bathroom and slammed the door.

I went down to *The Hatch* and out to the deck where I joined Luke and Brian. I sat heavily in a chair and spun an ashtray so hard that cigarette butts scattered across the table top as if flung from a centrifuge.

"I see *that* went well," Luke said.

I grabbed a towel from a passing waiter and cleaned up the mess. "So now that we've cast the white marbles we'd better damn well figure out a way to flush these fuckers into the open. Pray that Billy left us something on the boat to help our cause."

"She'll be in the water by eleven on Friday. How should we do this?" Brian's question was directed at me.

My mind was still jammed up on Jamie. I passed to Luke.

He reached for a cigarette, slid the ashtray in front of him then snapped the lid of his Zippo open and closed several times as he contemplated the problem. "Brian, how well do they know you at the boat yard?"

"Not well at all. I was there just the one time. And I don't look quite like I did back then."

"You *do* know how to skipper this boat, right?" Luke added.

"Licensed and everything."

"And they're just going let us walk in and *take* it?" I asked.

"I got the itemization when I called to have her made ready," Brian said. "Cashier's check was sent FedEx several days ago."

"We'll need proof of ownership to be on the safe side," Luke said. "A bill-of-sale showin' Cage as the new owner. Different name. Maybe a Groucho moustache and glasses?"

"Nothing's going to happen out there. It's too public," I said.

"That's not the concern, partner. Someone who works there could be watchin' to see who comes to claim her," Luke said. "By design or out of plain curiosity. So here's how she goes . . . ."

My head began to clear as Luke laid out his plan. Jamie would have to deal with this in her own way. "Then going straight in the way you described it sends our own little message, right? *Fuck you*, is what it says."

"And what if they had no idea that the boat was ever there?" Brian asked.

"Then we'll have had ourselves a few hours worth of fun," I said.

Luke finally lit up, taking the smoke deep into his lungs. "And I seriously doubt we'll have another chance before this is all over."

CHAPTER 18

WE HEADED FOR Fort Walton Beach Friday morning. The plan was simple. Luke would drop us at the yard. From there, Brian and I would take the boat inland across Choctawhatchee Bay to Cinco Bayou and rendezvous with Luke at the home of a lawyer buddy of his where we'd be able to search the boat in private. Then it was back across the bay to Destin Harbor where we'd dock, leave the boat and drive back to Panama City Beach.

Brian had been in Destin the day before to make arrangements for a week's mooring and ask around for the captain Billy'd worked for. But Captain Bob, it seemed, had left the harbor a year ago. Pretty much up and vanished and hadn't been heard from since.

We pulled into the boat yard at eleven and came to a stop outside a low building.

"Last chance to bail," Luke said.

"Let's do it," I said.

"I believe those were the words Gary Gilmore spoke just before they popped him," Luke noted.

"Thank you Norman Mailer. I feel so much better now. By the way, I appreciate the name on the paperwork. 'Bentley.' Cute. Billy and I put up with that shit all through high school."

"Next time we'll use 'Rolls' for variety."

"What next time?" I slammed the door.

"Break a leg, partner." Luke pulled away laughing, his tires spinning on the gravel.

"Here goes nothing," I said to Brian as we went in. I felt ridiculous in my concocted disguise consisting of a new white Panama hat, designer shades, Ralph Lauren Polo shirt with the collar turned up and a fat cigar stuck in my face. The get-up, like the name, had been Luke's humorous little idea.

Brian headed for the service department, envelope in hand. A young man behind the counter looked over the bill-of-sale then glanced in my direction and disappeared into an office.

Brian rejoined me. "She isn't launched yet."

My radar clicked on. "Sense anything out of the ordinary?"

"Nope. Boat yards always run late. I told him you were a real pain in the ass and asked him to hurry it up and make my life easier."

The clerk emerged from the office and walked over to us. "Mr. Bentley? I'm Mark. Sorry about the delay."

I champed down on the unlit cigar. "Won't be long, will it?"

"No, sir. She's already by the launch sling if you want to have a look."

Billy's fifty-two foot Hatteras Convertible rested in a cradle thirty yards from where we'd stepped out into the boat yard.

Brian stopped short of the gleaming white hull. For a moment he didn't say anything. "Like looking at a ghost ship. It was Billy's dream. He and Sam talked about living aboard once he'd finished his . . . commitment."

"How much?" I asked without really thinking, then clarified, "The price, I mean."

Besides dying? Oh I don't know, quite a few bucks, I'd guess.

"The way she's equipped, her age and condition? . . . half-million—maybe more."

We went back inside to wait.

Twenty minutes later Mark called from behind the service counter. "Good to go. I'll take you out to the slip."

We followed him across the yard and onto a section of dock with boats moored on both sides where he made the hand-off to a tanned and weathered man of about sixty, thickly built, with gray hair and a cropped beard of the same color that looked tough enough to burnish stainless steel.

"Mr. Bentley," he said, offering a hand with stubby fingers. He spoke with more than a hint of brogue. "I'm Tom Latham, yard foreman. She's a beauty, sir. Be assured that we've set her just so. You'd be takin' her out yerself, then?"

"No, no. I've hired a captain for that."

Brian had hung back a few paces to avoid direct contact with Latham who now looked in his direction.

"My first boat," I added quickly.

Latham's eyes lingered on Brian for a few more seconds, then returned to me. "Well, sir, in time she'll be your favorite lass, bring you great pride and pleasure."

"I'm sure she will."

Tom Latham's eyes wandered over the Gulf for a moment, as if he were awaiting the arrival of a ship long overdue or perhaps one that would never make port. "If you would, sir, there's some paperwork in my office to be gone over. And I'll be needin' a signature."

Latham's office was housed in a square, one-room wooden hut—more an outcropping cantilevered over the water near the gas dock.

Inside, it was damp and smelled of diesel fuel. Cedar clapboard nailed to the outside of exposed studs formed a common interior and exterior wall. Nautical memorabilia hung between the age-darkened two-by-fours. A brass coat rack draped with well-worn foul weather gear stood in one dim corner like a tattered and tarnished scarecrow.

Latham slid into an armless chair behind an old, marred desk and in that simple motion, became part of the room itself, confident in the comfort of his familiar surroundings—wolf and den, lion and lair.

"Please, sir," he said, indicating that I should sit.

I pulled a rickety old ladder-back chair across the worn plank floor and sat down opposite him.

"Shouldn't take but a minute. Now, where *is* that bloody thing?" He surveyed his desktop, then picked up a file folder, opened it and scanned its contents. "Ah, here 'tis. All in order. Yes, sir. All shipshape, as it were." He made no move to hand me any documents to review. Instead, he closed the folder and set it back on the desk with his hands folded on top of it, smiling crookedly in the ambiguous light.

There was something in his scrutiny, in the set of his mouth that caused my own mouth to go dry. It couldn't be happening here, I told myself. Not possible.

The door creaked open at my back. I forced myself not to turn around.

Latham raised his chin and looked over my shoulder. "Aye, what'll it be?"

"That fifty-six Viking Cruiser's due out at two and the port engine's still not running to my satisfaction."

"Okay then. Ask Ron if he'll take Mike off that little Bertram for a time—see what he can do, will ya, Smitty?"

Smitty left without a reply.

Latham's gaze found me again, light retreating from his features as the door was pulled closed behind me. In the dimness I imagined the face of a demented leprechaun. "Now, Mr. . . . Bentley, where were we?"

"The paperwork, Mr. Latham," I said. "Does something seem . . . out of order?"

"No, no, nothing like that, sir." He waited.

"Then perhaps I can sign and be on my way if you don't mind?"

"Oh I don't mind at *all*, sir." Still, he didn't move. "I just think you're bein' a wee bit foolish, Mr. Bentley—doin' what it is you're doin' here."

I leaned my arms on the desk. My heart thumped. "I beg your pardon?"

He held up a hand. "A poor choice of words, those. Let me explain. This boat you've purchased? Well, not to be pryin', but she cost a pretty penny I've no doubt. And yet you don't really *know* her. She's sat here for nigh-on a year. Don't mistake me; we've done all to be sure she's right. But that long out of water, sir. Well, things can happen. Things we can't always *see*."

Now where was he going? "What . . . *things*?"

He either chuckled or sneered; given the lighting and my state of mind I couldn't be sure which.

"Seals, hoses, electronics. Who knows? Boats are like ladies—temperamental under the best of conditions. I just don't want to see something unexpected happen."

"Your concern is touching."

He ignored the comment. "If she'd come out of *my* yard, let's say, or from any upstandin' broker, for that matter, you'd have a history of where she'd been and ya'd know what she'd been through."

I played along—as I though I had a choice. "Your opinion of her, Mr. Latham?"

"She's a real dandy, sir. Top to bottom. Pure as a virgin. Whoever had her treated her right. But you told me this was your first. Guess I was offerin' something for the future. Next time you might not get so lucky." He looked at me intently. "Do you know them, then? The prior owners? We never had the pleasure here."

"No, I don't."

"Your luck's holdin', then."

"I didn't realize I needed any," I said.

He winked. "Oh, but we all do, sir. Take this transaction for instance. Must have been five, maybe six months ago. Couple of gents came callin'. Here to have a look, see if they might want to buy her. Now, *they* brought a surveyor along."

They'd been here. I hung on every word as I began to sweat.

"Not that I was impressed with his work, mind you, him spendin' too much of his time elsewhere and not nearly enough on the essentials, in my opinion. And the gents—why, they seemed to fancy most what was in the cabinets and drawers and the stow-aways."

"What happened?" My question came too quickly.

Latham's eyes narrowed. He let me stew for a long moment "Said she wasn't exactly what they were after, but they'd think on it. They might have bought her. Your luck, you see, is that they didn't."

If Latham was on the wrong side, would he tip me off this way? Or was this a not-so-veiled warning? "You wouldn't happen to remember their names or what they looked like, would you?" It was too obvious. "Never mind," I said. "It doesn't really matter, now does it."

Latham spoke as if he hadn't heard a word I'd said. "They'd been referred by a broker down in Miami, they claimed. Asked for the boat by name. I thought it was a bit odd myself. If that fine craft had been listed somewhere there'd have been a number of inquiries over the past year. And names can be fickle things. Of course, none of that's any business o' *mine*, sir. Their faces I might well recall, tho' I'm not all that good in that department. But the one had lost an argument or had a nasty accident at some point, I'd venture. Porcelain smile that didn't work right. Droop to his right eye. Him, I'd know."

The hair on the back of my neck bristled.

He leaned across the desk. "*That* one, I didn't care for. No, sir. No *respect*, none at all. For the boat, I'm sayin'. Wore his street shoes right up on the decks. And his voice. *Cold*, sir. Cold as a nun's tit. *That* I remember even now. Voices—accents and such—are a specialty of mine, a thing I never forget. Not if I've engaged a person in a conversation of a length. Sort of like those that have tricks to rememberin' a room full of names." His eyes held assurance. "Looks can be changed. But a voice?"

He'd recognized Brian. I had no choice. "A voice for instance like that of the captain waiting out there with my boat?"

Latham's eyes crinkled into slits. "Now that you mention it, sir . . . aye. *Just* like that."

His words hung between us, suspended among the dust particles caught in the knife blades of sun that cut the room's muted light.

He slid the open folder across the desk. "Two signatures by those X's there are all I'll be needin'." He read my look. "Aye, we *could* have done this dockside in a wink. But then, we'd no 'a had our chat." He handed me a pen. "Be careful, sir. There's sharks in these waters."

"I'll be sure to watch where I swim."

I signed the documents with a shaky hand, collected the receipt off the desk and started to fold it. As I did my eye was drawn to the top of the blue paper, to the box marked, NAME OF VESSEL. In it was written, THE FREE SPIRIT. I'd not yet heard the name nor thought to ask what it was.

"The Free Spirit," I said out loud, testing the words that formed a name befitting Billy.

"Fine choice, Mr. Bentley. Fits her much better, don't you think?"

I looked up. "I'm not sure I understand. Fits better than what?"

"Than the name she came in with, sir. The one we were instructed to change at the former owner's request. The name by which those men inquired after her."

I folded the receipt and stuffed it in the pocket of my shorts. "What *was* she called back then, Mr. Latham?"

"Why . . . *Tate's Hell*, sir. Odd name for such a fine boat, wouldn't you say?"

My lungs turned to a vacuum.

In my mind, I saw a flash—then another—in a dark, remote place.

CHAPTER 19

I BOARDED *THE FREE Spirit* and entered the salon where Brian reclined on the white leather couch looking as if his gangly body had been dropped there from above.

I sat opposite him in a matching barrel chair and replayed my conversation with Tom Latham—replayed it for both of us, looking for anything I might have missed as I recounted the scene. I'd been numbed by the moment in Tom's office as a juror might be when the grizzly details of a killing are spoken for the first time in court. A re-reading of testimony in the safe confines of a jury room where the accused murderer's eyes are unable to probe menacingly into your head brings the event into better focus.

"They haven't been back," I said in conclusion. "But if Latham, or someone else is a watchdog they'll know soon enough that we've reclaimed the boat."

"And that I'm here," Brian said. "Maybe Sam, too."

"Maybe. If they don't already. Look Brian, we discussed the possibility of that happening."

He stood up and stretched, then said, "Not a problem. Just thinking out loud."

"Okay, so how does it sound?"

"Does it matter?" he said as he turned and left the salon.

We climbed to the flybridge and prepared to get underway.

Brian started the engines; a rumble passed through *The Free Spirit*. Then the timbre of the idling engines settled into a deep-throated growl.

I took the helm chair next to him.

"Twin seven hundred-twenty horsepower Detroit turbo diesels," Brian said as though I'd asked, his hand resting communally on the throttle handles. "She weighs close to twenty-eight tons. They'll push her through the Gulf at a cruise speed of about twenty- three knots." He finished his check list. "We're about ready. Could you signal down?"

I went to the port side and waved to a dock hand who waited by the stern. He loosened the line from its cleat then disappeared toward the bow. In a few seconds he returned and called up to the flybridge. "All clear, gentlemen. Have a good day."

I waved thanks, hoping, in fact that we'd have *several* good days and went back to sit next to Brian. "All set, skipper. Now how about getting us the hell out of Dodge before the posse shows up."

When we'd cleared the harbor Brian brought the throttles up, putting *The Free Spirit* into a comfortable cruise, like a jockey loping a thoroughbred through a light workout on a fall afternoon.

We headed north into Choctawhatchee Bay and thirty minutes later rounded a point of land and entered the narrows of Cinco Bayou.

A quarter-mile in on the south shore Luke waited at the end of a T-shaped dock that extended into the bayou from a sea-wall built of poured concrete that held back the water from the lawns and gardens of a large estate.

On Brian's instructions I went below, then forward on the starboard side to the bow. When he brought *The Free Spirit* to idle at the dock I snagged the line off the forward tie-pole, made it fast to the deck cleat, then moved aft and repeated the process.

With the engines shut down, Brian set the bow and stern lines as Luke tossed them to him from the dock. Lastly he retrieved a thick yellow power cord from one of the storage lockers in the cockpit and set one end into a receptacle on the boat. He handed the other end to Luke who plugged it into an outlet located on the dock.

With the flick of a switch, *The Free Spirit* hummed back to life courtesy of Gulf Coast Power.

"Nice shack," I said to Luke, looking over his shoulder at the house as he came aboard.

"Nice boat. Feels a little strange, I'll bet."

"More so for Brian," I said.

"How'd it go at the yard?"

"Not sure."

Luke drew on his cigarette and blew twin trails of white smoke out through his nostrils. "How so?"

"Tom Latham. The yard foreman. He had me going pretty good. A lot of double talk. A warning, maybe. Or just curiosity. Whatever it was, we've got to be careful."

"You just figure that out, did ya?" Luke said.

"Don't be a smart ass."

"I'll get Wesley to check him out. What else?"

"Billy renamed the boat."

Luke walked slowly to the stern, looked, then came back and locked eyes with me in silence. "Okay," he said after a moment, "I'll bite. Renamed her from what?"

"Tate's Hell."

"You got to be shittin' me."

"Crowley's little joke."

Luke flipped his cigarette butt into the bayou. "Christ-a-Mighty."

"It's seriously hot in there," Brian said as he emerged from the engine room, wiping beads of sweat that looked like tiny blisters from his forehead. "I'd give it awhile longer."

We'd been over *The Spirit* twice looking for anything that seemed the least bit out of the ordinary but came up empty. I'd thought from the beginning that what I had in mind would probably be below-decks—the closest thing to a basement—but I couldn't be sure.

While we waited for the engines to cool, Luke and I moved off the boat and onto the dock where we sat side-by-side dangling our feet over the water like overgrown clones of Tom Sawyer and Huck Finn.

"So we have the boat. Hurray for us," I said.

Luke chuckled. "Sorta like the damn dog that caught the friggin' car."

I picked at a splinter of dock wood lodged in my palm. "That about says it."

"Patience, partner. We're not careful, the next thing we chase might just up and run us over."

I squinted against the sun as I looked at Luke. "What the hell have we done, Luke? Just who do we think we are? No, better yet, who the *fuck* do I think *I* am?"

The room was barely large enough to accommodate more than one of us at a time with any comfort let alone the freedom to move about easily. Since I knew best what to look for, I went in first. The cramped space was still sweltering; within seconds my shirt stuck to me like a thin sheet of dark, melted plastic.

As kids Billy and I had our secrets, and our secret place. The overhead pipes and ducts in the basement of our house provided the perfect environment in which to build and hide a safe to stash our treasures: a stale pack of Camels; rubbers we'd bought from a vending machine in the men's room of a gas station; M-80's and Cherry Bombs from trips through the Carolinas; and our two copies of *Playboy*—'Tit Mags' in our slang—the *T-mags* referenced on the list Brian had retrieved from Billy's gear.

I began probing the various nooks and crannies looking over, around, and under the variety of pipes and wires and assorted junction boxes and fittings.

Something was here. I was sure of it. But five minutes of head-banging, knee-bruising search revealed nothing and I had the growing feeling that whatever might have been here had already been removed by the wrong people. The idea was as suffocating as the room itself.

Luke stuck his head through the door. "Anything?"

I straightened too fast from a crouch and smacked my head painfully. "Nothing."

"How about if I give it a try?" Brian said, leaning in. He stripped off his shirt and took my place in the sweat box.

I watched from the doorway as he went over the territory I'd already surveyed.

"Cage, squeeze back in here with me," Brian said after a few minutes search.

I squeezed.

He pointed to part of the overhead that was lower by some eight inches than the rest and joined at the forward bulkhead. It ran aft for about two feet and spanned the width of the room.

"So?" I asked.

"I don't think it's original. The fiberglass is close, but not exact. And it's faced in teak—a little fancy for an engine room. And this placard . . . ." he said as he pointed to a five by ten inch sign that read: *Warning: Blowers On Before Starting Engines.*

"You blow the engine room out as a precaution. There's a reminder up top at the helm. The one in the engine room is usually riveted next to the starter switches. Could be this whole part of the overhead was added after she was built. Funny that I never noticed it before—or did, but never thought about it." He opened a tool box and extracted a screwdriver. "Let's see what we've got."

Although six screws were visible only two actually held the plate in place; the others were fake heads allowing for quick access in just a few seconds. Behind the plate was the recessed dial of a combination lock with a small lever next to it.

"Well I'll be goddamned," I said.

"Now all we need is the combination," Brian said.

"Try four . . . fourteen . . . seventy-seven."

"His birth date?"

"He used it on everything from bike locks, to his football locker in high school."

Brian turned the dial as I repeated the numbers.

The lock gave on the second try with a *click*. He pulled the lever and the front of the rectangular section of the overhead dropped about an inch. Brian looked at me in anticipation.

"Be my guest," I said.

It took a few seconds to determine how the catches held; finally he popped them simultaneously and the section dropped slowly open to a forty-five degree angle on the type of slim black pistons used on the glass half of SUV tailgates.

The first thing my eyes rested on were the guns: a 9mm semi-automatic pistol and a short-barreled twelve-gauge pump shotgun with a pistol grip.

Brian read my question. "They're damn near mandatory. Modern day pirates. I'm sure you've heard the stories."

And not a bad idea if you run drugs for a living, either.

I blotted out the thought and turned my attention back to the drop-safe. The interior was lined with a foam material with custom compartments cut into it. One held the weapons securely in place. Three others held aluminum containers.

I removed the one on the left, set it down on the engine room floor and flipped open the latch, revealing, by my count, fifty-thousand dollars in banded bundles of one hundred dollar bills.

"Escape fund," Brian said.

"Might have been."

He removed the center box and handed it to me. I placed it on the floor next to its twin. This one held a collection of important papers—everything from Billy's passport and birth certificate to the documentation papers for the boat, to a copy of his will. And a small black sack.

I removed the leather drawstring pouch and carefully emptied the contents onto the floor. Our mother's diamond engagement ring emerged first followed by some of the coins our father had collected. A sapphire tie pin was next, then a pair of jade earrings. Last was another, smaller cloth bag that held an old gold pocket watch that had been handed down to our father from his father. I remembered the display Grandpa would make out of removing that watch from the pocket of his cardigan sweater when we'd ask the time—something we often did as a small boys just to see the revered timepiece and the way Grandpa handled it.

I held the watch now like a talisman, wishing there was a way to turn back time. That given a few more minutes of thought, Billy might have made a different decision.

I slipped the keepsakes back into the bag and set it aside with a sudden sadness that originated in a place and time in life that I could no longer visit, one that awaited my return on a day in the future I could not predict.

Brian handed me the last of the containers.

I'd never thought of Billy as the sentimental type. He was embarrassed by overt displays of affection and waved off acts of love or kindness on his part as nothing special. But the third box taught me something about my brother that he'd kept to himself besides his troubles. Something that I might have seen had I bothered to look. It lent testament to a drunken night in Boston when the Royce Brothers had kicked some serious ass.

"What are they?" Brian asked.

I thumbed the thick stack of envelopes and folded sheets of paper. "Letters. Must be every one he ever received that meant anything to him."

"You boys takin' a snooze in there?" Luke bellowed as he crammed his body through the doorway and into the stingy space. I heard a thud. "God*damn*! This place is made for midgets," he said, rubbing the top of his head. He stopped short. "Slick. What's in it besides the arsenal?"

"Cash, papers, some personal items . . . and a stack of private letters."

And newspaper clippings. A collection of words and pictures that captured the athletic achievements of my high school days. Of these, I said nothing.

"Any of it of any use?"

I sat back on my haunches. "Depends on how you'd spend fifty-thousand. The jewelry's not bad either," I said with a healthy measure of rancor.

"Chill out, Cage. We're on your side here."

"It's just that I was hoping there'd be more."

Luke found a paper bag in the galley. I emptied the letters into it along with the cash and the small sack that held the watch, coins, and jewelry, then added the papers from the first box.

The guns I left secured where they were; Jamie is not a big fan of household artillery. She's heard too many sad stories from too many broken-hearted siblings and parents seeking understanding of what went wrong at playtime.

I returned the containers to their spaces, closed the safe and replaced the small plaque. I was completely frustrated.

And totally unaware that for the past year, Billy's secret place had held what was to be the key to the syndicate—our link, locked away in a box we'd exhumed from the dark hold of his boat like a coffin dredged from the earth.

CHAPTER 20

BRIAN COACHED ME through the maneuvers that cleared the dock, turned us into the bayou and brought *The Free Spirit* out to Choctawhatchee Bay for a southeast crossing to Destin Harbor. I felt like a kid learning to drive a car with soft tires and too much power-steering.

"The key is to think ahead to where you want to be, not concentrate on where you are," Brian said with encouragement.

Prophetic words that in time were to have life-altering application to issues far more important than piloting *The Spirit*.

Our passage settled into a soothing combination of senses— the tangy smell of salt air, the piercing clarity of the October seascape, the engines' throaty exhaust mixed with the sound of rolling water as it fell away from the hull in tumescent, blue-white waves.

I relinquished the helm to Brian and turned to the rail behind me, facing west. The late afternoon sky was a rich deep blue, the sun lowering, taking on the illusion of growing in size, of moving nearer the earth. It was all so placid—so perfect.

Without Billy, so goddamned empty.

A change in the engines' speed brought me back to the helm. A short distance ahead I saw the Route 98 bridge as it spanned the East Pass. Traffic streamed across like ants on the march.

Brian piloted *The Spirit* through the channel and into Destin Harbor, then docked her in a slip, stern-first.

Luke was waiting to meet us. He secured the lines then came aboard.

I said that it had been a long day and we ought to be getting back to the Beach. But that was only part of it. The bigger issue was with Jamie, in finding a way to break down the emotional barrier that was building like a wall between us one stone at a time.

Luke rubbed a hand along the stern rail, his eyes set on the Gulf beyond the harbor. "I 'spose. But long as we're here, let's nose around a bit first. Go on up to the Café and have a beer. Ask an innocent question or two about Billy, about the boat—whatever."

I checked my watch. What would a few minutes change? "Why not. Hell, at this point what can it hurt?"

We walked past the circular bar in the conical, high-ceilinged lounge and went to the back where we selected a table that looked over the harbor below and the dock where *The Free Spirit* sat at her moorings in the early evening, still as a picture.

A cute young waitress with flirtatious eyes and a pretty mouth with upturned corners chatted freely as she took our drink order, lingering at Brian's elbow as she did.

"By land or by sea?" Deanne—her name according to her badge—asked.

"The watery highway, young lady," Luke said.

"I *love* boats. One of the big ones in the harbor?" This she addressed to Brian who stole a glance in my direction.

"Not as big as some," he said. "She's fifty-two feet."

"That's *big* where I come from." Deanne moved to the window, pulling Brian off his stool by the hand. "Point her out for me."

"Fourth slip to the left of that big sail boat with the black hull," he said.

Deanne tapped out the count on the glass with a manicured nail. "She's gorgeous! Yours?"

Brian looked at me for help. "Brian's the captain," I said.

"Then I guess that you're the owner?"

"That's reasonably accurate."

"What's her name?"

"The Free Spirit," I said.

She held on to Brian's hand for an extra moment then started for the bar. "Describes me perfectly. Be right back with your cocktails."

"I was you, I might just stay on the boat tonight," Luke said to Brian.

"Speaking of which," I said, "if I don't call Jamie and let her know that everything's okay, *I'll* be the one staying aboard. Alone."

I headed toward the alcove between the bar and restaurant, called Jamie on my cell then went into the men's room where I stepped to one of the urinals and unzipped.

I heard the door open behind me.

I held eyes-forward as a large shape moved into my peripheral vision to stand at the urinal next to me. His shoulders were square to the wall but his head was turned in my direction. His breath reeked of whiskey and cigarettes. I shifted my eyes slightly.

"That's right fuckwad, it's me." He was weaving uncertainly as he spoke, pissing who knew where. "Drain that minnow of yours motherfucker and let's have at it. I've waited a long time for this."

"I beg your pardon? Did you say something?"

He continued to stare, jowls reddened with anger. He was my height, heavier, beyond his prime, muscle buried under a layer of fat but there nonetheless. Without another word he shot a hand out and knocked the forgotten Panama Hat off my head and onto the floor.

I zipped up and flushed. Reason first, I told myself as the initial hit of adrenaline raced through my system. "Look. I don't know what your problem is, but—"

He grunted as he threw a round-house right.

I leaned out of range.

His fist smashed into the tile in front of my face.

I stepped back, spun and pinned him against the wall with my weight, forearm pressed against his neck, grabbed his damaged hand and yanked it up behind his back as far as I could, grinding the bone that had shattered beneath the brass knuckles he was wearing.

"*Christ!*" he managed through clenched teeth. I worked his hand harder. "All *right* . . .okay already. Fuck!"

I eased off but held him with his left hand trapped between his body and the urinal. "Why don't you tell me what this is all about, friend."

"Why don't you bite me instead."

He pushed hard against me, trying to free himself. I let up just enough for him to believe he had a chance then shoved him back against the wall. His head impacted with a thud and his knees went rubbery. He snorted a burst of air through his now-broken nose, sending out a spray of blood. His body language told me his will to fight was gone.

"Let's try it again," I said, tweaking his hand. "What's your fucking problem?"

Resignation. "Shit . . . don't. Aren't you that—?"

The door smacked open. Luke walked into the men's room and assessed the situation. "What's all the fuss about?"

"I believe I was just about to hear the answer to that," I said.

"I'll handle it. The skipper's already aboard. I'll join you when I'm finished here."

When I stood back the drunk tried to bolt. Luke caught him in the middle of the chest with an open hand and propelled him backward with a force that sent him crashing into the wall near the toilet stall.

"Go on, now," Luke said to me. "I'll be along shortly."

Brian sat at the dinette table opposite the galley, his right hand wrapped in a towel full of ice. I slid in next to him. "What happened?"

"Two guys at the bar had been eyeing you pretty good. Luke noticed it. When the one tracked you to the men's room Luke told me to walk the other one outside and keep him there until he brought his friend out. We get to the parking lot, the dude makes a comment about my earring and takes a swing at me. So, I dropped him. That's about the size of . . . ."

"Interesting," Luke said as he came aboard and into the galley. "Seems the two gents hired the boat that Billy crewed when he worked out here. They come down from Birmingham twice a year. Chartered it for the whole day but Billy cut 'em short. The big one got boozed up and out of control. Your brother rode him pretty hard all the way in. They tried to find the same boat again next trip, but couldn't. Then they saw you, Cage. Little help from the booze and they mistook you for Billy—and, pow, payback time."

"And *you* said . . . ?"

"Neither confirmed nor denied it. Said I didn't give a winged-shit who he thought you were but if he sees you again, it might be best to go the other way on account of I might not stop you next time. Or go so easy on him myself."

A thought had been banging around in the back of my brain like a ping pong ball in a metal box since I'd first met Sam. For a second, she'd seen Billy standing there, not his look-alike brother. Now this guy reacts the same way. "Do you know what would be really interesting? What would be *really* interesting is if Billy wasn't dead," I said.

Luke looked at me strangely, as though he thought that I was about to lose it—or already had.

"Humor me here. Just hear me out, okay?"

"Whatever you say, partner."

"Okay. So what if Billy got away from Crowley—something Crowley hid from the syndicate to save his own ass. Everything after that, including the article in the paper about Billy's body being discovered could have been a deception."

"And why would the authorities make up a story about—?"

"Because when Billy got out on bail you urged him to tell Wes what he'd been up to and the trouble he was facing. Said you'd cut him a deal: if Billy'd talk, the cops would cover him with the story of his murder and give him the time he needed to disappear along with Sam and Brian."

"He agreed. The story was planted in the paper. But Wes pressed too hard. He wanted to move too quickly. So Billy balked. Sam and Brian were rattled enough as it was, so they bolted."

I had Luke's attention. "Alright," he said. "I'll play along—for argument's sake. But why would Billy come back *here* after he'd gotten clear of them?"

I thought it over. "Because a year in hiding and jumping at shadows drove everyone nuts. Because they could be around the corner, waiting. Billy figured he could make peace with the syndicate because of his friendship with Georgie. He'd get the word out that he wanted to make a deal—recant what he'd told Wes about working for someone else and take the fall in exchange for Sam and Brian's safety. If that didn't work he'd threaten to blow everything wide open. It was all dictated and witnessed.

"If they agreed they'd be the ones to realize the biggest gain: Billy would be in jail for a good stint, and Sam and Brian would keep quiet to stay alive."

Luke gave the idea a moment of consideration. "I think you're crazy. I also think you're on to somethin'. They're gonna hear enough as it is to maybe wonder a bit. Might just push their buttons enough to flush 'em out."

He was right. A story about the men's room fight would make its way around the Destin waterfront—drinker to drinker, boat to boat. Embellished of course.

Add that to the appearance Brian and I had made at the boat yard.

Billy Royce? Back in town?

Could be.

With that idea, docking the re-named *Tate's Hell* in plain view, announcing that she was in fact *The Free Spirit* and was available for curious eyes became central to making contact with the syndicate. And for now, that was the primary goal.

I dug out my Blackberry and entered the number printed on the copy of the work order I'd signed. Tom Latham, good guy or bad, had cast himself as a key player.

Two rings and I had him on the line. I was matter-of-fact. "My captain says it's nothing serious. Some little vibration I can't even feel. But he's anal, and hell, this chunk of plastic cost plenty and I got to thinking about what you said . . . you know, about things happening with her being in dry dock for so long."

"Anything's wrong, Mr. Bentley, ya got my word we'll make it right."

"Great. We're going to hang around here in Destin for a few days. See if it goes away or gets worse or whatever. Thought I'd check now and see if we'd need to set an appointment to bring her in if we have to."

"Just call and let me know that y'er on the way."

We closed up *The Free Spirit*, leaving a small light on in the salon and some empty beer cans in the cockpit giving the impression that we'd be returning later, then climbed the stairs and came around to the parking lot.

Deanne was waiting with my pretentious Panama hanging on the tip of one finger. She set the hat on my head. "Hope nobody peed on it," she giggled.

"What a lovely thought," I said.

Luke swung the Jeep around and stopped a few feet away.

"Thanks for the big tip!" Deanne said, not moving from Brian's side.

I walked to the car.

Deanne and Brian stood talking quietly.

Luke tapped the horn.

Deanne raised up on her toes and kissed Brian on his cheek, then glided back toward the café door.

About five miles beyond Sandestin, Route 98 had been narrowed from four lanes to two for nearly three miles, traffic re-routed into an alley-like, head-on corridor that we'd passed through earlier on the way to the harbor. The westbound lanes were in the process of being repaved.

From where we were located to the outskirts of Panama City Beach several miles ahead, the population was exploding, the road bisected by widely spaced intersections that segmented commercial mini-malls and residential developments with cute little names into evenly spaced strips. For long stretches the pavement ran straight as a ruler, dotted here and there by what remained of once-dense stands of pine trees and a ground cover of scrub palm.

The headlights of LuAnn's Jeep bathed the empty road ahead in yellowed light.

Brian sat quietly in the back seat.

Luke hummed along with a vaguely familiar Reba McIntyre song about tail lights fading in the dark, and her broken heart.

I closed my eyes, leaned back against the headrest and began to drift among partially formed thoughts, images of Billy floating behind my lids like smoke on a windy day..

And then Reba stopped singing. Luke's voice took her place. "I think we got ourselves a problem, boys."

I sat up quickly. Luke's eyes were fixed on the rearview mirror. The Jeep was filled with light. There was a vehicle twenty yards behind us, its high beams blazing.

"Been closin' on us for the last half mile," Luke said as he accelerated the Jeep to seventy from the work zone mandated forty-five.

Our tailgaters did the same.

He slowed to thirty-five; the other vehicle dropped its speed as well. Luke stepped on the gas until we reached sixty-five and held it there. The vehicle following us matched the speed while maintaining a twenty yard gap between us.

Suddenly the headlights veered to the left. The vehicle started to pass then slowed and pulled even with the Jeep. It was a dark-colored Suburban with heavily tinted windows.

"Christ," Luke muttered. "This is all we need."

The Suburban dropped back in behind us.

Luke moved the Jeep up to eighty. "Best bet's to beat 'em back to the four-lane. They got any firepower we're in shit up to our waders."

We hit ninety. Orange-striped barrier barrels whipped by us in a blur inches from my window. We caught an RV within a quarter of a mile. The headlights of a vehicle in the opposing lane shone in the distance.

The Suburban couldn't have been more then ten feet off our rear bumper when Luke pulled out to pass the motor home at the last possible moment.

Our pursuers stayed glued to our tail.

Once safely by the RV Luke started to cut back in, but the Suburban beat him to it and trapped our Jeep in the wrong lane.

The oncoming vehicle bore down on us, lights flashing frantically, air horn blasting. It was a truck. By the sound of it, a big one.

"God*damn!*" Luke yelled. "Hold on!" He pulled the wheel to the left and careened through several of the rubber construction barrels and into the grass along the shoulder of the road. Dirt and gravel splattered against the underside of the Jeep as he fought for control.

A semi blew by us with the sound and concussion of a muffled cannon shot.

Luke skidded the Jeep to a stop. By then the Suburban was nowhere in sight.

My heart rate dropped back into the countable range. "That would have been ugly."

"There's a truth," Luke said, pulling back onto the blacktop, knocking two more barrels onto their sides in the process. "Might want to keep this part of the day to ourselves, gentlemen."

JAMIE AND SAM were at the Careys' house when we arrived. Out on the deck, the cool of the evening air mixed in uneven currents with the heat emanating from the outdoor fireplace. We'd circled our chairs like campers about to tell ghost stories. I had a good one to share—about just how close we'd come to being reduced to a tangled mass of steel, blood and bone—but recited my deceptive fairytale instead.

Jamie hated my idea. Plain and simple. "What if they already know about you, Cage? About The Hatch? What if they decide to check up on you in New York and you're not there? If Billy *were* alive, don't you think they'd figure he'd try to reach you, or that he might have *been* with you for the last year?"

"All good points. Assuming they knew Billy had a brother. Anyway, it doesn't make all that much difference. We're only trying to raise some doubt. We don't have to be totally convincing."

"Then why this made up story about wanting to make a deal?" she persisted.

"Latham recognized Brian, but never met Billy. If he asks someone he'll get a description of Billy that fits Cage," Luke said. "We need something plausible to offer if they run our flank."

Jamie huffed. "You make it sound like a war maneuver, Luke."

Luke shrugged. "Call it what you will."

"What about the boat?" Sam asked.

"We'll give it a few days in Destin then move her," I said.

"Move her where?" she asked.

"Over to St. Andrews Marina," I said. "If the syndicate doesn't show in Destin, chances are that's where they'll be given what you've told us."

Sam drew her feet onto the chair and wrapped her arms protectively around her knees. "It's too dangerous there. Way too creepy. Think of something else. Please."

"Sam's right," Luke said. "Treasure Island Marina on Grand Lagoon's where she was when Billy bought her. It'll do fine."

We finished a late dinner of grilled steaks with little more said on the subject, then said goodnight to Luke and LuAnn and headed for *The Hatch*. Sam and Brian walked the beach thirty yards ahead of us. I suspected the slow pace Jamie set came with a purpose.

"Luke's pushing too hard."

"This was my idea, Jamie, not his. If anyone fucked up, it was me."

"Did he try to talk you out of it? Because I sure would have." She stopped and turned to me. "Why do I get the feeling you think this is some kind of a game? That if you get in over your head, it's Luke to the rescue and everything has a happy ending."

"Why do you feel you have to constantly try and bring him down. Maybe it's *me* you're really mad at and it's easier to project that anger on Luke."

"So now you're an analyst, too?"

"It rubs off."

She glared at me. "I'm frightened. I have a right to be. This isn't like you. You're not . . . ."

"I'm not what, Jamie? Go ahead and say it."

"I don't know. Something's different, that's all. And I think somehow Luke's the one behind it."

"Like I'm the little perfect kid whose mommy doesn't want him playing with the neighborhood bad boy? Please. If I'm different," I said, "it's because of Billy's death. Luke's a friend to both of us."

"That doesn't mean I have to like everything about the man, does it?"

"No, it doesn't. Or about me either, as far as that goes," I said. "But you can trust him as much as you do me. That is, assuming you still do."

"Don't fish for reassurance. I can be pissed off as well as afraid at the same time and still love and trust you."

"Nice to know. Anyway, maybe you're right. Maybe he is pushing a bit. Maybe he has his own ghosts to contend with."

Jamie's expression changed. "You asked him, didn't you."

"Yeah. I asked." I took her hand and told her about Luke's sister as we strolled the beach toward home.

When I'd finished, we walked the rest of the way in silent thought to the sound of waves lapping against the shore, then receding in long sighs as though they meant to carry the weight of the ages out to sea.

CHAPTER 21

B Y ONE IN the morning the crowd at *The Hatch* had thinned. The last of the crew offered to handle the stragglers and lock up. The night manager said I looked tired. And I was. Dead tired. Tired in ways I'd never experienced. Tired to the point where I felt as though small weights had been hung on my bones like ornaments on a tree, but without any joy or anticipation. Still, I doubted that an easy night's sleep lay ahead of me.

Jamie said goodnight and went up to bed. I stayed and tended the outside bar, drew a few beers and chatted with a pair of regulars I knew would stretch our conversation to the two o'clock closing without the need for more than a dozen words on my part. I mixed myself a wicked Margarita in the process. Then another, this one with the best tequila in the house poured in even greater measure.

By the time the last tab was closed out I'd managed to construct a mighty fine buzz, one that morphed into the constant whirring of a thousand insects as I closed up.

I refilled my glass one more time and began to drain my feelings along with the tequila into the pit of self-pity until they slipped all the way down the slimy slope to wallow in the muck that lay on the bottom. I was drunk and getting drunker, my thoughts heavy, macabre, old memories tainted with self-loathing at the mistakes I'd made in my life. Pissed off at the things I'd missed or had simply been too self-absorbed to see or care much about.

On some lesser level of intoxication, my plunge into spontaneous depression would be recognized for what it was—

more fakery than fact—a pathetic little jig on the dance floor of unhappiness and insecurity set to the tune of woe-is-me. But at the moment there was too much perverse enjoyment to be had in playing the profound loser to consider it. Which only called for more alcohol.

Oh, what a bucket of shit and misfortune has been dumped upon Brother Cage's head! Let us gather together in song and lift his downtrodden spirits unto the Heavens! Salvation and forgiveness shall be his! Can I get an Amen? Well, can I? Come on people, how about ONE FUCKING AMEN!

And then the world spun crazily on its axis and I lay down on the deck and closed my eyes.

Just for a moment . . . .

. . . only to see . . .

a truck bearing down on Billy who lay on the road tied hand and foot as in an old silent movie. When the truck had passed, there he was again, this time lying on a metal table, white as powder, eyes glowing with a greenish light, face stitched together with thick black thread. I tried to shake myself awake, but it was too late; I fell deeper into the grip of my dream . . . .

. . . *where Billy wasn't my brother at all, but a ghoulish distortion, a caricature of Tom Latham.*

I was on a bus painted in rainbow colors and covered in shamrocks.

Latham got on and sat in the driver's seat.

I began to walk down the aisle, but his bowed leg blocked my path. "You want to play, sir, then you've got to pay."

Jamie and Luke sat in the back and didn't see me even though I called to them.

Brian and Sam waved at me from their seats, then plunged needles into their arms and laughed.

The door opened, and a burly figure with no face appeared.

I yelled to Jamie to get down as a spray of bullets began tearing into the seats. Windows shattered all around me.

Then Latham exploded in a shower of gore, and there was only darkness.

WHEN I CAME to, it was first light. I was shivering, covered in both dew and sweat. My body ached as if all the fluid had been drained from my joints, my head pounding to the point where I actually braced myself for an explosion as I dragged myself up onto my hands and knees. With great effort I drew myself erect, stumbled into *The Hatch* and made my way up the stairs and into our bedroom.

A sliver of morning light fell diagonally across Jamie, covering the curve of her hip like a white silk scarf as she lay on her side. I reached out to touch her but missed and fell to the floor with a thud that was accompanied by no apparent sensation.

"Jesus Christ," Jamie said.

I turned my face upward toward the sound of her voice, brain sloshing with the sudden movement. "Wha— What time is it?" My mouth was dry and clicked as I spoke.

"Five-thirty."

I propped myself up on my elbows. "Good morning, my love."

"When you sober up you're going to wish you were dead," she said—or at least that's what I thought I heard.

"Billy . . . Latham . . . they . . . he blew up, they . . . ." In my head the words sounded hollow and weak, as if I were speaking from inside a bottle. Then a pillow landed on my head. Followed by a blanket.

WHEN I NEXT opened my eyes, I was still on the floor, the glow of the room signaling that the sun was on the rise.

I put the time at around seven as I sat up and waited for all the mental cogs to mesh, then struggled to my feet and went to the sliding doors, pulling them open.

Voices rose from the deck below; the sun was on the other side of the sky from where it should have been. It would appear that I'd slept away the entire day.

I showered and dressed with great effort, then went down the stairs and into *The Hatch*. Jamie was at the bar drawing a pitcher of beer.

"So how do you feel?" she asked with a noticeable lack of caring.

"What the hell was that all about? I don't *get* drunk."

"Well, cross it off your list of things to do 'cause you were. Thought I'd let you sleep it off and wake up on your own. By the way, you said some *very* weird things in your sleep."

"Drunken stupor, to be exact. And I don't remember," I said, although the nightmare I'd had about Billy was as sharp as a carving knife. "You don't look particularly happy with me, dear."

"And I should be?"

"No, I suppose not." Then a thought snapped into focus. "Where are Sam and Brian?"

"They went out to the boat," Jamie said, picking up a towel and wiping the bar hard enough to wear a hole in the copper.

"I don't know if that was such a good idea."

"I don't think you were in a position to judge much of anything. Anyway, he thought it might be best if it didn't look, you know, like it was just dumped there. It's Saturday, lots of people around. I'm sure they'll be fine."

"Back when if I may ask?"

"Before dark, they said."

I reached across the bar top and took her hand. "I'm sorry about all this. I know it's hard on you."

The tension went out of her. "On both of us. We'll get through it; I know that. It's just— It's just that I don't know what we'll find on the other side." She laid her fingertips on my cheek. "Now go eat something. Try a big Coke while you're at it. You look like absolute hell."

As I finished my life-saving hangover lunch--a big greasy burger and a double order of fries--Luke showed up.

"Back among the livin', I see."

"Barely. Don't let me near a gun. How'd you know?"

"Call from Jamie. She came lookin' for your sorry ass in the middle of the night. Found you out cold on the deck and couldn't get a response."

"And you said . . .?"

"Leave you right where you were. You'd come around eventually and the mess would be much easier to wash off the deck than the carpet."

"Swell. All heart. Anyhow, the food helped." I pushed back from the table and stood up, wiping what I hoped was the last of the cold sweats off my forehead with my napkin . "Might as well start going through Billy's letters. *That* I can do sitting down. And it requires no sharp instruments."

"Thought you and Jamie woulda already done that," Luke said.

"It's personal stuff. I don't really know who might have written him what. Lady friends, for instance."

"Do the same for me, would ya?"

"You have a secret box of some kind?" I asked.

"Not since LuAnn I don't."

***

MOST OF THE letters were from family; those I sorted by the return addresses. I divided the rest in two and handed a stack to Luke. Some were in envelopes, others weren't.

We read just enough to disqualify each one, looking for anything related to drugs, the syndicate, or the boat.

Thirty minutes later we were finished. Nothing.

"Might be what you were meant to find was the money and the jewelry," Luke said.

"You're probably right. What the hell did I think we'd find? Names and addresses, home phone numbers for all of Billy's drug pals? Shit."

Jamie came into the office to check our progress. She picked up one of the three stacks of letters I'd secured with rubber bands and set aside from the others. "What are these?"

"Rejects. Old family stuff. Nothing of value."

"You didn't look through them?"

"What's the point?" I said. "It's all ancient history. They have nothing to do with this unless Billy's career was a lot longer than Sam thought."

"The point *is*, if he took the time to hide the letters in his safe, don't you think it's possible that he might have hidden something else *in* the letters?" She patted the top of my head. "I believe you've succeeded in damaging more than a few brain cells, buddy" she said as she left.

I found it in the last stack between the pages of an old letter from our Grandmother Royce.

I held the single-page like a scroll of priceless parchment and read aloud:

My Dear Billy,

I would share these words with you in person, but the failing health of my beloved Lillian and my weakened mind dictate otherwise.

What I have committed is an act of treachery. If I could undo what has been done, I would. But greed touched us both, and I chose the only path of peace available to me. So, a lesson: remember always that a pact with the devil is by nature filled with deceit.

I have no regard nor hope remaining for my own life, in a very real way, a comfort. And certainly of no concern to you. What <u>is</u> of concern, my dear boy, is that you understand the nature of your predicament. What was promised should now be due. However, such shall not be the case.

These are the vilest of people, Billy. Their ship is tightly run; the monetary rewards, as you know, significant; the exit, as you have discovered, solely at their whim. Perhaps now you have your answer to the question of the peculiar name of my last command, and your first.

To ask your forgiveness for allowing you to be swept in with such empty promises sounds frivolous to my own ears, so I shall not insult you further. Instead, I pass on the request that you hold dear your own life and those of the ones you love and with God's help find a way to brook this insanity.

May you one day find peace.

Your servant in time,

Cpt. Tobias R. Tate, III (Retired)

CHAPTER 22

JAMIE WAS BEHIND the bar when I came out of the office and handed her Tate's letter.

"How could he stand by and let Billy be *trapped* like that?" she said after she'd finished reading it.

"It took both of them to make the deal happen."

"And what do you suppose he means about having no regard for his life—and this stuff about his employer?"

"That's for Tate to answer when we find him," I said.

"But there's no envelope with a return address."

"We'll find him."

Jamie frowned. "So, somehow you do. Then what? Force it out of him? Use a sad old man to help avenge Billy's—?" She stopped herself. "I'm sorry. That's not fair. It's just that he seems so remorseful. Not at all like a hardened criminal."

"I doubt he was—or is. No more than Billy was. So if we get to him and he balks we'll walk away—wait for them to show themselves. If they haven't already."

BY EIGHT THAT evening Brian and Sam hadn't returned; a call on the land line to *The Spirit* went unanswered. Jamie was worried. So was I and didn't try to hide it from her.

I picked Luke up at his place and headed for Destin.

The reflected glow from the dock lamps and the lights from the windows of the buildings above the harbor swam on the surface of the black water like scattered schools of illuminated fish as Luke and I descended the stairs.

Most of the boats were buttoned up; some sent the muted sounds of music and laughter floating softly out across the harbor like an echo from happier times.

A wash of light fell across the aft-section of *The Free Spirit*, painting the hull in monochromatic gradations from gray-black to stark-white.

We stopped twenty feet short of the slip looking for movement or any signs of life. She appeared deserted.

We walked to the transom door, opened it and stepped into the cockpit. The salon door was closed but unlocked.

Except for the low hum emanating from the refrigerator in the galley and the ticking of the maritime clock the interior felt as still as a crypt. I strained to hear or detect anything out of the ordinary. "Brian?" I called out tentatively. "Sam?" Louder this time.

There was no response.

I started forward toward the galley then stopped dead, as if I'd run into an invisible partition.

"Wha—?"

I raised my hand to cut Luke off. The walkway where I stood separated the galley on my right from the dinette booth on my left, then continued forward and became a passageway where four steps led down to the three staterooms and two heads. I'd heard a faint click, like the set of a lock. I mouthed the word *below* to Luke, at the same time pointing in that direction to be sure he got the message.

"What is it?" he whispered.

"Door closed," I whispered back, then tilted my head from one side to the other, checking the two staterooms that opened on each side of the passageway. The third was all the way forward and in the shadowy light that was cast down into the gloom, I could see that all the doors were shut. I thought of the weapons in the overhead safe in the engine room.

Luke tapped me on the shoulder. I jumped. He was smiling.

"What the *hell* are you—?"

He pointed to the dinette bench that faced toward the bow of the boat. My eyes followed his finger, the tension draining from my body. There sat a woman's purse and a name tag, and beneath the table a pair of small black flats. Luke and I back-pedaled into the salon.

"Figure we should just leave?" I asked.

"I think that would be the—"

"Hey there." Deanne greeted us in a sleepy Southern accent as she came up the steps and into the galley wearing a white Polo shirt that reached to her knees, the short-sleeves hanging almost to her wrists. "Wow, did *we* zonk out," she said as she walked into the salon, flicked on a lamp and collapsed into the leather barrel chair. She pulled the shirt over her knees and squinted at the brass clock. "Quarter to *nine*? Yikes!"

"Sorry about the intrusion," I said.

"No, no . . . it's a good thing you hollered. I've gotta be at work in half an hour. We were gonna all get up and go back to my place around six and get something to eat. And Brian said something about calling you. Then, out like a light."

"We'll just see him later."

"Don't be silly." Deanne sprang out of the chair. "I'll go roust him."

Brian came up the passageway a minute later, a lazy grin on his sleep-lined face. "Sorry, guys. I turned the phone off. Not very responsible on my part. I'm not making apologies for Deanne. But it's no excuse not to think."

"Can't argue that," Luke said. "We strolled in here like a couple hunters at a boxed-bird shoot. Coulda been someone not near as nice as us."

Brian walked to the salon door and looked out into the night. "We had a stranger stop by today. This afternoon around two-thirty. He was looking for the boat."

Spiders wearing track shoes made their way up my spine.

"A freelance mechanic. Hispanic, maybe, but no accent. Nice enough. Introduced himself as Carlos. Said he does part-time work at some of the yards—including the one where The Spirit spent the last year. He comes around Destin on a regular basis. Said if I ever needed anything done that didn't require a trip back out there he'd be happy to take care of it. I said I'd keep it in mind. That was it."

"Nothing that raised any concern?" I asked.

"Maybe, maybe not. It's hard for me to say, the frame of mind I'm in. But, no, I don't think so."

Deanne reappeared, her hair damp and combed straight back. She retrieved her shoes from under the dinette table and gathered up her purse. "Time to go make my fortune." She turned to Brian. "And you I'll see . . . ?"

"I'll call you tomorrow," he said.

A quick kiss and she was off.

Brian watched as she walked down the dock and began climbing the stairs to the café.

"Anything else about this guy that you can recall?" I asked.

"Forget it. He was fine—just hustling. You get these guys all the time around the marinas. Most of them are second-rate auto mechanics that the yards won't hire."

Maybe, I thought. If he was telling the truth Tom Latham would know him. Then again maybe old Tom had been the one who'd sent this Carlos to check up on us in the first place. I'd feel better after I had a chat with the little Scotsman.

"So where's Sam?" Luke asked.

"She went for a walk—you know, left the boat to Deanne and me. Tapped on our door when she got back and said she was gonna take a nap."

"Better get her up," I said. "We need to get going. Jamie's been a little concerned."

I went down the passageway and knocked on the port stateroom door. "Sam. It's Cage. Rise and shine."

No reply. I knocked again. "Sam?"

I opened the door a crack. The bunk had been slept in but was now empty. On a chance I checked the forward berth.

Empty.

Same with the head.

We split up and went in different directions.

A half hour of searching the docks, area shops, bars and restaurants netted nothing.

When I returned to *The Spirit*, Brian and Luke were standing in the cockpit. "Anything?" I called from thirty feet away.

"Nothing," Luke said.

Then as I closed the distance, something caught my eye—a silhouette in the pilot's seat up on the flybridge.

"Topside!" I shouted, then sprinted to the boat.

Luke bolted for the ladder; Brian scrambled up behind him; I hurdled the transom and followed Brian to the bridge.

It was a scene from a horror movie but all too real. Sam was bound to the chair. A ligature encircled her neck. A red silk scarf. Duct tape sealed her mouth.

I tore the adhesive from her lips, saw the flash of Luke's knife as he quickly cut the ligature and the ropes that held her fast.

In an instant she was free; I dragged her down onto the deck.

Luke stepped in beside me and bent over to breathe air into her lungs, leaned on her chest and compressed her heart. Again and again he breathed and pushed, breathed and pushed, breathed and pushed until sweat dripped from his forehead.

I stared in disbelief.

It was no use. Luke sat back on his heels. A rush of air hissed through his clenched teeth. "They will die for this, goddamnit," he growled. "I swear it."

Brian dropped to the deck and lifted Sam's lifeless body into his arms and rocked her.

Tears blinded me as I stripped off my jacket. I knelt beside Sam and gently coaxed Brian away, then covered her face and laid her gently back down onto the deck.

This was *my* fault. If only I'd left it alone . . . if only I hadn't gotten stinking drunk . . . if I'd watched out instead for you, Sam. I looked at Luke. "No more. It's over."

"It sickens me no end," he said, "and I share the blame for this. But it's too late, partner. What's done is done. It's gone too far now. No free passes. What matters from here on out is that we find these bastards before someone else dies." He cast saddened eyes on Sam's body, then hard eyes on me. "Are we clear on this?"

I could only nod, unable to speak another word.

"Alright, then. They'll sit tight for awhile, see what we do. Wait for the story on Sam's death," Luke said, his face without expression. "It'll give'em a better line on the chance of Billy havin' returned from the dead. So, we wait 'em out. Make 'em sweat. No headlines. No story of any kind. We don't have much choice if we're to find Sam's killer." He bent down on one knee and took Sam's limp and lifeless hand in his. "Forgive us, darlin'," he whispered, his words as dry and cracked as old paint. "Christ-a-Mighty, I am so sorry."

I knew then what had to be done. I called Jamie and told her everything was fine—that we had a few things to do and not to wait up. We'd be late. I had no idea what I'd say to her about Sam when I had to face her. None at all.

Luke called Wes and told him where to meet us.

***

IT WAS AFTER eleven when Brian throttled up the *Free Spirit* and headed west across the bay running at cruise speed. No other boats were in sight; no one had followed.

We tied off the lines at the home of Luke's friend on Cinco Bayou where we'd been only days before.

I carried Sam's body off the boat as a loving father would a sleeping child, silently begging my brother for forgiveness with each heavy step.

Wes's eyes flashed in the darkness. "Jesus, no," he said.

The night air had turned to acid in my lungs. "Her name is Sam. She was Billy's girl."

He lowered his head. "Oh, man."

"We can't let them skate," Luke said. "We need your help, Chief. We need whatever time we can buy."

"Luke, take the bricks out of your skull. I'm an officer of the law."

"There's no other way, Wesley. We're boxed in now."

Wes Harland—police officer, friend, now potential co-conspirator—shook his head slowly as if simultaneously refusing and committing to the same idea. "So I break every covenant legal and holy. Then what? What happens if you strike out. Or worse?"

"As far as it's gone, I don't see that it really matters," I said.

His eyes fixed on Sam's body. Then he turned to Luke. "I let friendship and emotion cloud my judgment. Let you two go off like a couple of rookies on my watch and this is what happens. My fault as much as anybody's. I'll take care of it. And answer for it later."

"Let's hope that's not necessary," Luke said.

Wes took the lifeless form of Samantha Graham and cradled her in his massive arms. "There's always that, right? When there's nothing else left, there's always hope."

CHAPTER 23

IABANDONED ANY PRETEXT of sleep and rose with the flat gray hue that precedes true sunrise, eased out of bed like a thief stealing time without waking Jamie, without having to tell her about Sam, then jogged east on the tide-pack past shuttered condos and nearly-vacant motels. The beach was as empty as a desert island, as lifeless as the void in my soul. My mind ached as thoughts of Sam slammed against my brain with each step.

A mile of sand passed beneath my feet as I relived the previous night, my thoughts at some point interrupted by an eerie sensation that I was no longer alone.

I glanced over my shoulder. The outline of a running man was cast out of the gloom a hundred yards behind me.

I forced myself to wait a full minute then looked again.

He'd cut the distance by half.

Lady in Red.

To my right lay the Gulf; to my left and three hundred yards ahead, a cluster of houses—the nearest spot where I could veer off and run the streets and lose myself down an alley if I wanted or needed to.

I'm paranoid, I told myself as my pulse raced. If I started reading things that didn't exist into every situation I'd go nuts, or do something stupid.

Lady in Red. Do you guys know that song?

A quarter mile further on I made a decision, cut a wide loop and headed back in the direction I'd come.

My terms, fucker. Let's do this.

The runner was there, holding his course along the water's edge. If neither of us changed our line we'd pass shoulder to shoulder.

Thirty yards. His head was covered by a towel that shaded his face like a boxer doing road work.

Ten yards. He dropped his chin and moved slightly to his right.

We closed to within feet, then passed each other, neither of us breaking stride.

"Morning," I forced out.

"Buenos dias," he mumbled. "Never saw you looking so good as you did last night."

It took five more paces for my mind to process fully what I'd heard. I stopped dead and spun around.

No accent when he spoke English.

He was facing me from twenty yards away.

I took a single step forward, then spun suddenly and took off after him.

He darted quickly to his left and ran full out, scrambled up the low dunes and disappeared before I made it to the street.

I climbed the stairs to the deck of *The Hatch*, heart pounding, vapor rising from my body like steam from an iron in the chill morning air. I plunked down into a chair and watched a line of pelicans glide by without effort fifty feet above the water line.

Brian walked out onto the deck from the kitchen. He swallowed coffee as if there were rocks in his throat. "Tell me this isn't real. Tell me Sam's not dead."

"I saw him. I tried to get to him but I lost him. I wanted to beat him to death. Would have."

"Saw *who*?"

"He mocked me—mocked Sam, for Christ's sake. I passed him on the beach. I believe you met him yesterday at the dock in Destin."

"The mechanic? Carlos?"

"The sonofabitch is marking his ground."

Brian walked to the deck rail. The morning light imbued life into the flat water as if breath had returned to a cadaver and a blush had begun to appear on its cheeks. "They could have killed the three of us on the boat. And you this morning."

"They could have tried, you mean."

"Then why didn't they?"

"I don't know. But you can bet they have their reasons."

Brian flicked a dried piece of birdshit off the rail. "We might as well walk into six lanes of traffic blindfolded. About the same chance of staying alive."

I showered, then slid back into bed, the knowledge of Sam's death a suffocating iron yoke fastened around my chest.

Jamie was awake. She rolled on her side and reached for me playfully.

My rebuff was gentle; my words—the simple truth—were not. "Jamie, look at me. There's no other way to say this. Sam was murdered last night."

She stared at me without blinking or breathing, her body going rigid turning cold where it touched mine. I reached for her hand but she snatched it away as if my fingers were tipped with fangs.

I searched for something to say.

"Don't tell me you're sorry. Don't tell me *anything* except that you'll give up this craziness." She broke down in deep sobs that shook her body.

"We can't turn back, " I said.

"You *won't* is what you mean." She sat up and wiped at her eyes. "I don't know who you are anymore. I can't stay here. I can't be part of this any longer. I can't watch you destroy yourself over Billy's mistakes. I can't . . . watch . . . you . . . destroy . . . *us*."

I offered no defense, "Go to Boston," I said. "Spend some time with your aunt. Come back when it's over."

She searched my face in silence, tears streaming from her eyes. "If it ever is. If it really ever is. And I don't see how that can ever be."

Jamie packed carelessly, material things no longer seeming to have value.

I tossed a few things into her suitcase that I thought she might need, then called Wes and asked him to arrange to have a deputy take Jamie to the airport and see her safely on a plane.

He didn't ask why I'd made the request.

A deputy arrived a few minutes later.

I held the door for Jamie as she slid listlessly into the front seat of the unmarked patrol car.

"Please understand. I . . . I just can't take any more right now."

I kissed her cheek. "Go. I understand."

The truth was, it was a relief to have Jamie out of the syndicate's reach. Had I plotted to drive her away from danger, it couldn't have been easier. Gosh, all it took was a little help from Sam. Christ. What degree of emotional distance now stood between Jamie and me? I wondered when or if I would one day learn the pain of its full measure.

"You okay?" Wes asked after the deputy had pulled out onto Front Beach Road.

"Sure. All that's missing is a bullet in my head," I said.

Brian left for Destin. We wanted *The Spirit* out of the harbor—wanted to keep *us* on the move and the syndicate off balance. He'd decided to take Deanne on a day-cruise along the coast then anchor or port somewhere overnight where no one could find them.

Wes and I went inside and sat by the windows where I could watch the beach, as if I expected Carlos to come up for breakfast and apologize for his actions.

"No last name?" Wes asked.

"Yeah. Dead," I said.

"You're a laugh riot."

"Then why aren't you smiling?"

He glared at me, his eyes clearly conveying the seriousness of his thoughts. "Carlos. That's it?"

"That's it," I said.

"Where's this letter Luke told me about?"

I got it from the office.

Wes read it twice.

"Find him—if he's alive—and you'll have a good chance to turn him. Especially when he hears what happened to Sam."

"Finding him is going to be a problem," I said.

"Not as tough as you might think," Wes said.

"Right. After he unloaded the boat on Billy he probably went off and crawled—"

"In a hole? Why? You don't think they'd keep a line on him? And according to what he writes here he's got a sick wife. That means medical care. And at his age he's got social security payments coming—not that I think he needs the money. But the government has this thing about mailing checks." Wes tapped his fingers on the table. "Let me think on it. I've got people. We'll track him down." He handed the letter back to me. "Don't go making things harder than they already are. Now about this

Carlos. He might be the killer, but someone else is pulling the strings. Time to make Latham play his hand. If he was warning you off, the question becomes why? And from which direction?"

I called Tom at the boatyard and asked for a meeting.

Was it about the boat? Latham asked. Were the vibrations worse?

Yeah, I said, the vibrations I was feeling had become *much* worse.

WE MET AT a burger joint halfway between Panama City Beach and Fort Walton. It was neutral ground, nice and public, a place that was always crowded. This time I skipped the hat and cigar. Instead, I told him that I had people who knew where I was going.

The pronouncement elicited a crooked little smile.

"Mr. Latham, let's cut the shit and get to the point. Do you know who I am?"

"Why . . . you mean there might be more beyond who you *say* you are?"

"Don't get cute. You know something about the boat—about its history. And you recognized my captain."

He stirred cream into his coffee. "Aye. No sense in denying that much. Things are not right. Someone's up to no good."

"Gee whiz, how observant."

His eyes sparkled and his mouth turned up at the corners. "*Now* who's the cute one, Mr. Bentley? Perhaps a bit more respect would help ya in gettin' what it is y'er after, sir. And clearly y'er after *somethin'*."

I leaned back from the table and studied his face. "The simple fact is I need your help. And you know it. So, tell me why you're here—what it is *you're* after, Mr. Latham?"

"Freedom, sir."

"From what, if I may ask?"

His expression darkened as though my question had taken him back to a black hole in his history that he'd rather avoid. "Ask ye' may, but it'll do ya' no good now."

"What won't?"

He chuckled. "To be mindin' y'er own business, sir. Bit late for that, though, isn't it."

I waited him out.

"To the point, then. Money, Mr. Bentley. It'll do us both a measure of good."

I sank back in the chair. Money. And why not? Money had been the root of the whole ugly mess, hadn't it? Everything reduced to its simplest form. "How much?"

"Twenty thousand."

"Ten."

The leprechaun grinned. "Don't be a fool. I could *double* the price and you'd pay." He started to rise from the table.

"Twenty, then . Just . . . please, sit down."

He hesitated, then sat. "Aye, sir. But I won't be doin' it twice."

"You'll have it tomorrow. But I need whatever it is you can tell me *now*. And I need your eyes on the inside."

"Now it's trust ya want from me, is it?"

"You'll *get* your money, Mr. Latham. On that, you have my word. But how do I know you're not playing both sides? How do I know that whatever you tell me is fact?. Or worth anything at all? That you won't sell me out?"

"You don't, sir." Latham studied a scratch on the surface of the table, running a truncated finger back and forth over its length. Finally he looked up. "Truth be known, yours is the second request for my able assistance." His eyes took on a different cast. "But the odds are in your favor, lad. Ya see, when

I was a young one my family moved to Chicago. My father joined the ranks of law enforcement. I followed the tradition. The rest were all girls.

"He lived to retire and pass at a respectable old age. But there was all manner of crime back then too, and too many didn't. Truth be known, Mr. Bentley, I was simply in no mood for dyin'. I quit the force and took to workin' the freighters that came and went on the Big Lake. From that day my father showed me no respect. He thought me a coward, although he never used the word. It's haunted me all these years, wonderin' how he might be lookin' down on me for my failings."

He leaned in toward the table and lowered his voice. "I've made my choice, lad. I'm old and I've got a disease and there's a graveyard in the Empire I've been wantin' to visit for years. Now's my chance. I'll play fairly. I'm judgin' that you'll do the same." For a moment his attention returned to the marred table top. Then his eyes caught mine in an icy hold. "Them, I'm not so sure about. They may pay me no mind, but I can't risk it." He straightened in his chair. "Tomorrow will be fine for the money, lad. Fine indeed. But I'll put what I'm about to tell ya on the tab and sleep better for it."

Latham said he had become curious about the boat—why no one came for it.

"No trick at all to findin' who owned her," he said, "long as some fancy trail of corporate names hadn't been used, that is. Documentation. Simple check of the number.

"I learned she'd recently changed hands, so it seemed even stranger to me that she'd been put up so soon, particularly as she was licensed for commercial charter. And there was the fact that most of the work that was ordered didn't need doin', if you ask me.

"So I dug a bit deeper, checked around with some of me mates along the coast, never sayin' she was here, of course. I wasn't in search of trouble."

"And what did you find out?"

He looked at me with surprise. "Then, you don't—Ah . . . but of *course* you do."

"I'd like to hear it from you," I said.

"Aye. Well, sir, the young lad what owned her turned up dead, robbed and murdered by one of his own deck-hands no less. The killer himself—a local boy—died of a drug overdose not long after. Stole the money to feed his habit. Happens all too often nowadays. People killin' and stealin' for the sake of an unholy addiction. Sad is what it is."

"Then you must have discovered who it was that sold the boat to this . . . young lad. For every buyer, Mr. Latham, there's a seller."

"That's the thing, sir. As I said, 'tis a simple matter when the ownership's clear. But the trail was covered. Came up a charter company no one in my acquaintance ever heard of—one that led to a post office box in St. Petersburg." He leaned back, chin resting on thick, steepled fingers. "Before we go further, could I inquire as to your interest in this, Mr. . . . Bentley? Police, or private?"

"Private—*intensely* private. But I suspect you already know that."

He nodded. "And what precisely have ya in mind for me to be doin' about it?"

I asked if he knew anyone at the yard by the name of Carlos.

He said he hadn't heard the name; but that didn't mean he wasn't an employee. Part-time turnover was high and the mechanics worked in shifts.

"I'll snoop around a bit in the personnel files. Might be it was a lucky guess, or the process of elimination, but somehow the others found the boat a while back, now didn't they? They never sat well with me. No sir, not at all."

I rose to leave. "I'll have the money delivered to your office by courier, Mr. Latham." I wrote my cell phone number on a napkin and handed it to him. "Call me when you have something."

"I'll do that, laddie." As he stood, a groan escaped his lips and a hand went involuntarily to his stomach. Then he staggered, nearly falling.

I reached out to steady him.

He waved me off. Then he was hit with another jolt of pain. This time he took my arm as we walked outside.

"Tom?"

He let out a deep sigh. "It'll pass, lad. At least today it will." Then a grin that would make the blood of a young child run cold came to his lips. "And this number?"

"What about it?" I asked.

"See that you're still around to answer when I call."

CHAPTER 24

THE PHONE RANG at six a.m. Monday morning. It was Jamie; she'd arrived without a problem; her aunt was happy to see her and had a thousand questions about us and our life in Florida.

Her uncle was out of town on business; she and her aunt were flying to Nantucket for the day.

I said again how sorry I was, how I was at fault—how saddened I was about Sam.

She'd said little more other than she'd call me in the evening.

It all seemed stilted. I wondered again if she'd ever look at us the same way after what had happened.

I HEARD FROM TOM Latham in mid-morning.

"There's nonesuch a mechanic, sir. There's not a shred of paper on him over in the office, and no one I talked to in the shop ever heard of the lad."

"He's an intermediary, then. Someone else on the inside who's not going to show his face is feeding out information."

The simple truth was that it might have been Tom all along. I had no way of knowing. But if it had been, then as he'd said, he'd made his choice and that was all that mattered.

"I've laid a bit 'a chum around the yard, like I'd somethin' to share with this Carlos. If it falls on the right ears, I suspect he'll be in touch. He'll get nothing by phone, you understand— face-to-face it'll have to be. For a fee, of course . . . that is, if you don't mind?"

"Credibility."

"Aye. You're a quick study. I'll let you know if the shark takes the bait."

I left the office with Luke late that afternoon and went to the police station at Wes's request. He'd sounded more than a touch wound. He was in his office wearing dark blue warm-ups and riding a stationary bike—a new addition to the cramped room.

"Some kid come steal the other wheel while you were in the can?" Luke asked.

Wes looked as if he'd been sprayed with a garden hose. "Funny." In another minute the timer buzzed. He dismounted and snatched up a towel and vigorously wiped his face and neck.

"What happened to the gym?" Luke asked.

"Damn desk time is what."

"Latham says Carlos is a ghost," I said.

"Bo Crowley all over again," Wes said. "They won't keep Carlos around long before he gets himself a dirt nap. If they've got deeper eyes in place, then I was wrong. They're still runnin' an operation around here. They'll guard it like a pit bull." He rubbed his hands over his face. "Step it up, boys— and I do mean *now*."

"And just how are we supposed to do that?" I asked.

Wes downed a full bottle of water then tossed the empty plastic container into the basket. "Bay Medical had Tate's wife's records. Cancer. Some oncologist in Jupiter wrote for her file last year. I got his name and called a guy who works that part of the coast. Confidential kind of guy, if you get my drift."

"I get it."

"Good. And you understand that all this has to stay off the record, right?" He paused and shook his head slowly as if he'd just remembered the answer to a simple question. "Of course you do. What the hell am I going on about. Anyway, he found an address—tracked Medicare claims through a source."

Wes snatched a slip of paper off his desk and handed it to me.

"It's your best shot. So for Christ's sake, don't blow it. Get down there and make the man sing for you. I don't know how gentle I'd be about it either if it comes to that. They're not gonna stop until they figure out why you're runnin' this sham of yours and then pick whatever time and place suits their fancy to dance on your heads." He stripped off his sweatshirt and started for the door, his torso looking as if it had been chiseled from hard coal. "Now let me go soak my head under the shower and get back to work before I come to my senses and call in the cavalry."

W HEN I GOT back to *The Hatch*, it was late afternoon. Brian was out on the deck.

Sunset in the Panhandle comes early in the fall, the cool sharpness of the air and the clear colors of the crystalline sky seemingly that of some other state less associated with searing heat and stifling humidity.

I changed to jeans and a heavy sweater then joined him, bringing along a full tray of extra dry martinis.

The overhead heater threw off a warmth that descended only as far as the table leaving my lower body feeling as if it were wrapped in a wet compress.

"How was the cruise?" I asked, relieved to see him sitting across from me. Where was Carlos? Had he seen Brian and Deanne as they boarded the *Free Spirit*? Watched as they left Destin Harbor Sunday afternoon? Noted their return today?

"Deanne couldn't stop talking about Sam. She thinks the two of them would make great friends. I had all I could do to hold it together. I said Sam would call in the next day or so, if you can believe that. I feel like I have spikes driven into my head." He drained his glass in one long gulp. "Anyway,

I moved The Spirit over to the Treasure Island Marina like you asked."

I watched as the colors in the sky thickened and spread across the clouds. "Carlos is a go-between," I said. "Tom's making a run at finding the main contact. I've got to trust him. I'll check with him in the morning before Luke and I leave for the airport and see if he connected."

"Airport?" Brian's brow furrowed as though the word were unfamiliar to him.

"Tate. We have an address."

"No shit! That's great. What do you want me to do?"

I took a healthy sip of martini then warned myself against a repeat performance. "I want you to keep your head down. Take another cruise with Deanne. A long one. Sitting targets make me nervous."

Brian stabbed his finger at an olive, dunking it again each time it resurfaced. "I wish I could take it all back— change it in a way that no one would get hurt. Bring back Billy and Sam."

"So do I," I said. "So do I."

I LAY IN BED, caught in the strange time warp between sleep and consciousness so that when the phone rang I was unclear as to what I'd heard.

I cleared my head with some difficulty, and answered it.

It was Jamie.

"He's here, Cage. That creep is right *here*!"

"Easy, babe. *Who's* there?"

"My cousin, that's who!"

"The one who—?"

"Yeah. *That* one."

I fought my way through the last of the spider webs that clung to my senses and came fully awake. "If he so much as *looks* at you—"

"He doesn't know that I'm here. It's a big house. My aunt told me. She's going to help me get out of here before he finds out."

"*Help* you? Why don't you just leave on your own?"

"It's not that easy. It's my uncle. He wants me to stay."

Jamie and her aunt had returned from Nantucket late in the evening. A driver was there to meet them at the airport. Michael Monahan's personal valet.

The unexpected greeting annoyed her aunt, or made her nervous. Jamie was unsure which. Perhaps, she thought, it was both.

"Thank you, John," her aunt said to the driver, "but I do not recall ordering a car. Jamie and I are quite capable of—"

"Yes, ma'am," John said as he looked at them in the rearview mirror. "Mr. Monahan thought you might be tired from your trip. He assumed you'd have gone shopping and sent me to help with the packages."

"How . . . thoughtful of him. But as you can see, we haven't any."

John glanced over his shoulder and smiled. "Yes ma'am. I noticed."

He drove to the house on Beacon Hill, swung the long black Cadillac through the remote controlled gates and passed under the side portico, then parked at the service entrance.

John held the rear door open for Jamie and her aunt. "Mr. Monahan has guests and wishes not to be disturbed just now," he explained.

"Mr. Monahan is out of town, John."

"Not any longer, ma'am."

Jamie and her aunt went in through the kitchen.

"Now there's a fine how-do-you-do," her aunt remarked. "You come all this way from Florida and your uncle can't set business aside for one minute to welcome you home."

"It's okay, Aunt Giselle. I'll see him tomorrow."

Her aunt laid a hand with skin as thin and fragile as fine china on Jamie's forearm. "Well, he'll have a piece of my mind all the same. Would you like some tea, dear?"

"No, thanks," Jamie said. "Actually, bed sounds good right now."

Jamie kissed her aunt goodnight then took the back elevator to her room on the fourth floor.

She showered, put on the robe and slippers that the maid had laid out on the bed, then went to the desk to get her cell phone to call me. As she did she heard the sound of angry voices rising up through the heat vent at her feet.

Although she couldn't make out the words, she knew there were two people arguing. One voice belonged to her uncle; it took a few minutes of listening before she was sure of the other.

It was her cousin.

Hearing his voice after all these years repulsed her, made her feel watery inside and caused her to involuntarily clutch her arms high around her breasts. She was startled by her own protective reaction, by the fear that had so easily returned from a place in her mind that had seemingly reached reconciliation but now, apparently, one over which she had no control.

Still, curiosity got the best of her. She got down on all fours and turned her ear to the vent.

The argument was escalating; they were shouting at each other now. She thought she heard her own name scattered among the blistering words.

Jamie listened more intently.

There it was again, spoken by her cousin in a tone of scalding accusation.

Now she became truly frightened. Why should they be arguing over her? Was it because she was in the house? Or was it over something that happened years ago? Whatever it was she wanted badly to leave, to come home.

As she started to get up, the house phone rang. At first, she was afraid to answer it.

"Jamie? Are you there?" It was her aunt. She spoke in a near whisper.

"Aunt Giselle?"

"Yes, dear. I imagine you can hear them all the way up in your room, can't you."

"What's going on? Why are they—?"

"Listen to me closely. I want you to turn off your light and lock the door to the hallway. Come down the back stairs to my room. You'll sleep with me tonight. Something's happened. I'm not sure what, exactly, but your cousin is in grave disfavor with your uncle. They've said horrible things to each other—things that I can't repeat.

"In the morning, I'll call the service and have you taken to Logan after your uncle leaves for his office. He wants you here, Jamie. For several days at least. And I don't think that's such a good idea."

"But why would he want me to—?"

"Hurry, dear, before they're through and one of them sees you." Her aunt hung up.

She threw together her suitcase and made her way down the stairs to her aunt's room. Then she called me.

Jamie was near tears, something that rarely happened and put me further on guard.

"I don't even know what *plane* I'll be on. My aunt doesn't think I should make reservations. She's worried that someone might check and find out."

I spoke evenly. "When you get on your flight, call Wes. Give him the airline and the time you'll arrive. He'll meet you. Luke and I are going after Tate. I hate that I can't be there for you but we're running out of time."

"Okay. And, Cage . . . ?"

"What, babe?"

"I just . . . I just love you, that's all."

"Come home. I'll meet you here as soon as I can. Everything will work out. You'll see."

CHAPTER 25

I CALLED THE YARD at seven the next morning looking for Latham. The answering machine said he was out but if I wished, I could leave a message. I didn't.

Next I called Wes and told him to expect Jamie's call.

"Quick trip," he said.

"Something happened—something not so good. Keep a close eye on her will you?"

"No sweat."

Luke showed up at seven-fifteen. Our plane was at eight fifty-five, arriving West Palm Beach at one-thirty.

Changing planes in Atlanta meant an hour layover. I tried Latham again but he wasn't in. It was almost ten-thirty.

I called my office.

No message there.

I had a bad sense.

We touched down at Palm Beach International at one-thirty.

Twenty minutes later we were heading north on Interstate 95. Low banks of dark clouds blew in off the Atlantic like a herd of mastodons on the run, sending intermittent sheets of rain across the highway, buffeting the rental car and cutting visibility.

Luke squinted through the spray on the windshield while I checked the directions Wes had given us.

"Two more exits," I said. "706 East. Jupiter—Indiantown Road."

Twelve miles further up the highway, we saw the sign. A mile after that we exited and drove east toward the Atlantic

Ocean for ten minutes through heavy traffic, turned north on U.S. 1 then cruised by the entrance to the townhouse complex that was home to Captain and Mrs. Tobias R. Tate, III.

A security guardhouse stood at the end of a landscaped drive a hundred feet back from the highway. Tate's unit, we'd been told, was in the section adjacent to a marina that provided direct access to the Intracoastal Waterway and the Jupiter Inlet.

Wes's investigator had confirmed that the Tates were in residence by calling then claiming a wrong number when a man had answered.

"The old Captain just can't stay away from the briny deep, now can he," Luke said.

We circled back south, pulled into the deserted lot of a public beach and parked under a towering pine. The rain intensified, striking the hood and roof of the car in loud splats as if an artery in the tree over our heads had been severed.

Luke called the Tates' condo and did the wrong number bit. The old man was home.

"So, what do you think?"

"I'm worried about Jamie."

"She'll be fine. Wesley'll see to it." He drummed the wheel with the fingers of both hands. "I mean, are you up for this? You don't look so good."

"I don't get off on roughing up senior citizens with sick wives."

"Not the plan. But don't expect an invitation to tea, either. Too late for that."

We'd noted several realtor signs stuck into the ground at the entrance and reasoned that the guard would be used to prospective buyers coming and going and wasn't about to stand out in the rain and ask for identification. Even so Luke left the wipers on high, throwing water in the guard's direction as he rolled down

his window saying, "real estate office" while pointing toward
the sign visible on a building ahead on the right.

The guard waved us through.

We parked at the realty office and walked several yards
back to the section of attached townhouses that fronted on
the marina.

Tate's unit was near the far end.

"Keep your face turned away from the door until after it's
opened," Luke reminded me. "Lookin' through one of those fish
eyes? . . . *I* might even believe that the dead had come back to
life. We don't want him havin' a damn heart attack before he
unlocks it." He pulled out a black leather ID holder from his
pocket as we approached the townhouse. He read the question
in my eyes. "Prop. People tend to pay attention when the cops
come callin'."

"Super. Impersonating a police officer. That'll sit well with
the Florida Bar."

"You really think that'll be the worst of it if any 'a this ever
comes out?"

I didn't have to answer.

Luke rang the bell while I stood in the rain looking in the
opposite direction. I heard the door open and then a man's voice.

"Yes?"

"Tobias Tate?" Luke asked.

"That's correct. Something I can do for you, officer?"

"Detective. And yes sir, there is."

At the sound of Tate's voice I'd involuntarily turned toward
the door. It was open less than a foot. Beyond it was the shadowed
face of the man who'd played a part in my brother's death.

Tate's eyes met mine with a look of astonishment.

Luke saw it happen and nudged the door open.

Tate backed up until he hit the wall behind him. His knees buckled and he sank slowly to the floor as if his legs were melting columns of ice. He was wide-eyed and staring at me, his cheeks as red as ripe tomatoes. His body heaved with the labor of rapid breathing and when he tried to speak, he managed to produce only unintelligible groans and whimpers.

Luke glared at me as he knelt beside him and laid a hand on his hunched shoulder. "Easy, Captain, we're not here to hurt you. This man is Billy Royce's brother, sir. We know about most things that happened. We're just lookin' for answers to some others."

His light green slacks began to darken at his groin.

"Cage," Luke said, "give me a hand with the Captain here, would you?"

I squatted down next to Luke. "Come on, sir, let's get you to your feet."

Tate winced as though my hand had burned through his shirt where I grasped his upper arm. He stood unsteadily for a moment, supported on either side by two men he didn't know, his face streaked with tears, his own waste running down his leg.

Then remarkably, he straightened and freed himself from our grip and ran his hands back through his gray hair. When he spoke his voice was deep and sure. "Gentlemen. If you'll excuse me for a moment? Please, have a seat. I'll return shortly. You caught me quite by . . . surprise, shall we say?" He moved toward the stairs, head erect and ascended to the floor above without a backward glance.

Luke followed closely behind.

In a few moments I heard the sound of a shower running. And then singing, a kind of chant that brought back memories of the hymns I'd heard as a young boy but whose meanings were lost on an inattentive child who wished hard to be anywhere other than church.

Something didn't make sense.

I walked into the living room and sat on a floral-patterned couch.

The rear of the high-ceilinged room was a wall of glass that looked out over the marina where a variety of expensive power yachts and sail boats sat like useless toys in the rain.

Tate came down the stairs a few minutes later. He'd changed to fresh clothes and bore a look of confidence in his eyes—and something else I couldn't quite put a name to.

Something I *felt* more than saw.

Luke was a few steps behind him. He came over and sat next to me on the sofa. "He's an officer," he said quietly, "Navy. Most likely he'll ignore what just occurred. So will we. Just so you know, his wife's upstairs. She's dead."

We stood as Tate walked toward a chair that was obviously his favorite: On the small table next to it sat his pipe stand and humidor, reading glasses and a large glass ashtray.

"At ease, gentlemen, at ease," he said, lowering himself into the leather recliner. He selected a pipe from the rack with much consideration, added tobacco from the polished wood box and tamped the bowl as he spoke. "How's the ship, Billy boy?"

The hairs on the back of my neck stood at attention. I shot Luke a glance and saw his quick nod. My mouth felt full of sand. "The ship? The . . . ship. Ah, fine, sir, just fine."

"Never thought she'd end up in the command of a *ghost*, but then she's not the first and won't be the last, I imagine. Quite a fraternity there when you think about it. Centuries of lost sailors. I'm honored that you've chosen to pay me a visit." He lit the pipe with a silver lighter and drew the smoke in deeply. His eyes lost focus and he began to hum a nonsense tune.

The stillness in the room and the sound of his humming seemed to widen and grow as the realization of his mental state gained proportion.

He came around again. "Nasty bit of business you went through as I understand it, Captain Royce. Nasty. But that's all behind you now. Yes. All in the past."

"Captain?" Luke said. "Sir, we've come to ask for your help."

That seemed to capture his interest. He cast his eyes on Luke as if he'd only now become aware of his presence in the room. "I see. And you are . . .?"

Luke hesitated, looking to me to continue.

Tate's sanity, or what remained of it seemed tenuous at best. I felt as if we were walking along the rim of a deep canyon peering uneasily over the edge. One misstep and down we'd go. And we might not get him back if we lost him. *Think*, Royce. "Sir, ah, this is my . . . my escort. Yes, my escort—the gatekeeper to the other side. To the Lost Fleet, sir. I've asked him to accompany me here today."

"Yes, yes, of course. And what is it you wish of me?"

"Sir, I'd like to find the enemy and square things. I'm counting on your help." I produced the letter he'd written to Billy and handed it to him.

Tate read intently, his mouth working in silence as if he were straining to break a cipher. Then he looked up at me and nodded.

I began to breathe again. "Sir, the problem is that we've been unable to discover the enemy's port," I said.

He leaned forward. "For years I was held as a prisoner of war. They thought they'd turned me. But all the time, I was a spy. Oh, I kept their secrets, all right—carried out their missions. But I had them fooled. I kept records, don't you know. All carefully coded, of course."

"Records, sir?" Luke asked.

"*Detailed* records. Times, dates, coordinates—names as well when they were careless enough to use them. It's all in my private journal, you see, secured in my quarters. But, until . . . ." He faltered and his eyes dimmed. "Until Lillian . . . until Mrs. Tate . . . ." He sat back, lost to us for a moment.

"Captain?" I prompted.

"I'm sorry. You were saying . . . ?"

"Mrs. Tate, Captain. You were speaking of Mrs. Tate. And your journal."

He stood and paced. "Yes. Mrs. Tate."

"Captain," Luke said. "Mrs. Tate has . . . passed on, sir."

"Yes. As the gatekeeper, you'd know."

"I do, sir. And I'm sorry."

"Only a short time ago, as I recall. And now you see, now . . . well, now . . . ." He went blank, sat again and re-lit his pipe.

"Now, sir," I said, "now we can move against the enemy. Find our peace. Both of us can."

His mind worked to process my words, assembling them in whatever order it chose while his face slackened.

When he next spoke, he was no more than a sane, weary old man who'd captained a long battle and in the end, lost. "Yes, Mr. Royce. I suppose we must. It's my only hope of salvation. It was too much for her—for my Lillian. This whole business. It ate away at her until there was nothing left inside and the disease took hold. *I* did that, don't you see?" He dropped his head into his hands and pulled his gray hair into tangled spikes. "The shame of it!" And then as if a switch had flown open in his brain cutting off a momentary circuit to reality, he shot out of the chair and stood erect. "To war then, gentleman! To war!" He turned smartly to address Luke. "But first, sir, a question."

"Yes, sir?"

"Accommodations. For the dearly beloved of a captain who has served long and well. Can you make them?"

"I'm sure I can, sir."

"Come, then, and we shall discuss the matter."

Captain Tate led us up the stairs and into the master bedroom.

Lillian Tate's frail body lay on a hospital bed beneath a sheet tucked neatly under her chin. An intravenous tree stood in place next to her as the lone sentinel to the exactitude of the one certain equation in life.

"Arrangements must be made with Mr. Hendricks," he intoned softly. "But I'm no longer certain of the protocol."

"Mr. Hendricks, sir?" I asked.

"The undertaker, son. He lays claim to all of us at some point, don't you know."

"I'll take care of everything, Skip," Luke said.

Tate looked on the face of his deceased wife as he spoke. "Thank you, sailor. Remind me to put you in for extra leave when this is over."

Luke smiled. "Thank you, Cap. I believe I'll need it."

CHAPTER 26

CAPTAIN TATE CHATTED privately with Luke for a brief time before I took him back down to the living room where he promptly fell asleep in his chair.

Luke went to search Tate's den for the journal—the skipper had been unable to remember its whereabouts—and descended from the second floor a few minutes later with a book clutched to his chest like Moses holding a tablet.

"It's gibberish, nonsense ramblings. Every word of it. He'd hidden it under Lillian's mattress. He wrote a passage to her yesterday. Must be when she died. Might be her passin' pushed him over the edge but he was on his way to gettin' there as it was. There's a bunch of publications up there on Alzheimer's and dementia. Some medications, too, for whatever good they do."

"So what happens now?"

Luke opened the cover of the ledger and handed me a piece of paper. On it was written a phone number in the 561 area code and a loving note from Lillian with instructions to call Mr. Hendricks after she died as they'd promised each other he would, so they could once again be together.

"There's no 'Hendricks' in the phone book in the category," Luke said. "And I don't see any family pictures around, and no numbers or addresses of a personal nature in Mrs. Tate's book. No dates marked on her desk calendar for birthdays or anniversaries and such. I think the two of them are it. No one left to keep an eye on him after she was gone."

"And nothing to use to threaten him with if he suddenly developed a conscience and went running to the police. So they take him out."

"She knew his head was goin' so she set the time and place—wrote it out for him. Soon as she dies, he calls. This way it's quick and painless. He knows what's comin', and that's all right. Or maybe he doesn't. Nothing left for him to live for either way. Judgin' by all the religious knickknacks and whatnots, I'd guess him to be a pretty good Catholic. In his mind he's sinned enough for one lifetime. Even so, he can't end it himself."

"Looks like we found him just in time," I said.

Luke turned the book over in his hand. "Or maybe the subconscious will to survive kept him from callin'. The mind's a funny thing, Cage. Just when you think dyin' wouldn't be so bad somethin' inside tells you livin's the most precious thing you can think of. Anyway, now he's got another reason to keep breathin': The Old Man's got it into his head that I'll get Mrs. Tate buried in Arlington National. I told him there'd be papers to sign. Might take a week or two." He started back up the stairs. "Meantime he's got a call to make. And I'm guessin' that whoever this Hendricks is he's gonna be delighted to hear from him."

"Gentlemen, you're quite sure this is the proper course of action, then?" Captain Toby asked from the chair behind the desk in his study adjacent to the master bedroom.

I had to keep reminding myself that this wasn't some cruel game we were playing on a feeble mind. This was meant to save his life. "Those were your orders, sir."

"Yes. Of course. No harm, I suppose. You'd know, wouldn't you?"

"Yes, sir, I would. Just say what we rehearsed."

Luke tapped in the number on the desk phone and handed the receiver to Captain Tate.

I picked up the extension in the bedroom. The space was shuttered and smelled of medicine and sickness. Luke had covered Lillian Tate's face with the sheet. On the night table sat a small tray where pill bottles stood like captured chess pieces, the game finally conceded.

From where I was I could see Tate at his desk. When the call connected the phone rang twice, then was answered by a machine with a computer-generated voice that said, *Leave your message after the tone.*

Tate spoke calmly. "This is Captain Tobias Tate speaking. Mrs. Tate has left us, and as agreed, I wish for your services. You have my number. I'll be here, waiting for your call." He hung up.

"That was fine, sir," I said, coming back into the study. "Now it's time to pack up and move ahead with the mission."

He looked bewildered. "I . . . see. Yes, all right then. A little rest would be good, perhaps." He started toward the door. "Lillian. Mrs. Tate? You won't forget the arrangements?"

"No sir," Luke said.

"Carry on, then. Wake me when the watch changes, sailor."

We went through drawers and closets, piled shoes and clothing, toilet articles and medicines into two suitcases. We didn't know how soon they'd arrive but it was a safe bet that they wouldn't be calling first.

We hauled the suitcases down to the garage and threw them into the trunk of the Captain's ship-sized Cadillac.

A stack of newspaper sat in one corner of the garage. I found the number for the *Palm Beach Post* circulation department, called from the kitchen and canceled until further notice.

Luke woke the Captain and coached him through a note for the mailman, then put it in the box by the front door.

"What about Lillian?" I asked.

"Wesley'll get his guy here to cover it. Or our mysterious Mr. Hendricks will. That bit of bidness is going to have to take care of itself—no disrespect to the dearly departed. Fact is, the good captain will accept whatever I tell him."

"Captain," Luke said as we stood in the garage, rehearsed and ready to go, "I can't tell you how important this is, so please, if you have *any* questions at all . . . ."

"No, it's perfectly clear. You've explained it quite well."

Captain Tate had to be seen by the guard leaving the property on his own, not with us—a situation that might raise unwanted questions. And we sure as hell couldn't risk security placing a call to the police.

Tate would drive out in his Cadillac. We'd follow in the rental car and join up at the public beach where Luke and I had stopped earlier.

The rental would be turned in at the airport, then a second call would be made to Hendricks—whoever he was—only *this* time, the message would say that we were in the company of a living, breathing, if not slightly delusional link in the syndicate's food chain.

From there we'd drive the nine hours to Panama City in the Cadillac. What we'd do after that was anyone's guess: Discovering Captain Toby in the state he was in, and his wife dead was not what we'd expected.

"All right, Captain," Luke said as he opened the driver's side door for him, "give us a minute to go get to our car, then back on out. And remember, sir, close the garage door with your remote control there once you're out and in the driveway."

"Not to worry, Lieutenant." Tate had taken to calling Luke by that rank. "All is in order."

We closed the downstairs blinds and took one last look around. As an afterthought I grabbed the Captain's pipe and tobacco from the ashtray in the living room and stuck it in my pocket.

Then, it was out the door and into the fading gray light of the early evening.

CHAPTER 27

TWO MINUTES TURNED to three. Three to five. Still no Captain Tate.

"I was hopin' he'd get it right the first time. I'll go back and light a match under his ass," Luke said. He jogged toward the building and disappeared around the corner.

I still hadn't reached Tom Latham and wanted to check on Jamie as well. By then she was back from Boston, safely picked up at the airport and delivered home. I hit the icon on my Blackberry and speed dialed Latham's office.

The answering machine again took the call.

Next I tried our private line at *The Hatch*.

When it was Wes Harland who answered, my throat tightened. "Where's Jamie?"

"Right here," he said, then quickly added, "Not to worry. She's fine."

There was something in his voice. "Then tell me what's wrong," I said.

"It's Tom Latham. He's dead."

"No. Ah, shit." But I'd felt it all day.

"They found his body under the gas dock at the boat yard. He'd been in the water for awhile. Local sheriff thinks he got tangled up somehow in a dock rope and tripped, hit his head on the piling on the way down."

"Godamnit, Wesley. Here we go again. Another local Sherlock solves a—"

"Ease up. We know he didn't trip. I've got the proof right here."

210 Murder On The Whiskey George

"How?"

"I'm standing in your living room looking at a scumbag named Carlos. He tailed Jamie and my deputy from the airport. I'd parked my ass out there on a hunch that someone might know something about who was traveling where. So I picked up on him and tailed him back here."

"Lucky for us."

"No luck involved. You underestimate my skills."

"No. I do not. Thanks, partner. But how did he know she was flying in?"

"Somebody tipped him, he says. Nobody with a name. Carlos might be a little higher up in the pecking order than we figured but that doesn't mean his fate would have been any different than Crowley's. I'm confident that he's gettin' to where he sees that."

"Wes, please. In plain English. I'm having a little trouble processing all this as it is and we've got to get out of here. And fast."

"From Tate's?"

"Right. I'll explain later," I said. "Now tell me about Carlos."

"He was told to go to the airport and confirm Jamie's arrival, grab her when he could and then sit tight and wait for further instructions.

"So he shadowed her back to The Hatch as directed. I was watching him and I could tell that something was about to happen. He says he got another call telling him to move quickly—get to her and do whatever necessary to find out what was going on. So in he went. Only I got to him before he got to Jamie."

My mind was reeling. "What are you going to do with him?"

"Keep him right here. And one more thing, Cage: No surprise. They've known about you from the start. Carlos tells me you've been on their radar from the day you moved here.

And somebody at the top they call Crazy Jimmy has a real hardon where you're concerned. Carlos said this guy can't get clear on exactly what you're up to and he's rapidly running out of patience."

"Then they know I'm here with Tate. They wouldn't have sent Carlos after Jamie if I'd been there."

"Wrong. They knew you and Luke went to the airport but couldn't tail you past security. So they don't know where you went. The guess was up to Boston to be with Jamie. He said that he had no reason to suspect that you knew about Tate or where he was. I think he blew it on that one, and I believe he knows it. One more reason to cooperate. I don't imagine mistakes like that are acceptable."

I took a deep breath. "That's a help," I said. "Now, put Jamie . . . ."

Headlights swept over me as a car pulled to a stop several yards away at the corner of Tate's street.

"Cage? What is it? What's going on?" Wes asked into the sudden silence.

"We've got company is what. I'll call back."

I deadened the phone as I watched a man step out of the car. He came around to talk to the driver for a second then turned and walked slowly toward the Tates' townhouse. The car pulled away and passed within a few feet of the parking area where I sat hunched down in my seat.

I flicked on the overhead map light and searched frantically for the paper where I'd written the directions to the Tates' along with their phone number. I grabbed it and fumbled to quickly punch in the numbers on my Blackberry, hoping against reason that either Luke would answer or that Tate would, and he'd be lucid enough to understand the warning.

After four agonizing rings an answering machine kicked in. At the tone I shouted, "Luke! If you can hear me pick up. Now!"

Nothing. "Goddamnit, they're *here*! On the way to the fucking front door." I started to get out of the car.

"I hear you." Luke said as he picked up. "How many?"

"One on foot and one in a car who just drove away."

"Okay. Stay on the phone. Move fast. When you get to the corner, tell me what you see but stay out of sight."

I was there in a matter of seconds. "He's going up the walk towards the door."

"Okay. Stuff the phone in your pocket but don't turn it off. Let me know right away if things change. My bet is he rings the bell just like the Avon Lady. When you see the outside light come on it means he did just that. Move in hard and take him down. If he's only sellin' insurance, tough shit. We'll apologize later and buy a policy."

I saw a light come on in the foyer a moment later through the frosted windows on either side of the door and in the spill, made out the silhouette of a man standing square to the entrance twenty feet ahead of me.

The outside light would be next.

The rush of adrenaline was so strong that a sharp pain raced across my lower back when a second later, the light shone and the door cracked open. I shot forward, running low and hard on the balls of my feet.

By the time my target sensed what was happening, it was too late.

I drove a shoulder into his ribs and sent him through the door and smashing into the wall on the far side of the foyer. His head impacted the decorative marble with a sound like the beat of a drum. He crumpled immediately to the floor on legs made of cooked spaghetti.

Luke rolled the would-be assassin onto his back and went through his pockets and removed a brown plastic pill bottle. "It's even got the Captain's name on it. Sleeping pills. Just an old man who lost his wife and couldn't go on alone. These boys are all hearts and flowers."

It was then that I noticed the Captain standing off to the side. From the look in his eyes he might have been on the blind side of a two-way mirror. Something else was different, too. I realized that it was his clothes. He was wearing Dress Whites.

"It's what delayed him," Luke said, noting my surprise. "I found him upstairs gettin' changed. Only reason I got to the phone when you called. Looks good though, don't you think?"

"Captain Tate? Sir, are you all right?" I asked.

The question seemed to awaken him. "What? Yes, yes, of course. Nasty fall, that. Is he . . .? Do we know . . . ?"

"Not one of ours, Cap," Luke said.

"Oh, dear. Well in that case, shouldn't we send him to the brig?"

"We'll take care of it, sir. But it's gonna change things a little bit. We still got one out there."

After the Captain went into the living room I told Luke about Latham, and the tail they'd put on Jamie.

His mood darkened. "Bottom of the ninth, partner. We need us a hit. About now I don't give two shits how we go about getting it."

It took a full minute for the thug to regain consciousness. When he did, he brought himself to a sitting position and leaned back against the wall. He fingered the lump on his head as if reading Braille. "Fuck," he muttered.

Luke squatted down next to him. "Fuck what, honey?"

"Fuck you, is what."

"Where's the Captain?" Luke asked without looking up.

"In his chair. Humming away."

"Good. There's no need to upset him more than he already is." Luke patted the punk's cheek. "Now, what say we try this again? And no more knock-knock jokes. Who are you, and who's out in the car?"

Our prisoner considered Luke—measuring his chances, I thought. He was in his late twenties, well muscled but looked seriously unsettled. "I'm the Lone Ranger, and that out there is Tonto. And you're all about to be dead."

Without a word Luke clamped a hand on the man's throat.

Tough Guy's eyes bugged out as he clawed at Luke's fingers. In a second he began bucking up and down on the floor as if he were sitting on hot coals.

When his face turned crimson, Luke lightened his grip. "Next time, *Kimosabe*, I'll crush your fuckin' windpipe. People are already dead. I've got no time here and no patience for games." Luke removed his hand. "Now let's have a name."

"I can't . . . fucking . . . breathe. I think you—" He lashed out and shoved Luke, knocking him off balance.

I was out of position and couldn't reach him as he scrambled to his feet and turned to bolt toward the door.

Luke caught him with a kick square to the kneecap then rolled toward him and hauled him down by the belt, pinning him under his full weight. "A *name,* I said."

He spit at Luke who slapped his open hands over the punk's ears. "I do it harder, one or both are gonna rupture and you'll go deaf. Your peepers are next. How far you wanna go with this?"

Pain seared in his eyes. "Alright, alright. Get off me."

Luke let him up.

The punk sat once more against the wall, one hand at his throat, the other rubbing his right ear, saying nothing.

Luke lit a cigarette. "I haven't made myself clear, have I? Okay, I'll spell it out. You got five seconds to shape up. You don't, I'll finish off the voice box . . . then the ears . . . then I'll put this tobacco stick out in your eye."

Tough guy smirked, but it seemed weak. "You some kind of psycho or something?"

Luke took a deep drag on his cigarette, pinched it between his thumb and finger and jabbed it toward tough guy's right eye. "Card carryin'certifiable."

Tough guy flinched, his bravado fading. "Okay. So it's Tony. So what?"

"Alright. That's better." Luke sat on the floor and leaned against the wall next to Tony—two old friends shooting the shit. "So now I'm gonna tell you a story. Anywhere along the line you think I got it wrong, you just stop me. Be sure to listen good because when I'm finished, you'll have a decision to make.

"So here it is. Once upon a time there was this low-rent punk. Thought of himself as bein' pretty righteous. I'll call him . . . Tony. Anyway, Tony never did anything really bad or heavy. Petty stuff, mostly. Then one day this hard-core bad dude type offers him a job. A big buck deal. Got his name from a friend of a friend. Do this *one* thing, he says, and you're on your way. All you gotta do is pop this old guy's cork—deliver some pills and make sure he swallows. Watch him fall asleep, and that's it. Nothin' to it.

"Only thing is, Tony's so dumb ass stupid that he's got no idea about what he's gettin' himself into. He's not even smart enough to ask, 'Hey, why are you trustin' me with this?' Well, the answer is, they don't.

"See, what Tony doesn't understand is that after he caps the old guy? . . . well, they cap Tony. Why? 'Cause they don't like loose ends and they got a thousand Tonys to choose from in the future so who really needs this one dickweed hangin' around braggin' on what he did and maybe talkin' to the wrong people?"

Luke grabbed Tony's face in one hand and wrenched it toward his own. "Tony? You ever kill anybody?"

Tony shook his head, *No.*

"Didn't think so. And you wanna live to see tomorrow? . . . see your mamma again?"

This time, *Yes.*

"And the story's not wrong, is that a fact? Sounds about right, does it?"

Tony found his voice. "Not wrong . . . no."

"I wouldn't shit you, son. Not about anything as precious as life and death. It's way too serious a subject."

Tony had begun breathing harder as Luke talked. The reek of nervous sweat permeated the air around him.

"Now," Luke said, "about that decision. Either you help us get *Tonto* in here where we can get real personal with him—in exchange for which you'll get his car keys and a chance to disappear forever and turn your sorry life around—or I'll slit both your goddamn hamstrings right down to the bone and toss you in the street where you'll flop around like a fish outta water until Tonto comes drivin' by and finds you. Then the two of you can have yourselves a little private pow-wow about what happened in here."

For a moment I thought Tony would vomit. "I'm . . . I'm supposed to call the car after the old guy's conked. Then the one that dropped me off comes by to check it out, picks me up and we're gone. That's it. I swear. It's all I know."

Tony sat next to Luke on the living room couch rubbing his throat. He'd been carrying a .38 in a shoulder holster. I sat in a chair facing him with the gun in my lap and at the ready although I doubted we'd need it. At least not where Tony was concerned. Clearly, he'd found religion.

"This the same guy that hired you?" Luke asked.

The Captain hummed in his chair, oblivious to what was going on.

"No. Never seen him before today."

"How much time do we have before he expects to get his call?" I asked. According to my watch almost thirty minutes had gone by since Tony first arrived in the foyer.

"Anytime now, I guess. Not sure how long the pills were supposed to take." Tony turned to the Captain. "Hey, man, look, I didn't really—"

"Leave him alone," Luke growled.

"S-sure. Sorry."

Luke put a hand on Tony's shoulder. "Now listen up good, son. You wanna win your freedom then you've got a job to do. And you'd best do it right. Mess it up or get cute, and I may have no choice but to take your life. I won't hesitate. Not one bit. You believe me now, don't you?"

Tony went pale. "Yeah . . . I do. I believe you."

For that matter, so did I.

CHAPTER 28

THE CAPTAIN HUMMED his happy tune while Luke coached Tony on how to handle the call.

I programmed the phone number Tony had given me into my Blackberry and went into the kitchen for some privacy to call *The Hatch*. I spoke briefly with Jamie. She sounded numb; there was little I could do other than offer words of comfort that seemed pointless and hollow.

Wes came on the line. I told him about Tony and pulled up the phone number he was to call.

"Same number that Carlos has. That means they must have sent him in after Jamie when the Captain left the message about his wife dying. That's what changed the plan," Wes said. "Perfect time to force your hand. If they had Jamie and the Captain was dead, all the cards go to them. The last possible connection to Billy would be gone.

"But the way it's playin' out, if the call comes from this end *first* sayin' Carlos has Jamie all wrapped up, then when Tony's man walks in and finds you there he thinks he's covered."

"You can get Carlos to lie?"

"I most certainly can."

"Tell Jamie that I love her."

"Will do. And . . . good luck, partner."

I punched off and went back into the living room. "They're about to believe that Carlos has Jamie," I said to Luke. "We'll give them ten minutes to get the message through before Tony makes his call. Then, we wait."

Luke's grin could have melted a polar ice cap.

Tony's phone conversation with his man was brief and to the point.

Within five minutes, I heard the tap on the front door.

The Captain was sequestered upstairs with Luke.

I stood to one side, out of the line of sight as Tony opened the door. It was the point of highest vulnerability but Tony did just as he'd been told: As soon as the door was opened, he started walking toward the living room. "The old guy's upstairs in bed just like you wanted it," he said.

I heard the door close and in a second, the man entered my field of vision, passing the common wall shared by the foyer and the dining room where I was concealed. I stepped out behind him, locked him in a sleeper hold the way Luke had demonstrated and pressed Tony's .38 to his temple.

"What the fuck?" It was all he managed before he went slack and slipped to the floor.

By the time he began coming around, I'd found the automatic pistol holstered in the small of his back and conducted a quick once-over of his pockets where I found a ring of keys and a roll of Certs and a switchblade knife.

Tony sat hunkered down to one side, staring wide-eyed at his semi-conscious employer.

Luke came down without the Captain. I tossed him the car keys I'd taken from the unconscious man's pocket. Tony watched them longingly as they flew through the air and into Luke's hand.

"A promise is a promise," Luke said, handing Tony the keys. "Now get on I-95 and drive north until you're ready to fall asleep. Grab some coffee. Then head west a good distance and get lost in some town or other where they grow wheat and eight o'clock makes it a late night. Make somethin' of yourself, son. Not many get to see a livin' lesson like this, then get a second chance."

"I don't know what to say."

"Not a fucking word would be appropriate. You're still a sack a' shit to me. Go on, now. Just git."

CHAPTER 29

"WELL, NOW. IF it isn't Mr. Royce. My name is James," he said smoothly as he looked up from the living room floor of the Tates' townhouse. "What an unexpected pleasure."

His eyes had betrayed a moment of astonishment as he studied my face but quickly took on a superior cast. I pictured his internal computer feeding back a situation analysis confirming that no matter what we believed our advantage to be, he had Jamie under Carlos' thumb in Panama City Beach.

He rotated his head in Luke's direction. "And Mr. Carey, your dear departed brother's attorney and your companion in this little adventure. Or should I say one of them. One that's still alive, that is."

Luke grabbed him by the belt and shirt front and yanked him to his feet.

James stood six feet tall with the build of a middleweight. We were close in age. He had a curly mop of jet-black hair, pale green eyes set closely together in a face that gave the impression of having been taken apart and reconstructed without the benefit of having the original blueprint.

I reasoned that the damage had been inflicted by my brother in a parking lot outside a bar in Panama City Beach—that he'd been the architect of this particular Frankenstein. "So it was *you* Billy fought with. Or should I say, pounded into an ugly pile of—"

I saw the punch coming, blocked it and delivered a counter with speed and purpose. It caught him flush in the mouth.

His lips smashed against fancy dental work that broke like cheap crockery.

I ducked low and hit him again, this time in the gut, pivoting at the hips and driving my fist all the way to his spine.

Then again, splitting the skin over his right eye.

"That's enough!"

I was suddenly paralyzed by a pain that started at the base of my neck and raced up the left side of my skull like a jolt of electricity. I turned my head with great effort and saw that it was Luke's hand that held me strangely immobilized.

"Keep it up and you'll kill him. You don't want to do it."

But I did. In that murky corridor of the brain where dark thoughts lurk—ones that are weirdly fascinating to consider—I wanted to beat him straight to hell. For Billy. For Sam. For Latham.

Luke lessened the pressure of his grip "Let it pass. There's no purpose to be served just now."

I pushed James away as a bizarre blend of nausea and euphoria passed through me, realizing that I would have done it: I would have killed him if given the chance.

James tried to conceal the pain as he sat defiantly on a chair in the kitchen holding an ice pack to his mouth. According to him the damage I'd leveled was for the most part superficial: The broken caps could be replaced, he said, and in time the lip would heal.

"Few more stitches over the eye won't mean shit where *this* face is concerned, now will they."

"You're lucky I didn't let him finish the job," Luke said.

"Ah, but think of all the excitement you would have missed without me." James dabbed at his lip, studied the blood-soaked towel then shifted his eyes to mine. In a micro-second his calm turned to fury. "I'll fucking kill you for this!"

I sat on my haunches and looked him squarely in the eyes. "Just like Billy, huh? Didn't dare try it yourself.

If you had? . . . trust me, you'd be the one in the ground. The truth of it is that you've had your sorry ass bailed out twice now—once by Mr. Carey here, and once by a nice fellow who happened to come to your defense that day when you and Billy had your little run-in. I don't know what it was you said that got him going, but by the looks of you I'd say he was well on his way to taking you out."

He laughed at me. What he said next and how he said it chilled me like frozen air. I had to force myself to remember that Jamie was safe—that the advantage was ours as long as I didn't lose my cool and blow the ruse. "Whatever chance you and that bitch of yours had, Mr. Royce, is gone. You'll both be dead and rotting in a hole somewhere before you see another day."

Luke pulled him to his feet. "I've heard enough of your crap."

James stood his ground, the veins in his forehead pulsing like live snakes under his stretched skin. "I think you need to understand something here, you fucking ape. *I'm* in charge. Not you. Not Mr. Royce."

Luke stepped in close to James, dwarfing his size. "Is that so?"

James smiled, his teeth tinged red as if he wore clown's lipstick. He turned his eyes on me. "Your little fuckmate is mine, now. And there's *nothing* you can do about it other than to save her a bit of pain and suffering."

Again, I told myself that Jamie was okay—that Wes had it covered. "Just shut up. You don't frighten me. You don't know what you're talking ab—"

"She's with my associate. The little lady is back from Boston and all wrapped up like a fucking Christmas present. He's a man of special talents. I've watched him bring an hysterical woman to orgasm at the moment of her death. Quite extraordinary, really. So, to be gentlemanly about it, let's say . . . the more pain you endure the less I have inflicted on her. Pretty fair of me actually, don't you agree?"

"You're out of your mind. Bluffing."

"Call her."

I stared him down, then let just enough doubt enter my eyes.

"Go ahead."

I dropped my eyes and studied my smart phone for a time as if I had never seen one before, then with hesitancy hit the speed dial for *The Hatch*. Wes answered. "Jamie?" I said. "Honey? What's going on? Are you okay?"

"We're cool," Wes said, then began to sing.

I let my face slacken, then disconnected the call.

The smile on James' face broadened to a point where his wounds opened and fresh blood flowed.

"Don't hurt her," I said, trying like hell to appear contrite while struggling to block out Wesley's off key version of *Zippidy Doo Dah* at the same time.

"*Don't hurt her,*" James mocked. "Is that the best you can do in the way of a last fucking request, big man? Is that all you've fucking got?"

I raised my chin from my chest. "No. It isn't."

"What then, Royce, you fucking slug. What *is* your last fucking request?"

"I want to know why you had my brother killed."

James winked. "There! Now, that's more like it."

CHAPTER 30

"LET'S SIT DOWN, shall we? After all, we're civilized men and Cage here has asked the question of the century."

We moved to the living room where Captain Tate was once again asleep in his chair, blessedly oblivious to his surroundings.

James observed him as if he were a disobedient child. "Then there's the matter of what to do with the good captain. We'll get to that later. For now, allow me to enlighten you on the demise of your dear brother Billy and a few other items I think you'll find to be of interest."

As James regaled us with his sick and twisted narrative, I visualized what he recounted with growing rage.

He was crazy, all right. And when I found out just who he was and what he'd done, I wanted a second chance to make him dead.

And this time there'd be no stopping me.

JAMES "CRAZY JIMMY" Monahan was Jamie's cousin—the same one who'd tried but failed to rape her years earlier.

He'd resented her from the time she'd come to live with his family, barely enduring the affection his mother smothered on her, growing quickly tired of hearing how difficult her young life had been and how she deserved to be treated with special care.

"For Chrissake, Mom!" he'd shouted one afternoon in a fit of anger, "Uncle Jim was a drunk, and Aunt Carrie was nothing but a slut who got what she deserved—some disease for letting him screw her after he'd been out fucking whatever walked. Jamie's playing you and Dad for fools. The money you give her! Jesus! What are you trying to do, *buy* yourselves a daughter because you're all dried up and never had one of your own?"

His mother struck him across the face. He was pure evil, she said, and she hated him.

In return, he struck her back, splitting the skin above her right eye and knocking her to the floor.

When his father came home that evening, he'd taken James down to the basement. He'd tried to intimidate him. But it hadn't worked. Two weeks later, James said, he'd raped Jamie for hours to prove a point: No one, *no* one would threaten him and get away with it. Not then. Not *ever*.

I knew he was lying: It was an *attempted* rape; and whatever had happened that night in the basement, I'd bet my life that his father had made his point.

He'd have at her again, he went on—to spite her, he said. But he decided that she wasn't worth the trouble. Instead he'd wait, no matter how long it might take for the chance to get to her in some way his father couldn't see.

In time, Jamie's relationship with me provided that opportunity. He began to scheme. It had to have the right *look*, had to *mean* something. Killing me just to kill me was too easy. There had to be mental suffering, humiliation, the kind he'd had to endure—that feeling of helplessness, of outrage over seeing Jamie get such special treatment. And she'd have to know, have to hurt, have to be the cause of my death and live with that knowledge forever. But there was no way to make it work. She'd go to his father, and he'd be royally fucked.

And then, along came Billy.

Like each of his two younger brothers, James said, he was in charge of a division of his father's empire, Monahan Enterprises.

The company was divided into three businesses: an import concern, an investment concern, and a marine and aviation company that dealt in the brokerage and syndication of high-end private and corporate yachts and aircraft. All were under separate names and lost to each other in a maze of sub-corporations, partnerships, and off-shore affiliations but were in fact closely related—vertically integrated. And while a vast majority of their business was legitimate, the heart of it—the real money— was in the drug trade.

It was simple, but slick: The import division set up and administered the relationships on the drug production front; the investment arm moved the proceeds in and out of the country; transport—marine and aviation—took care of trafficking. This was James' division, the fool-proof easy-in-but-out-only-if-and-when-I-allow-it setup, his own brainchild. The main component, Southeast Marine Operations, was overseen by a Cuban named Jorge Vasquez—Georgie, as he was known to his friends.

Jorge's parents fled the Island in advance of Castro, leaving behind most of a sizeable fortune but retaining enough to start a business in Miami and send their son to college.

Jorge received his MBA from Boston University where he'd met Billy at a party during their senior year. They'd become friends at a time when Billy and I were going separate ways. After graduation, they'd cruised down the Intracoastal Waterway together with some other friends to Miami where Billy worked for Jorge's father at his marina for most of that summer.

When Jorge's father sold his business suddenly and without explanation, Billy left for a job at the Pier 66 Marina in Ft. Lauderdale, never knowing that the company that forced Jorge's father to sell was in fact owned by the Monahans who were busy expanding their Southern transport operations in cocaine and marijuana.

Jorge stayed on and made his pact with the Monahans: He'd do whatever was expected of him—with no argument, and not a word to anyone—and make a good living while he was at it.

In time Jorge moved up in rank and once he'd proven his loyalty, was assigned more responsibility. He liked his new job, especially when he got to bust a few heads among the troops. He was feared, respected, and well paid. But not as feared or respected, and certainly not as well paid as his new boss, James Monahan.

Whatever Crazy Jimmy wore or drove or ate or drank or fucked, you didn't. Even if you could afford it. If you were smart, you steered clear of Crazy Jimmy. If you couldn't, you worked hard to kiss his ass and get along. After all, he was heir-apparent to his father—*the* boss.

Crazy Jimmy sensed that Jorge knew the affection he had for him was no different from what he might feel for a pet dog who in this case happened to walk upright and could speak two languages. So he never let on that he knew Jorge was a college graduate—not until the day they discussed the referral that had come down from Tobias Tate, the old fucker in Panama City Beach who was losing his coconuts and wanted to be replaced— *needed* to be replaced.

Jorge, he thought, seemed unduly nervous that day.

And well he should have been: If you petitioned Crazy Jimmy to let one of your runners retire, you'd better have three things going for you: a good reason, names and locations of living relatives, and someone in mind to take his spot. With Tate, Jorge had only two: the reason, and the replacement.

Item three—the critical part about the relatives—turned out to be the problem.

When Tate had been recruited, Jorge had the computer search done in the usual way. But somehow, it got messed up.

Jorge signed off, thinking he was getting a guy with lots of debt, a willing attitude, three kids and five grandchildren. But as it turned out, the Tate they profiled, while deeply in debt with his charter business and most willing to make a few harmless runs for a bucket of money, had no one else besides a wife. What he *did* have was the middle initial R, not A. It was a major fuck-up.

When he'd found the nerve to tell James about the error, Crazy Jimmy had been uncharacteristically calm.

"Mistakes sometimes happened," he'd said.

Had Jorge properly and permanently taken care of the researcher? Yes? Good. Then everything would be all right.

The next day when Jorge's girlfriend called from the hospital where she'd been taken after a paper shredder accident cost her the index finger of her right hand, Jorge had been in a meeting with Crazy Jimmy, about to review the Tate replacement and lay out the details of how it would be handled.

Jorge listened with growing nausea to his girlfriend's cries on the other end of the phone, then hung up and asked James, *why*?

Crazy Jimmy said he thought that counting fingers was a very effective way of keeping track of Jorge's fuck-ups.

Jorge promised that no more mistakes would happen.

James was sure that that would indeed be the case.

With that piece of business concluded, James picked up the Tate file and scanned it. When he saw what it contained he was stunned. It was all there: replacement's name, personal profile, family profile, friends, girlfriend, financial information—everything. And the name. The *name*: Royce, William T.

"You sure about this, Georgie? This Royce? About his family and all? About his brother and this woman he lives with in New York?"

"A hundred percent, Boss. Tate said he and Billy had a nice casual conversation about his family, especially his brother. Checked it out every way there is. You think I'm gonna do it twice? Fuck up again?"

"Billy?"

"I ah . . . I know the dude personally—from, ah, some friends in Boston and from when he worked for my ol' man here in Miami. He wants a boat bad. He'll do just fine. No kids yet, though. That a problem?"

"Fuck the kids. Then, you've made him an offer?"

"No way, Boss. Not until you approve this thing with Tate and his wife."

"Yeah, yeah. Sure. Approved. It's your fucking balls if it goes wrong. So, tell me about Boston."

"Oh. That. Yeah. I, ah, you know, went to . . . ."

James laughed. "You don't think I know about your fucking degree? Give me some fucking credit here, okay? You humble yourself for me, you little spic. It's amusing, really. It's also why I trust you and why I only took a finger and didn't fillet that girl of yours. I like you, Chico. And I know you respect me and would never cross me."

"Never, Boss."

"Good. Fine. Now, let's do some business. I want this Billy Royce on the hook big time. Pull him in by his fucking dick and nail it to a fucking post. No way out. But do it tenderly. Don't spook him. Don't lose him. Let him think that he's got an out. And for *Chrissake*, don't let that old douche bag up there screw this up."

"Sure, Boss. Whatever you want."

"This is *very* important to me. Do you understand that, my friend?"

"Si."

"Extremely important. So when the time comes and he's wanting to quit and count his money like they all eventually do, he's gotta believe. And do you know what I think would make him sit up and take notice?"

"What's that, Boss?"

"Maria. That sweet piece of Columbian ass I've been banging. She's a lousy blow job and she's getting on my nerves. When the time comes, I'm gonna send her to you. Use her, my trusted Cuban friend. Use her to bring it home."

After the pre-dawn meeting with Brian following Maria's murder, Billy called Miami demanding to talk to Georgie. The call was routed instead to Crazy Jimmy.

"Calm down, Billy. Business is business, and the sense was you weren't going to accept things for what they were."

"Who the hell are you? Forget it. It doesn't matter. I don't want anything more to do with this crap. I've done my bit. I want out. You'll never hear from me again. But Christ, why the girl?"

"Not my fault. Don't you see? *You* caused that. If only you'd gone along without all the fuss. Now I'm afraid you've seen too much. You're in—permanently."

"You can stick it up your sick ass. I'll go to the authorities."

"You'll do nothing of the kind. Not until we've had a chance to talk. Tell you what. I'll come see you. Maybe we can reach an understanding and avoid all this unpleasantness."

"I don't need to—"

"Just hear me out. What have you got to lose?"

When Billy walked into the Sea Goddess Tavern, Crazy Jimmy signaled him over to his table.

"You Georgie's boss?" Billy asked.

"*Every*body's boss. Please, take a seat. Let's not make this more difficult than it has to be."

Billy sat. "I don't see that it's difficult at all. You people are out of your fucking skulls. This isn't what I thought I was getting into when I agreed to the deal."

"Let's dispense with that, shall we? Frankly, I don't care *what* you thought you were or weren't getting yourself into. Fate has smiled on me, and if her teeth are rotten it's not my fault, is it?"

"What the fuck are you talking about?"

"Choices, Billy. Choices. It's a sad story that's about to have a happy outcome. For me, anyway. It's like a fable. In the end one dies for the good of all."

"If you don't start making sense, I'm out of here. And I'll take my chances."

"With your brother's life? Or your sweet little Samantha's, perhaps?"

Billy rose out of his seat. "I've had enough."

"No you haven't, Billy. Not *nearly* enough. I'm giving you a choice. You should be grateful. Now sit back down."

"Get to the point. You've got about thirty seconds, asshole."

"You came to us to syndicate your boat. Now you know the nature of how our business works and *I* know the nature of your family. It's a trade-off, Billy. You've gotten your boat, and I've hit a home run. While you don't need to know all the details, I have a great interest in hurting someone close to your brother. In order to do that I need to kill someone.

"Initially, I thought it would *be* your brother. Now I'm not sure. Since it's you who dragged everyone into this, maybe it should be you who decides who lives and who dies."

Billy stood. "Your fucking head's on fire. I'm leaving. And if I hear one more word of this crazy crap coming from your mouth, I'll shut it for you." He left the table and headed for the parking lot.

James caught up with him. "It's not that easy, Billy. Don't you turn your back on me, fucker! And don't you *ever* call me crazy! It's your brother who dies, or that little bitch cunt of yours. It's up to you."

Billy turned on James Monahan, a deadly calm in his eyes. "*What* did you say?"

"I said, nominate your brother for cemetery duty, or your punch. Actually, I hope it's your brother. That way I'll have the pleasure of fucking your pretty little Samantha. If she complains, I'll slit her throat from ear to—"

And that was it. Billy started to reorganize Crazy Jimmy's face.

More likely, to kill him.

THE SCENES CRAZY Jimmy drew for us through his oddly animated and detailed account were mind-numbing.

But after all that had happened, I finally had my answer.

"My brother was different. He wouldn't be intimidated because he was a good man. He had courage—something you wouldn't understand. So you had him killed. He still won. You wouldn't understand that, either, you sick fuck."

"My father went batshit when it made the local news," Monahan said, as though he heard nothing I'd said. "I denied having anything to do with it of course. I pinned it on that nothing—on Crowley. Had Daddy Dear known what I had planned, he would have stopped it. Not good for me.

"It was so perfect. I was certain Billy would give up the girl to save you. In a way it was even better than having you dead. He'd tell you, you'd tell Jamie . . . . She'd have you only because some other slut had paid with her life. The guilt would be too much for both of you. Her happiness would be destroyed. She'd leave you. But I misjudged. Your brother would have ruined my plan if he'd lived.

"Public murder isn't good for business. So my father put the rest of you under his protection. Anyone connected with you or that bitch of yours was out of bounds. A year, and nothing happened. So I let it ride.

"Then Billy's old coze shows up. Then his buddy. Next, you go after the boat." Crazy Jimmy laughed. "Absolutely perfect. I *love* what you've done for me. If you'd just left it alone none of this would have happened. You've made my day—my whole fucking *life!*"

The truth of his words nearly split my head in two. "You couldn't kill Jamie, so Sam was her stand-in. Jesus."

"I'd had enough of my father's candy ass crap. *That* one nearly cost him a stroke. I wanted her to be first—wanted you to have the chance to see me at my best. I wanted you to see how badly you fucked it all up for them. I tried to convince the stupid fuck that all of you had to die—that you were a danger to the entire enterprise. He's getting old—wouldn't listen. His judgment sucks. From now on, *I* call the shots. And that is why, Mr. Royce, you and your spoiled little whore are growing nearer to your God by the minute."

Luke looked with contempt at James Monahan. "Why some people are ever born is one of life's great mysteries."

It took all I had to keep control as I punched in the number for *The Hatch* on my cell and tossed it to James, who looked instantly confused.

"Remember to push the little red icon there when you're finished, asshole. My battery's running low."

"What are you trying to pull here? Whatever it is, it won't work."

"Just do it."

James stared at me as he put the phone to his ear. "What the hell is th---?" And then the color began to slip from his face like wet paint from a cracked mirror. When he'd finished listening, his eyes looked as dead as if a circuit breaker had suddenly tripped in his brain and the lights had gone out.

"The flip-side of arrogance, is cowardice." Luke said to me, his tone professorial. He spoke as if James wasn't there. "The idea is to put these little fuckers in a position where they're helpless. Add the right kind of encouragement and all their pluck goes right out the window. You break 'em by forcin' 'em to face their own mortality. The thought of dyin' scares the shit out of 'em. Confront 'em with it, make it real and you own 'em. No matter the outcome, they'll never be the same. Inside they're ruined. And that, my friend, is the one place a man can't hide."

In the garage, I found a roll of electrical tape and some rope and used them to bind James Monahan hand and foot on the kitchen floor. He offered no resistance as I worked, or when Luke injected him with a strong sedative from a vile he'd found on Lillian Tate's night stand.

"At some point, I suppose you plan to kill me," James said with seeming disinterest.

"Let's get the place straightened up and the Captain ready," Luke said, leaving Crazy Jimmy with his question unanswered. "Soon as you figure out what you want to say about all this to Jamie, we'll call back up to the Beach."

We turned to leave.

James' stopped us with one word.

"Georgie," he said.

"What *about* Georgie?" I asked.

He smiled as his eyes fluttered closed. "What are you going to say to him when he calls? What do you suppose will happen to the others?"

"Calls *where*? What *others*?"

"When he calls me for orders, you asshole."

As it hit me, I turned slowly to Luke.

"The Spirit, Cage. The goddamn boat," he said.

"Brian and Deanne. Christ, Georgie's got them."

CHAPTER 31

I FISHED CRAZY JIMMY'S cell phone from the pocket of his raincoat and switched it off.

The sedative had taken effect and there was no way to bring him out of his stupor to answer Georgie's call when it came in.

And no way for us to risk answering it until we'd had a chance to think things through.

I used my own phone to reach Jamie, dreading what I had to tell her.

But she already knew. "It was the name," she said. "Crazy Jimmy—what his brothers called him. This Carlos creep used it when he was talking to Wes. When I heard it I thought, no way. It can't be. But then there was all this weird stuff that happened in Boston with my uncle. And then, oh God, Cage, I heard him say something about The Spirit."

I saw Sam with a ligature wrapped around her throat; a man hanging upside down from a rope with his head submerged beneath the water; a girl no older than Deanne with a knife plunged into her heart. I pushed the images aside like scenes from a half forgotten nightmare—had to, or it might happen again.

"You've got to get a call through to your uncle. He's the only one who can put the brakes on Georgie. Tell him that we have James. But be sure he knows and believes that he's not dead. Tell him we know about the drug operation—that James gave it all up, told us everything about the entire setup. Have him give you a number that I can relay to Georgie so he can call your uncle for confirmation on what he's to do—which is exactly *nothing* other than to follow my instructions. Tell your uncle— Tell him that if *anything* happens to those people on that boat I will personally kill his son and then we'll all make a run for it. Tell him that I realize we'll probably end up dead because of it but I think we're as good as that anyway unless we can strike some kind of bargain."

It took a brief moment for what I'd said to sink in. "Kill him? But . . . you're not *like* that. What's *happening* to you?"

"Jamie, this is no goddamn time to go passing judgment on me. These are murderers. You said so yourself. If he's not home, have him found. I doubt very much that he's ever out of reach."

"We never did anything to deserve this."

"Maybe not. But it's up to us to put an end to it. Now please, just *do* it!"

Jamie's conversation with her uncle had been cold, business-like, no confirming or denying anything. She was emotionally dried out, she said—felt like a stone. But she had a number for us to pass on to Georgie that would connect him to Michael Monahan when Crazy Jimmy's underling checked in from *The Spirit*. Unless Crazy Jimmy Monahan had been lying about that, too.

But he hadn't been bluffing. Less than five minutes after I turned James' cell phone back on, its synthesized chirp broke a silence that filled the Tates' living room like poison gas and set the blood rushing in my ears.

"Yes?" I said.

"Boss? That you? Christ, I've been trying to get you for the last—"

"Shut up, Georgie, and listen carefully. I'm about to give you a number. Call it. Then call back here." I repeated the number twice.

There was no response. The phone clicked dead.

Several minutes passed. The cell phone remained silent.

Luke taped James' mouth then slung him over his shoulder and deposited his slack body in the cavernous trunk of the Cadillac next to the Captain's luggage.

I rushed around the living room and kitchen, wiping prints, straightening up, then did the same upstairs.

"They'll try an ambush," I said to Luke as we hustled the Captain into the car.

"Doubt they'd risk it. Not with James here. But you can bet your ass they're contemplatin' a whole lot of things. Our best move is to head for the airport and dump the rental. Once we're on the road we'll be able to spot anything suspicious and figure out how to deal with it."

I drove the Cadillac, Luke the rental. It was dark and still raining. The guard at the gate never gave us a look.

On the way out Indiantown Road to I-95, James' cell phone finally rang. I grabbed it off the seat next to me and flipped it open.

"Who've I got?" Georgie asked from aboard the *Free Spirit* somewhere in the Gulf of Mexico.

"Cage Royce."

"Whoa. Impressive. The man has a move or two. Okay. So first things first. Anything funny happens, like helicopters or the Coast Guard come snooping around the boat, things like that? They're both dead. Believe it."

"Anything funny happens? . . . like someone goes swimming with their hands tied behind them or stops breathing for some reason, things like that? Crazy Jimmy ends up in little pieces spread all over the fucking state and you'll answer for it to his father."

"You got mine, I got yours. Like that?"

"Just like that. Only neither of us is going to squeeze, right?"

"I've got my orders. No squeezing."

"Good. Now here's what I want you to do. At noon tomorrow, bring The Spirit into the marina at the Clearview Gulf Resort. Stay on board and act like everyone's having fun when you sign for the slip."

"Oh, but we are!"

"Shut up, Georgie, or I'll call Mr. Monahan and tell him you're not helping."

"That won't be necessary. Go on."

"That's it. It's all you need to know. We'll take care of the rest. You'll get a call from Monahan telling you what to do after that. And, Georgie . . . ?"

"Yes?"

"Keep your hands off Deanne, you hear me? Think about it. You've got ten fingers but only one dick. And up to one is as far as I'm going to count."

While Luke returned the rental car, I called Jamie again from the Palm Beach Airport and told her about my talk with Georgie. It was time for her to place another call to Michael Monahan in Boston.

"Tell your uncle that I said he's got to be here by noon tomorrow."

"What if he says no? What if he can't?"

"He won't say no. He'll come. You're here. And it's his son we're talking about. Even if he doesn't give a shit about him he's still got a problem that's critical to his business. And it's a problem that demands his personal attention. We can't let him stall, Jamie. I don't know how much time we have until they come up with some plan of their own—if they haven't already."

"Okay, okay. Let me be sure I've got this right. Reservations at the Clearview—a three-bedroom villa in a quiet location under the name *Buford* for tonight and tomorrow. Guaranteed late arrival."

"Right. Very late. Luke came up with the name, by the way."

"I could have guessed. Okay, so my uncle is to check in by noon tomorrow under his own name. I'm to tell him you'll call."

"That's it. Except for you."

"Glad you remembered. You'll phone . . ."

" . . .when we're about a half-hour away. You sure Wes doesn't mind bringing you over?"

"You think you could stop him?"

"Nope," I said.

"He said to tell you he's taking Carlos out of play—locking him in a holding cell at the station under some phony name on a drunk and disorderly."

"One down," I said.

There was a brief silence. "With all this . . . with my uncle and my cousin . . . with what happened to Billy . . . can you . . . do you still love me?"

The question nearly ripped my heart out of my chest. "Does that really need an answer?"

"Right now? Yes."

"With every beat, lady."

We left the Palm Beach International Airport in the Captain's Cadillac at eight, estimating making the Clearview Gulf Resort at about four in the morning, local time.

Luke gave the Captain one of the pills I'd taken from Lillian's collection; it had him snoring away in the back seat before we were ten miles up I-95. At Fort Pierce we cut over to the Florida Turnpike.

When we hit Gainesville, we stopped for gas and coffee, hit the men's room and then set out again.

"How you holdin' up?" Luke asked.

I gazed out the window at the passing darkness. "Running on fumes. We're really hanging ourselves out here, aren't we?"

"Have been from the start. It's the way it works sometimes."

"Jamie's family being involved in this is the last thing I would have expected to find."

Luke fished a cigarette from the pack that sat on the dashboard and pushed in the lighter. "You ever hear of 'Six Degrees of Separation'?"

"A play. Sure. I saw it years ago on Broadway. Why?"

"Then you know the theory about bein' linked by a few acquaintances to everyone else in the world, right? Used to be it was on account of friends and family mostly. Now it's all this high-tech instant-this and instant-that computerized shit. At times I believe it's brought more harm to the world than good— like a superhighway of potential trouble. Way too easy to know everybody else's bidness and find a way to use it against them— credit card rackets, psychics, home equity scams, title loans . . . . Hell, there's a thousand of 'em. And if you end up gettin' suckered in, sometimes the best you can do is find a way to cut your losses."

"I get your point. But there's got to be more. There has to be a way to *hurt* these people."

He turned his head to look at me. The illumination from the instrument panel cast a pale green light on his face. The lines around his eyes took on the appearance of deep cracks in aged wood as he grinned. "Findin' a way to do just that is what brought you here in the first place, idn't it?"

The unmarked Panama City Beach police cruiser was parked under the front portico of the Clearview Gulf Resort and Marina when we pulled in at a few minutes past four in the morning.

Jamie got out and ran into my arms. The nineteen-odd hours since I'd last seen her felt more like a decade. She held me tightly.

"Almost over," I whispered. "Let me go get the villa. I'm beat. I believe we all are."

I crossed the two-story hotel lobby, the leather heels of my shoes striking loudly against the hard marble flooring.

The young lady behind the registration desk put down her book and came over and ran my card, made the name change on the reservation without a question, then handed me the computerized key with a fabricated smile and tapped a silver bell that sat in front of her on the counter, the intrusive sound of what seemed to me an unnecessary act harshly amplified by the nighttime emptiness of the enormous lobby.

A porter rousted himself from his stand not twenty feet away, rubbing a hand over his eyes and blinking himself fully awake.

"If you'll follow me?" he said cheerfully, as if it were suddenly noon.

We followed him as he drove his little electric cart through a curving maze of darkened streets, at last parking beside a two-story villa encrusted with climbing vegetation and overhung by palm trees.

I tipped the porter handsomely, explaining that we'd take care of our own luggage.

He bid us good-night, then hopped back onto his electric buggy and disappeared around the corner.

"We need to get our guest out of the trunk," I said.

For a second Jamie looked confused. "Oh. Him. God, please, keep him out of my sight."

I knocked on the trunk of the Cadillac. "You heard what the lady said."

Wes got into his car. "I gotta go make sure Carlos is all snuggly."

"Thanks," I said. "For everything."

"Don't thank me yet."

I watched him drive off, wishing he could be with us in the morning but knowing that he'd already let himself get far too involved as it was, wondering what would become of his career and his family because of it.

"One more issue," Luke said to Jamie. "Tate's mind's a bit disorganized. Maybe you'd be of a comfort."

She woke the Captain, introduced herself as his personal envoy and escorted him inside to one of the three bedrooms while we tended to the luggage.

Crazy Jimmy barely stirred as we carried him up the stairs, laid him down and tied him securely to one of the twin frames in the smallest bedroom.

Luke flopped down on the other bed and was snoring mightily before I finished double checking the knots around Crazy Jimmy's wrists and ankles and turned off the light and closed the door.

Jamie was under the covers when I came into the master bedroom. I stripped off my clothes and started to head for the shower.

"How sad about Mrs. Tate. The Captain's worried about some . . . arrangements. As hard as I try not to, I feel sorry for him," Jamie said.

"I understand."

I'd been under the spray for only a minute when Jamie pulled back the curtain and stepped in.

The incoming air stroked my warmed flesh like a cold hand.

She leaned against me, shivering despite the hot water that sheeted our bodies.

"It feels wrong," she said.

"I told you. It's all going to work out," I said, unable to muster much conviction.

She studied my face. "Did he tell you?"

"Why Billy was killed? Yeah. Because your cousin couldn't . . . . Because Billy wouldn't make a choice."

"You're talking in circles."

"I'm thinking in circles. I still need more answers. And some serious sleep."

"Don't hide anything from me, Cage. No secrets, right?"

I stuck my head under the spray and rinsed the shampoo from my hair.

CHAPTER 32

I WAS DRAGGED FROM a deep sleep as the last stanza of *Lady In Red* blared over a loud speaker while I chased a hooded figure down an empty beach and through an obstacle course of tilted headstones and fresh graves.

Gradually, my brain worked to set the sensors and fire up the memory chips that would give me a clue or two as to where exactly I was.

A shaft of light knifed its way into the room through the center of the drawn curtains. I saw that the other half of the bed was empty.

I found Jamie, Luke, and the Captain sitting out in the villa's small, privacy-fenced courtyard looking as though they were on vacation but not having much fun—all except for Tobias Tate, that is.

Luke read the morning paper with a scowl; Jamie sat at the glass-topped table with a bleary stare, sipping coffee.

"Cheery group," I quipped.

"Got time to kill," Luke replied, "but no one felt like a game a' lawn darts."

I poured myself a cup of coffee. Tate sat to my right, dressed in shorts and a brightly colored Hawaiian shirt, oblivious to the prevailing mood. The morning sun was already high and warm.

"Morning, sir," I said.

"Good morning to you, Captain Royce. Splendid day for it."

"Splendid day for what, sir?"

He looked around quickly then spoke in a conspiratorial tone. "For the mission, sailor. Clear skies and calm seas. Couldn't be better."

Jamie patted the back of his hand. "The Captain and I talked about lots of things this morning. He's had quite the life."

"Nothing so spectacular, Jamie dear." His bright mood lessened a shade. "And there are surely parts of it I would rather forget, if I could only remember what it is I'd rather not. Which makes no sense whatever, I'm afraid."

She reassured him that it did.

"Yes, well, I suppose it might. Tell me, how's Mrs. Tate this morning?" he said to me.

"Sir, Mrs. Tate is— She's . . ."

"Yes, yes, I know, sailor. Mrs. Tate is quite dead." He dismissed the thought with a wave of his hand. The Captain turned to Luke with a concerned look. "The arrangements, I meant to say."

"Taken care of, sir."

"Good, good, good. In that case, I think I'll go take a constitutional."

At twelve-thirty, I called the front desk and asked to be connected to Michael Monahan's room.

"Yes?"

"Cage Royce, here."

"Jamie tells me that we have some business to transact."

"That's a bit of an understatement, Monahan."

"No need for hostility. I assure you, that will get us nowhere."

"And just where is it we're going?"

"I believe finding an answer to that question is precisely why I'm here, is it not?" He was calm. His inflection never varied.

"There's an open-air terrace off the upper level of the main lobby, to the back. I'll meet you there in five minutes," I said.

"Fifteen. I had to catch a rather early flight. I need to tend to some other business first."

The phone went dead.

"It's like talking to a fucking vampire. He thinks he's invincible."

"Don't let it eat at you," Luke said. "He'll try to rattle you into showin' your hand. When he looks at you, listens to you, he's gonna make a call about how serious you are."

"Dead serious."

"I believe it, but *I* don't count. Make sure *he* knows you are."

"And how am I supposed to do that? With a cross and wooden stake?"

"Think about Billy. Trust me, it'll come to you, partner."

MICHAEL MONAHAN ROSE from his chair as I approached the table. I'd delayed my arrival, wanting to establish my own brand of control.

"Commendable, Cage. I would have expected nothing less." He appeared taller somehow than he had at Billy's funeral—handsome, well-tanned, his suit perfectly tailored.

What had once been a distant respect on my part was now hatred. "Don't fuck with me," I said evenly.

"My apologies, then. It was meant as a compliment. Please, be seated."

The chair he indicated faced the sun; I sat in the one that didn't.

He conceded the point with a nod. "Old habit. Too many hours of tedious negotiation."

"Somehow I get the feeling that you're a far better negotiator than you are a man."

The change in his demeanor was almost imperceptible. "I don't intend to explain myself to you, Cage. In fact, I find all this . . . this flap about drugs that Jamie spoke of to be of little interest. I'm a businessman. I move product. Fill a need. What happens at certain levels in the process is the responsibility of middle-management and really none of my concern."

"No, I'm sure it isn't. Any more than what happened to my brother."

"That, I'll confess, was unfortunate for both of us."

I nearly lost my composure. "Unfortunate? I'll tell you what's *unfortunate*. It's unfortunate that it wasn't *you* standing in that mortuary looking into the open skull of a member of your family instead of me. My brother's head was half blown off. Most of his face was missing. And do you know why? I'll *tell* you why. Because one of your managers—your own *son*—made a mistake and decided it would be best for business if Billy died. *That's* why. And if things don't go well here today and *I* happen to decide that James is bad for business—the business of living a long life where Jamie and I and two of our friends are concerned—I'll gladly arrange a similar fate for him."

He eyed me closely. "My son is an idiot. More to the point, your brother's death was completely unnecessary. Jorge should have been far more careful about using a punk like this Crowley fellow to keep an eye on the business. From what I've been told, your brother was allowed a very fine boat and Crowley judged that he must have deep resources and thought he'd steal a little for himself. When your brother caught him in the act and dismissed him, Mr. Crowley . . . what's the phrase? . . . lost his cool. But that score has been settled."

This was torture. "Allowed? Settled?"

And then a tumbler fell into place. I stared at him for a good ten seconds.

"So your idiot son was telling me the truth. You really *don't* know, do you?"

"Know *what*, Mr. Royce?"

"No. Go ahead. Tell me what you thought was happening. I want to hear it from you."

He shook his head, his impatience showing. "Very well. I thought the fact that your brother became involved in our business was rather ironic. All in the family, if you will. It was a fact I discovered later, however, after it was . . . too late."

"What's so *ironic*, Mr. Monahan, is the fact that Billy's involvement gave James a way to get at Jamie. Billy was killed because he refused to play Crazy Jimmy's version of Russian Roulette, *not* because some punk wanted his wallet."

Monahan's look expressed genuine confusion. "What in blazes are you talking about?"

"Your son hates Jamie. Obviously, you know that. But I also know he wasn't able get to her directly because of you—because of something you did or said a long time ago. So when Billy dropped into his lap, he decided to use him to hurt her."

I told him what I'd learned from his son. When I finished he sat looking at his hands. "I'm sorry. I had no idea. He told quite a different story to me. And I'm sorry about this Sam person as well."

"What the hell does it matter if you're sorry? Would you have stopped it? Is that why you sent Carlos in yesterday? To grab Jamie and . . . *guard* her?"

"What? No. I mean, yes, I would have. I know it sounds easy to say now and is of little consolation to you, but I would have seen that your brother was released from his obligation to us—free and clear—and that his lady friend was—"

"You're right. It's too easy. You're negotiating—bargaining for your son."

"Not true. You have my word."

"Now that really holds a lot of value, doesn't it? Billy's dead. Your word is worthless."

He cleared his throat and looked into my eyes. His gaze was chilling. "No matter what you might think of me—and that really isn't the issue here—my word is my honor and far from worthless. It will keep you—*all* of you—alive. I sent no one after Jamie for *any* reason. That, too, had to be James' doing. In fact, I tried to keep her in Boston to *protect* her."

"But, why? Why should I take you at your word? Things can happen, you know. Odd things. One at a time. It's business, remember?"

His face softened. "Not this, Cage. This is . . . personal." He straightened his shoulders. "May I see her?"

"Not until I know why you're so willing to do this. I'm not stupid, Monahan. You know we can't beat you. Too many people would die in the cover-up before anyone got to you. *If* they got to you. And Jamie's not willing to be the cause of that. Neither am I. So, what is it? What really happened that night in the basement? I got Crazy Jimmy's version, but I think it was bullshit. What was it you said to make him hate her so much?"

He leaned forward. There was no threat in his eyes now. "Accept my word, Cage. Some bits of history are better left undisturbed. I should think you would have learned that lesson by now. If you'll recall, I tried to wave you off when we spoke following your brother's funeral. Life is for the living, remember? In any event, what happened in the past won't change a thing. You'll still be protected—all of you. I promise."

"I don't remember asking for your protection. I also realize that you're not doing this for me. This is for Jamie."

"It is. Yes. I won't deny that."

"That's only part of it, though, isn't it? I think it's just as much for you."

He slammed his fist on the table. "Why is that so *damned* important?"

"Because I need a goddamned good reason to trust you! She's my life, Monahan, and I find you a little short on credibility."

He sat quietly for a moment. When he finally spoke his tone was weary. "Yes, I can see that she is. And so maybe you do deserve to know. Then it can be *you* who decides whether or not to tell her. I never could—a promise made to someone long dead."

"Tell her what, Monahan?"

"That . . . she . . . is . . .my . . . *daughter!*"

The truth was there, deep in his eyes—in the tremor of his hands. And in that truth lay the reason we were still alive.

"Please. Allow me to explain . . . ."

When he'd finished, Michael Monahan stood, his figure blocking the sun, casting me in shadow.

I felt a chill. From the inside.

It feels wrong, Jamie had said.

"Hard as it may be for you to understand, Cage, I dearly love my daughter. I've maintained that love in the most difficult of fashions. From a distance. I will see that no harm befalls her. Ever."

"You're a regular fucking hero, Monahan. Now get out of my sight."

"Just as soon as we've settled on the arrangements. Or have you forgotten?"

CHAPTER 33

DESPITE WHAT MICHAEL Monahan believed, to keep the truth from Jamie would be a betrayal of trust, even given the possibility that what I had to say might break her spirit, if not her heart, and in the end, would give James what he'd wanted all along.

I found her in the courtyard reclining on a lounge and flipping through a magazine.

"Where is everybody?" I asked.

She laid the magazine on the ground next to the lounge. Her anxiety was palpable. "The Captain's upstairs writing in his log book. Luke's working on making James presentable."

"Your . . . uncle will be here in an hour to confirm that James is in one piece and still breathing. Deanne a little after that, followed by Brian once Georgie gets the all clear."

"You were gone a long time."

I went and sat on the end of the lounge, took one pedicured, bare foot in hand and began to massage it.

I felt her tense. "Cage. Look at me. What is it? What happened?"

How could I do this? Where should I start?

"Cage?"

"What happened is, I wouldn't let it alone. And I wish to God now that I had."

"No secrets, right?"

It was our promise.

"Go ahead. I'm listening," she coaxed.

I took a deep breath, told her first that I loved her—that nothing could ever change that. And then I calmly recounted Michael Monahan's story.

JAMIE'S MOTHER HAD married into the Monahan family believing life had finally been good to her. Her own family, while not poor was middle class Boston-Irish; she'd had to work and save for her own education.

She'd met her future husband—Michael Monahan's younger brother—by chance at the pub where she worked. He was a dashing man of considerable wealth, adventurous, with a quick-witted sense of humor. They fell madly in love and within a few months, married.

But shortly after their second anniversary the union began to fail. The flamboyant young husband's problem with alcohol and his lack of business acumen were set on a collision course. Before long they'd gone through his money and fallen in debt to his family. His frequent binges became a public embarrassment; at home, he was a private disaster.

With her love and patience fading and the prospect of a return to the life she'd worked so hard to escape a growing reality, she turned to her husband's brother looking for help.

What she found was a man with problems of his own. His wife was cold, he said, more interested in where their name fell on the society pages then she was about falling into bed.

What *he* found was a woman willing to do whatever was necessary to protect her financial well-being. And so, they struck an accommodation.

The affair lasted until she became pregnant with Jamie. They agreed that she would claim the baby as her husband's and Michael would provide clandestine financial support. But then a strange thing happened. When Jamie was born, Michael

Monahan discovered an unexpected joy: He loved his new daughter.

In time, Michael and Jamie's mother discovered a deep love for each other as well. After her husband died, for a time Michael considered divorcing his wife in favor of her—no matter the consequence.

But in the end the cost and the business implications were too onerous; he could never bring himself to do it. Instead, their relationship endured the way it was.

When Jamie's mother was diagnosed with terminal cancer Michael was devastated. He anguished over the coming loss and pledged to her that Jamie would be well cared for. He would bring her into his home. She would be loved and protected, although their secret would remain just that. She could never be told the truth.

In the beginning things went well. His wife took to Jamie as her own. Michael was careful to hide his affection but saw to it that Jamie was financially secure. Privately, he established a trust fund in her name, and she was included in his will.

Then as his eldest son, James, moved into his teens, the boy's personality changed and the trouble began. He became moody, often showing displays of temper, oft times violent. He resented Jamie, sensing an unnatural bond between her and his father. He was incessant in his complaint that she didn't belong, repeatedly asked why she was so special.

Michael thought maybe the boy already knew: There had been talk over the years, bits and pieces here and there he'd believed at the time too indistinct for young ears to comprehend. Perhaps he'd been wrong.

And while he wasn't yet aware of the full nature of the family business, his father suspected that James believed it to be a source of vast riches and underneath, not completely legal. Perhaps James was afraid that Jamie might unfairly share in that wealth, diminishing his own cut; even at his young age, his son had a sense of what money could do—of what it could *control*.

On the day James hit his mother, Monahan had meant to punish his son physically. He'd taken him to the basement—to the room James and his brothers had converted into a small gym where they lifted weights and boxed, honing the defensive physical skills that the privileged children from Beacon Hill often needed in the less affluent streets of Boston.

As Monahan began lacing his gloves, James suddenly lashed out, his voice near a shriek. "She's *yours*, isn't she? Yours and that dead-whore mother of hers. Well, I'll tell you what *Father*, if you so much as touch me I'll make sure Mother knows everything." He was shaking and looked as if he might cry. "Jesus, Dad, we don't need her. We're family. She'll ruin everything! That's what they do. All of them!"

Michael Monahan was speechless. He'd come to accept that his son was disturbed, perhaps even dangerous. The boy asked endless questions about the business and seemed to know or sense more than he should. But it was always about the money and who you had to threaten to get it—to keep it.

He was aware that James' brothers were growing more and more afraid of Crazy Jimmy, as they called him. They'd talked about it quietly. The other boys showed promise, had business sense. One day they would run important areas of Monahan Enterprises. James was a potential problem, but cutting him out altogether might present a bigger one.

After much thought Michael saw a place for Crazy Jimmy. Over the years he would use it, play on it, control it. And now was the time to start. Molding people to his own use was one of his special talents, a skill he'd use without reservation even on his own flesh and blood.

"All right," he intoned, "you want to talk man-to-man? Fine, let's do that. You're right, son. Women *are* difficult. But whatever you think of them, they do serve a purpose, each one different from the next. That's the way it is with your mother, the way it was with your aunt and the way it is with Jamie.

"You're smart in ways your brothers aren't. But even so I can't expect you to understand some of the things I do, some of the things that are . . . necessary to the business. What troubles me is that in trying to figure out Jamie's importance—in spending so much time and energy on the subject—you're missing the bigger point. What about James? *That's* what you should be thinking about. *Your* future, not hers."

"B-but, I *am* thinking about it. That's why—"

"I know you didn't mean what you said. You were emotional, upset. Teenage years are hard. I understand. Believe it or not, I was one myself once upon a time."

"Dad, it's just that . . . ."

James had calmed, softened. It was the right moment. "It's all right, son. And now there's something I want *you* to understand. In order for you to be as important to our family business as I know you someday will be, I have to know that I can trust you completely with the deepest of secrets."

"But you can! I'd never tell any—"

"I know, son. I know you don't *think* you would. But sometimes stress is difficult to manage. We say things we don't mean to say, divulge things we don't mean to divulge. So we're going to enter into a contract, you and I. In fact, I'll have it drawn up tomorrow."

"What do you mean? What . . . what *kind* of a contract?"

"It's a very simple one. And it will be written in such a way as to be completely legal and incontestable. So, here it is, my boy. Should you ever again mention anything about Jamie, me, and your aunt to anyone under *any* circumstances whatsoever, or should any physical harm come to Jamie by your hand or because of something you might order someone else to do, you'll be cut out of my will. You'll lose your inheritance. And upon my death what would have been yours will go instead to her. And if she's deceased, it will go to your brothers."

"You'd *do* that to me?"

"Oh, yes indeed. And there's more." Michael Monahan's voice took on an ominous tone. He knew his son would never forget what he was about to say—that he'd believe. Because it was true. If it hadn't been for James, he'd never have had to marry that cold woman upstairs. His life would have been so much better. "If anything unnatural happens to Jamie after I'm gone, your fate will be determined by committee with only the best interests of the company considered." Michael moved close to his son, close to his face. He could read cowardice in the boy's eyes. "Wrong her, you little shitting pup, and I'll see you dead or know it from my grave."

"THEY NEVER SPOKE of it again. The next day, both of them acted like the whole thing had never happened."

Jamie had lain with an eerie impassiveness, listening quietly as the wrenching truth was unveiled. Now she bolted from the lounge and ran into the villa.

I started after her, then realized that the last person she needed with her at that moment was the messenger.

She came back into the courtyard in time, eyes reddened, and sat on the lounge twisting a tattered tissue in her fingers.

"So now I know why he tried to rape me. He was testing his father's control over him by tempting fate. If it hadn't been for his father's threat he would have been back at me time and time again until one of us was dead. But that one time was it. He'd lost his chance.

"I was afraid of him, but he wouldn't have touched me physically after that. He'd been stripped of his manhood. I served to confirm it. So all of this is because of me. Because of my own family—my own . . . father."

"None of it's your fault."

She pressed the tip of a finger against my mouth. "Thanks, sport, but I have to deal with this one on my own terms."

I'd never seen her look so defeated.

Nor had I ever felt as helpless or inadequate as I did at that moment.

CHAPTER 34

MICHAEL MONAHAN KNOCKED on the door of the villa at two-thirty, looking every bit the father. He was dressed in tailored black slacks, a pale yellow oxford cloth shirt buttoned at the neck and a gray cardigan sweater with leather-wrapped buttons.

"Nice touch, Ozzie," I said, "but she doesn't want to see you."

He ignored the sarcasm. "Does she know? How is she?"

"She knows. And how do you *think* she is? Gosh, let's see. All these years you thought your father died a drunk and your mother had worked hard raising you. Only now you discover that your *real* father is a heartless gangster who had an affair with your mother and you weren't supposed to happen along, but you did. Add it up, Pop. She's just fucking great."

"Rather a sordid way of putting things, don't you think? And I'm not heartless any more than I am a gangster."

"I really don't care what the hell you are. What I care about is Jamie. I'd suggest that you live up to your word and see that our friends are released, then take your son and get the hell out of our lives."

He looked at me—*into* me. "I'll never be fully out of your lives. And for that you should be grateful."

It was a simple, ugly truth. "I'm just thrilled at the prospect, Dad."

"Where is James?"

"He'll be down in a minute. Make allowances for his appearance. We had a slight altercation and he didn't travel here in First Class."

"Just as long as he's alive." Monahan's words were sharp and cold, like cracked ice. He unclipped a cell phone from his belt and entered a set of numbers. After a brief wait, he said only three words: "Bring the girl."

Crazy Jimmy trailed Luke down the stairs five minutes later, a hand resting on Luke's shoulder like a prize fighter leaving the ring after a one-sided loss. The bruises on his face and mouth had turned a dark purple; the cut over his eye was crusted in dried blood. He looked better than I'd expected but much worse than when he'd walked into the Tate's townhouse twenty-four hours earlier.

Monahan stared at his son, but said nothing.

James' eyes were downcast, like those of a contrite child caught stealing money from his mother's purse. "Hello, Father."

"Sit," Monahan ordered. "We'll be leaving shortly."

James did as he was told, unquestioning in his obedience. I imagined that he'd not be easily forgiven for plotting revenge on Jamie, nor for Sam's death in defiance of his father's directive.

Jamie had come in from the courtyard, quietly and unnoticed. She looked proud, undaunted by the revelations of the past few hours. She walked to where James sat then stood silently facing him.

"Jamie? Honey?" I said. She ignored me. Then in a flash, I recognized the calm for what it really was.

She struck Crazy Jimmy across the face with all her might then turned toward her father who stood barely five feet away.

"Jamie, darling. I don't know what to say. All these years I've—"

"Don't say a goddamn word! Haven't you caused *enough* pain? Haven't you already done everything you could do to ruin my life?" She rushed her father and began pummeling him with her fists.

Monahan offered no resistance, instead absorbing blows as if each individual strike he was dealt served as just punishment for a corresponding year spent in deceit.

I moved quickly to step between them.

And that's when the front door flew open.

What happened next took only seconds in real time but played out in my mind in slow motion.

Deanne was sent flying across the room and into Luke as Georgie shoved her clear from behind. He spun toward Jamie and her father just as I'd reached them and begun pulling them apart.

Georgie misread my intentions. He pulled a gun from his belt and leveled it. There was a small spit of sound when he jerked the trigger.

The shot missed me and punched a small round hole in the wall only inches from Jamie's head. I pushed her to the floor.

Monahan was now in the line of fire.

Georgie swung the pistol toward me, the acrid smell of cordite hanging in the air between us.

I dove forward and tackled his legs, pulling him to the floor as he squeezed off another round. I scrambled on top of him and pinned his gun-hand against the tile.

Jamie screamed. *"Cage! Look out!"*

I held fast to Georgie's arm and flattened down against him, my head turned to one side. In the edge of my field of vision I saw a man come through the door from the courtyard with his gun drawn and pointing in my direction.

He saw Luke too late. The punch took him in the throat, crushing his wind pipe. He fell to his knees gagging, his eyes bulging in his futile, death-throe attempt to suck in air.

Georgie struggled fiercely beneath me. Suddenly, I lost my strength to a sharp pain as something stuck me high in my back and grated against my shoulder blade. I rolled away to avoid another strike.

Georgie regained his feet and swung the sights of his pistol at my chest.

Monahan's booming command caused him to freeze. *"Enough!"*

Everything stopped, as in a game of musical chairs.

Luke stood over the body of Georgie's accomplice. He was a man I recognized from a fight I'd had in a men's room.

Jamie looked pale and leaned against her father for support.

James sat motionless on the sofa, a wet stain spreading slowly over his blue shirt from the wound in his chest, turning it brown. His eyes were open but looked on some other world. He was dead, taken by the shot Georgie had meant for me.

"Jesus Christo!" Georgie yelped. His eyes darted back and forth between Crazy Jimmy's lifeless body and Michael Monahan.

"The gun, Jorge. Bring it here," Monahan said in a calming voice. "It's all right. I'm not going to do anything to you. Now please, bring it to me, son."

But Georgie was having none of it. His face said it all: He'd killed James. What chance did he have with his father? Before anyone could react, Georgie turned tail and rushed out the door, running for what he must have believed to be his life.

I went to Jamie. She fell in my arms.

"The boat, Cage." It was Jamie's father, his voice urgent but analytical, as if he'd at last found the solution to an important corporate problem. "We must stop him before he does something foolish."

Monahan and I made our way quickly on foot toward the main hotel. When we reached the entrance he clasped me on the back as we went by the doorman, as if we were two old friends going in for an afternoon drink.

C'mon, son, let's get a brew and discuss the terms of the dowry. You'll be good to my little girl, right?

"Blood," he uttered like a ventriloquist. "The stab wound. Smile."

Pain or not, I'd forgotten completely about it.

We crossed the tiered levels of the lobby and went onto the terrace where we'd sat earlier. From there we could see the footbridge that spanned a lagoon and ended far out in the water at the restaurant and marina complex where *The Spirit* would be moored.

Georgie was more than halfway out, speed walking. We were only seconds behind him, but seconds might make all the difference.

At first I thought it was a backfire coming from one of the large boats that sat in their slips on the smooth, calm water.

We were thirty yards from where the boardwalk ended at the marina. A few people were scattered around the outdoor bar. One of them was looking in the direction of *The Free Spirit.*

She was moored in a slip well away from the other boats.

Monahan and I walked at as near a normal pace as possible, not wishing to draw undue attention to ourselves. As we approached, I saw Brian standing in the cockpit.

When we reached him, I realized that what we'd heard had not been a backfire. It had been the sound of a single gunshot.

Georgie was lying face-up on the floor of the cockpit, his eyes frozen in time, blood seeping from beneath his still body.

The door to the engine room was open.

In the light that angled through from the afternoon sun, a smoky haze drifted in front of the mouth of the safe as it hung down from the overhead looking like the jaw of some cave-dwelling predator.

CHAPTER 35

MONAHAN RETURNED TO the villa. Brian and I worked Georgie's body into the onboard fish box with some difficulty, then gave the cockpit a fresh water wash-down until the last of the diluted blood that had turned to a thin pinkish solution became clear as it ran to the scuppers and drained into the Gulf..

When our work was complete, I replaced the pistol in the safe and locked it, then went into the salon where I retrieved two beers from the galley, handed one to an ashen-faced Brian and lowered my weight onto the leather sofa next to him like an old man whose bones ached without relief. "Drink it," I said. "It'll help."

He emptied half the can. "When Georgie got the call to bring Deanne to your villa," Brian said, "Vic—the other guy—was supposed to stay with us. But Georgie started second-guessing what James would want him to do and what the old man was up to. That's when he decided Vic would go along. They locked me in the engine room.

"I wasn't about to chance something happening at your end and not being ready, so I got the pistol from the safe. When Georgie came back, he was nuts—waved a gun in my face and started yelling at me in Spanish. I thought he was going to shoot me. So I pointed at something imaginary over his shoulder. He turned to look and when he did I raised the pistol and pulled the trigger. Christ, I didn't even hesitate."

"You had no choice."

He looked down at the open beer can held between his knees as if waiting for a genie to appear and solve all our problems.

"What happens now? What about the body?" he asked. "I suppose the police will want to—"

"Bodies," I said. "We had some trouble at the villa. But not the kind Georgie expected. His boss is dead. So is Vic. But there won't be any police—not officially."

"Wes? He knows what happened here?"

"Not yet," I said. "But he will soon enough."

ICLEANED THE BLOOD from the sofa as best I could while Jamie sat in the courtyard with her father.

I could see him talking intently while she looked past him, perhaps reflecting back to some moment or event in time that if revisited could be altered in a way that would cause her world to spin on a slightly different axis, and all the pain in her life and the evil of these past months would be magically erased.

What could he possibly say to her after all the years of dissimulation and the devastation of the day that would carry any weight with her, or offer any solace? Perhaps what he spoke were words of self-indulgent pity that reached her as no more than deaf tones as he sought to lighten the guilt and shame that rested heavily on the dark and vile gristle that was his soul.

Maybe one day she'd tell me. Maybe not. Whatever the choice she was owed an exception to the rule of no secrets, a right upon which I would not intrude.

Luke moved Vic's body into the kitchen, helped straighten up the living room then went up to look in on the Captain.

In seconds, he called down to me, his voice somber.

I climbed the stairs with a knowing sadness, any residue of hate or anger toward the man who had been a cog in the wheel of death that had run down my brother, gone.

Captain Tobias R. Tate, III, United States Navy, Retired, was dead. He lay on the bed in his Dress Whites, his hands crossed over the brim of the cap that sat squarely on his chest.

He looked serene, his release complete, his torment over, Tate's personal Hell and all the baseness it had brought to bear on too many lives forgiven by the merciful God to whom I'd heard him pray in song beneath the running water of a cleansing shower.

At least, that's what I wished for him.

Luke laid a hand briefly on Captain Tate's shoulder, then gently straightened the collar of his uniform, although I saw nothing out of place.

"The mind is a powerful thing, Cage. It can will most anything into comin' about if you truly want it."

When I went down to tell Jamie about Captain Toby, Michael Monahan was gone.

CHAPTER 36

I HAD TO PASS by the kitchen on my way out to the courtyard and glanced at the humped shape of Vic's carcass where it lay on the floor, my gaze drawn to his open, glassy eyes and the discoloration on his throat that appeared as a blue-black smudge of oil against the chalkiness of his skin, the telltale bruise the mark of a fatal blow delivered with the speed and hardness of a piston by a man who could take a life with dispassion in one moment, then mourn the death of an old man he hardly knew in the next.

Beside Vic's remains lay the body of Crazy Jimmy Monahan, the would-be king of his father's criminal enterprise, a bedspread thrown over his corpse, black garbage bags spread beneath him to catch any latent blood that might seep from the wound in his chest opened by a whipping boy whom he kept tethered to him by fear, a menial servant who had taken his master's life even as he'd meant to protect it.

These were things that happened to other people in a place with which I had not been familiar but had now become a part of my landscape.

Evil remains a dark fantasy to most people—an oddity observed in graphic pictures or told through embellished stories whose level of appeal seems dependant on the equation of safeness-of-distance, of the level of brutality and the degree of disbelief.

So when the Devil comes and sits upon your windowsill and peers inside your house, your best recourse is to pull the shades and turn on as many lights as you can in order to keep a hold on your sanity. Jumping through the window and tackling the monster for most of us is not a prudent option. The world is a better place for it. Trust me on this.

I went out and sat next to Jamie on the lounge she occupied with all the relaxed casualness of someone who thought the structure might fail at any moment and send them crashing to the ground—put my arm around her shoulder and held her close to me as I shared the sad news.

"Hon, it's a blessing," she said of Captain Tate's passing. "About the only thing I can think of right now that is." She wiped a tear from her eye with the sleeve of her white cotton blouse. "But really, I do know that in time there will be things to be happy about again. Better days lie ahead, and all that."

"Maybe the world's not such a bad place after all," I said.

Her smile was thin, and private. "Maybe not. But it's full of bad people, isn't it."

Luke joined us a minute later.

Monahan had called.

"He's sendin' a crew. They're comin' for the bodies and to clean the place up good as new. They'll take care of the Captain while they're at it. I think that's alright."

"What about Georgie?" I asked.

"When they're done here, they'll meet The Spirit at Treasure Island and take care of that as well."

Jamie fell against me, tremors rippling through her body like gentle waves. "And what about Sam? What happens to her?"

Luke rested his forearms on his knees. "I expect you'll be unsettled by this, Jamie, but Wes didn't have a lot of options. He's risked everything for us. If any 'a what he did goes public, not only is his job gone but he goes to jail to boot. I'm serious about that. So his brother is seeing to the arrangements. We'll be there for her."

***

O N FRIDAY EVENING, Luke, LuAnn, Jamie, Brian and I drove six miles north of the Beach to the small town of West Bay.

Deanne stayed behind, preparing for the cruise we'd planned for early the next morning. She'd come apart when she'd learned of Sam's death and simply couldn't face what we were about to do.

At the foot of the bridge that rises high over the narrows at the west end of the bay, I turned left and followed Wes Harland's directions along the south shore to a narrow lane. A quarter mile later, the path became no more than a tire-rutted track that led to a small dirt clearing. I parked under a big oak tree with thick limbs draped in a lacey crochet of Spanish moss.

We followed the beam of a flashlight under a sky as black as tar with stars stuck to it like rhinestones thrown by the handful as we ambled along a footpath through thinning trees. The evening was October-cool and smelled of earth as we walked toward the sound of voices drifting ever closer on the night air like gathering spirits.

Ahead, the footpath swung to the left around a stand of pine trees. Forty yards further on, we came to Bone Harland's fishing camp.

We moved together toward a cabin whose door stood open on a single large room with a bar running the full length of the back wall. Ceiling fans turned lazily overhead. Tables of card players crowded the warped wood floor.

One of the players—a man with hair as white and nappy as lamb's wool—looked up at Luke and nodded. "Wes n' Bone out to the pit. They lookin' for y'all."

The barbecue pit was off to the left of the building. A group of men stood around a cooker shaped like a small steam locomotive; smoke billowed from a two-foot high stack at one end. The smell of roasting pork permeated the air with a sweetness that moistened your mouth and softened your thoughts.

As we drew closer Wes said something I couldn't quite hear, and the others drifted off.

A man four-fifths a replica of Wes opened the cooker, chased the smoke away with a flap of his apron and basted meat with a paint brush full of thick sauce. "Y'all doin' okay?" he asked Luke.

"Better when that sow's done," Luke said.

"Luke, you know well as me that ya cain't hurry a good pig no more than you can a pretty woman."

Wes made the introductions. "This here's my brother Boneparte—Bone. Bone, meet Cage Royce and Jamie Shea. The friends I told you about. And Brian Martin."

Bone Harland closed the top of the cooker and wiped his hands on the front of his apron. "Pleased," he said, shaking hands with us. "My sympathies in regards to the young lady. The Lord 'll look after her now." He fixed his eyes on Jamie as if absorbing the depth of her sorrow. "We gonna send her on her way. Billy's waitin'. You can count on that. Don't you worry none, Miss Jamie." He opened the lid of the cooker and swabbed the pig with more sauce. "Sweet Lord Jesus. Everythin' gonna be alright."

Wes led the way around to the back of the building, to a heavy door wrapped in tin that opened on a large, walk-in cooler.

Sam's handmade wooden coffin was inside, sealed and set on cement blocks.

The cemetery was nestled among a stand of old oak trees whose twisted trunks looked in the darkness like tired old men on a last march home.

We set Sam's coffin atop four planks that spanned the newly-dug grave, then gathered in a circle and held hands, each with our own thoughts, all of us feeling a profound

sadness as Bone preached of life and death and salvation—
of a heaven filled with children and winged angels in a way
I'd never heard.

When he'd finished, I truly believed that Sam and Billy
were now joined together for all eternity in a place of glory.

B Y THE TIME we returned to the camp the pig had been
carved and the card games suspended. It was time for Sam's
wake—time to celebrate her life.

Soon, everyone was elbow-deep in barbecue and
beans, coleslaw, and thick white bread that had been toasted
over the coals.

The laughter was hearty, and full of hope.

At midnight, we said our good-byes, then walked toward
the path that led to the parking area, the poker games once again
back in full-swing.

"Cage? See you a minute?" It was Bone. We moved off to
one side. "Need for you to do me a small favor, you don't mind.
It's about my brother Wes. It's this cop thing a' his. He's a good
man an' a good chief—don't read me wrong. But it's gettin' to
him worse all the time. Cain't half do his job. Feels like he cain't
do no good, the way it is."

"He's talked about his frustrations. Government and
politics."

"Used to be mostly that. Not so much now. It's more 'bout
what y'all been doin'. Whatever it is has gone an' changed him
some."

"It's changed all of us, Bone."

"Life has a way, don't it? This trouble y'all had? Wes don't
say what it is to the word, but he says the law couldn't a' done
it by the book. They try, and y'all woulda got burned for sure."

"I'd say that's a fair assessment."

"So that's what I'm gettin' at. Wes don't need to be like that—he need to be on the edge a' things. My favor is, maybe you can find a way to make him see that. Help him move on somehow before he blows hisself up. He's one proud dude, that man. Worked hard to get what he's got. Now it don't taste so sweet, but he's afraid to push back from the table. I tell him he needs to, but sometimes it's hard for a brother to help a brother, know what I'm sayin'?"

I knew. All too well. I waited for the hitch in my throat to pass. "That's something to consider, Bone. I'll see what I can do."

CHAPTER 37

WE IDLED OUT of the Treasure Island Marina aboard *The Free Spirit* at seven on Saturday morning. An hour at slow cruise would put us well out into the Gulf of Mexico.

I sat up on the flybridge with Brian, bundled in a heavy sweater, drinking coffee from a thermal mug in the cool morning air.

As the sun broke the horizon the first shades of pinks and reds touched a line of thin clouds that spread like drifting smoke on the horizon. Steadily, the sky became clearer, as if the haze of sleep were lifting.

We rode in an easy silence, the deep rumble of the engines in the belly of the boat offering a comfort that I sensed we shared.

After a time Brian checked the synchronizers and engaged the auto pilot. He got up and stood at the rail. "It's been some year, hasn't it ?"

I joined him. "That it has. Everything other than these past couple of weeks seems like a blur to me."

"I know what you mean," he said.

"So have you given any thought as to what you'll do now that this is all behind you?"

Brian drank from his mug. "Not much about it, no. Only that I miss the Gulf. And now, well . . . now there's Deanne, too."

I ran a hand over the rail. "Jamie and I talked last night. We really don't want to sell this tub but we don't see the sense in keeping her—not unless by some chance there's a captain somewhere who might run her as a charter business for us. Say, on a percentage deal of some kind? Might even live aboard, if he liked. I don't suppose you happen to know of anyone like that, do you?"

I climbed down the ladder and went into the warmth of the salon where I was greeted by the smell of frying bacon.

The dinette table held all the things that went into making up one of Luke's famous weekend breakfasts. Scrambled eggs, thick toast stacked ten inches high, and of course a big bowl of cheese grits.

LuAnn made the coffee.

Deanne fixed plates for Brian and herself and went up to the flybridge. I wondered if he'd tell her about his new job now, or wait for a special night. Maybe one spent aboard.

Luke and I, LuAnn, Wes and Tisha Harland all ate ravenously. For some reason food tastes better when the surroundings are different from the norm—like a hot dog at the ballpark, popcorn at the movies or hamburgers on a picnic.

Association, so I've been told.

Jamie picked at her food for awhile in silence and then excused herself and went below. She returned wearing a heavy jacket and carrying the bag she'd brought onboard.

I followed her out to the cockpit.

She stood at the starboard rail with her eyes closed and her head held high in the breeze of the boat's forward passage.

I slipped an arm around her waist and listened for a time to the sound of the water as it fell away in sheets from the sleek hull.

"I wanted this to be a special moment," she said, "as special as Billy was to us. And Sam. Sweet, sweet Sam." She leaned into me. "We'll mark this moment as a passing, and as a kind of celebration. The freeing of the spirit. We'll live life differently because of them, because of who they were and what they taught us about love in the short time they were together. I imagine them looking down on us. Happy. Holding hands and laughing. That's what I see, babe. That's what I'll always see."

She picked up the bag. I held it open while she removed two wreaths of roses. She raised one to her lips, then cast it over the side. "Red for Billy," she said, "his favorite color." Her mouth trembled, but she held back her tears.

And then the second. "White for Sam. For her unselfish love," she said.

We held each other. and watched as the flowers drifted aft, as the wreaths touched together and disappeared beneath the wake.

"Now . . . it's over," she whispered. "Let it go, Cage. Don't burden yourself with something you think you should have known or done."

She kissed me lightly on the cheek and went back inside.

I turned my face into a rising breeze—salt spray burning my eyes.

Billy's voice floated to me on the wind. *"I screwed up. It's just that simple. There* isn't *an answer beyond that. Sometimes, Big Brother, there doesn't need to be one. It's time you understood that. I'm okay, now. Sam, too. You can let us go. Our turn to watch out for you."*

My eyes filled, then spilled over. "You're right, Billy," I whispered to the wind. "And so is Luke. The mind's a powerful thing."

Sometime later, after Brian had turned *The Spirit* for home, Jamie returned with fresh coffee.

We stood together at the aft rail. A north wind had kicked up as it often does in the late fall; *The Spirit* made way against an angled chop.

Jamie leaned back against me, shielded from the brisk air as we watched the foamy spray of the boat's wake toss and tumble. Whitecaps broke in diamond-white slashes along the emerald-green surface of the Gulf of Mexico.

"I'm a wealthy woman. That's what my father said to me. And I am. But not in a way he could possibly understand."

"He said there was a trust. That you were in his will. I said he shouldn't mention it and that you'd never accept it. I told him that we were just fine with what we have."

"Pretty much what I told him. I refuse to touch a cent of it," she said. "Can't we just give it away?"

"Not without a lot of questions being asked. The way he's set it up, you're sort of stuck with it, even if you just let it sit there."

She frowned.

"But there might be another way. I've been working on an idea. Let's see what you think."

I explained.

Jamie thought my plan was perfectly wonderful.

By nine-thirty, the *Free Spirit* was back in her slip at the Treasure Island Marina, everything buttoned up and shipshape.

Brian and Deanne went dockside for a long walk. As they were getting off the boat Deanne stopped to give me a big hug and whisper her thanks. He'd tried, she said, but Brian couldn't wait to tell her about our offer.

Jamie and I helped Luke and LuAnn load the Jeep with the extra dishes and utensils they'd brought to make and serve breakfast. While we were at it, we told them about the money and what we'd decided to do with it.

Luke clapped me on the back, beaming, just missing the still-healing knife wound. He put an arm around Jamie's shoulders. "Billy'd be proud."

Twice she started to say something, then stopped. Finally, she stood on her tiptoes and put her arms around Luke's thick neck and whispered something in his ear.

He smiled in response to whatever she'd said, then kissed her gently on the forehead.

I thought I heard him say, "You're welcome."

Wes and Tisha sat alone in the salon. We'd asked them to stay for a few minutes after everyone left; there was something we wanted to talk to them about.

"Wes," I started, "I've been talking to—"

He held up a hand. "I *know* who you been talkin' to. And I know what he said. Brother Bone worries too much is all."

"Not Bone. Jamie. She's come into some money that neither of us wants. It's drug money, pure and simple—laundered until it's squeaky clean. But that doesn't change its origin. The thing is, she doesn't have the option to turn it down without a lot of legal wrangling that might prove to be very unhealthy.. So we want to use it to set up a type of fund. For Billy. Private. Very private. And we'd like you to run it."

He leaned forward, elbows on his knees, big hands clasped together. Next to him, Tisha wriggled closer. "I'm flattered. Really, I am. But why not have some organization that's equipped for this sort of thing deal with it? It's not exactly what I'm qualified to do."

"No one knows better than you what it's like trying to go after bad people head-up through normal channels. You said it yourself—not enough manpower or funding. And you keep tripping over the rules.

"We want this money used in a different way. To buy a little justice here and there where the system fails. You know how to do that. We don't. Money talks, and with it we can go after drugs or anything you want or think we should. Go outside of the rules, work around the edges of the board. Like darts. It's good strategy."

We all waited.

Wes stood, setting his jaw.

"The edge of the board counts just as much as the bull's-eye," I said.

"Now, where the *hell* did you come up with that?"

"Billy," I said. "And he was right."

He shook his head; a grin touched his mouth. "He just might be at that." He held me at arm's length by the shoulders, his eyes sparkling. "It's somethin', ain't it?"

"What is, Wesley?"

"The things we can learn from our brothers," he said, "if we'll only take the time to listen."

EPILOGUE

FALL IN NEW England is unlike anywhere else in the country. Sporadic days and nights that tease the autumn spirit with cooler temperatures in late September become a promise fulfilled as October begins. The air turns dry and crisp; the skies take on a crystalline clarity that remains hidden much of the year under the veil of Atlantic humidity, and the taint of commerce.

By mid-month, the summer greens have begun to fade, gradually giving way to the early touches of color splashed randomly among the trees and bushes like splattered paint, soon to be finished in a masterpiece of flaming foliage, as if the sun had fallen to earth and set the land ablaze in a brilliant display of oranges, yellows and reds.

It's a time of Ivy League football played before sparse crowds warmed by hot chocolate and Bloody Marys—traditional rivalries between old universities known more for their academic standing than their athletic triumphs.

My favorite season.

We've promised ourselves that next year we'll take a week's vacation, fly to Boston, then drive to Vermont to see the colors. We'll find a country inn with a great stone fireplace, knotty-pine paneled walls, bedrooms furnished with antiques and four-poster beds with down-filled mattresses and big lumpy pillows.

By day we'll bike across covered bridges and through villages with cobblestone streets where old churches with white-washed steeples have stood unchanged since the Revolutionary War.

At night we'll bathe together in a claw-footed cast-iron tub set on a floor of pegged-oak planks, fall naked into bed and make love to the sounds of squeaky springs and the groans of aged timbers, then succumb to the embrace of a deep and healing sleep, snug beneath muslin sheets, an old wool blanket and a hand-sewn quilt as the sweet smell of the woods passes through an open window and scents our dreams.

That's the way Jamie describes it. That's the way it will be. Next year.

B RIAN TRAVELED TO Michigan to visit with Sam's parents shortly after her funeral—to try and explain the tragedy of what had happened to their beloved daughter.

At first they were in shock, despondent and unbelieving. They were devastated and demanded a full investigation be conducted by the authorities.

Brian pleaded with them to consider what that would mean, to think about their own safety and to understand why it was that he'd come forward at all. The reach of the syndicate was beyond the law. Nothing could bring Sam back, but her death had been avenged. Her killer was dead. She was at peace.

Finally and with great pain, they relented. They would contact the authorities regarding Sam's disappearance only to say that they'd received a phone call in which Sam had told them that she was deeply depressed. And then, she'd simply disappeared and they now feared the worst. That somewhere alone, she had taken her own life

They'll visit her grave soon.

We'll all be there.

As carefully as the Monahans ran their organization, mistakes had to happen.

In Tobias Tate's case, it had been the lack of an extended family sufficient to maintain the threat that would hold him bound to the secrets of the syndicate even beyond his own death—although in the end it was the old man himself who had conjured up a final path to freedom that lay well beyond their reach.

With Billy, it had been to misjudge his iron will—his unshakeable determination to protect those he loved and atone for his misdeeds. For his one moment of greed and thoughtlessness in an otherwise selfless life.

Where Carlos was concerned, it was an old criminal sex charge in the State of Louisiana uncovered when Wes ran a computer search for outstanding warrants for one Juan Carlos Ramirez, acting on an anonymous tip that cost the Monahans a loyal soldier.

As Juan Carlos was being transported back to Baton Rouge, he was shot dead as he attempted an escape. The deputy had stopped the police cruiser along an empty stretch of country road so that he and his charge might unzip and relieve themselves.

Juan Carlos looked at it as a chance to beat-feet, the deputy had reported. The bullet had taken his prisoner in the back of the head.

It was a convenient story, as old as the public cemetery where Juan Carlos Ramirez would be buried in a numbered grave. No one had claimed the body.

A month later, the deputy who'd shot him vanished without a trace.

A week after the incident, Wesley Harland resigned his position as Chief of Police, Panama City Beach, Florida, citing a lack of confidence in "Just about every damn thing having anything to do with the damn justice system."

Follow-up questions from the local press asking about his future plans went unanswered.

Brian accepted our offer and re-started the charter business. He's already in demand.

Deanne quit her job at The Marina Café, and the two now make their home aboard *The Free Spirit*.

They feel Billy's presence, they say.

And Sam's.

I don't doubt it for a minute.

The days following the melee at the villa were difficult for Jamie. She was moody, at times distant and depressed. But it wasn't the disaster I'd feared.

We talked for hours about mistakes, about guilt, about all things fair and unfair in a world without reason.

About family—brothers, and fathers, and mothers. And about promises.

Often the conversations were more a monologue as she worked through the emotions of the past year and contemplated what she'd learned about her life. Slowly, she began to find understanding, to accept things, to discover a sense of peace.

Me? I think it's fair to say that I've made my peace with my brother's memory, and for the most part all that happened.

But I'm not the same as I was. At times I have the sensation that I've shed a skin of some sort—that I can cross the established lines of civility without touching them.

Jamie says that it's brought on by the move, by our new way of life.

But, she senses there's more—far more. That part, she leaves alone.

Luke and I talk about it sometimes after the sun goes down and those we love and care about are safe for the night.

Or on the days following the worst of the nightmares where the cast of players return in fractured scenes and I wish to Almighty God that I'd simply gotten up and closed the window on the Devil.

***

O N THE SATURDAY following Thanksgiving, Luke and LuAnn threw a "leftovers party." It was an annual tradition, a bash that started at four in the afternoon and continued until the food was gone and all the liquor was consumed. Rules of the house.

Jamie and I ran the beach at two, then together took a long, lazy shower.

I dressed and went downstairs to help stock the bar for the coming evening and check on a late delivery of kitchen provisions while Jamie did her nails and finished getting ready.

By three-thirty, she still hadn't made an appearance; I went back up to see what was keeping her.

I found her on our bed wearing a smile and a sheer negligee, black, the color of her hair, the covers pulled back. Her green eyes danced. She looked radiant, completely alive for the first time in weeks.

She patted a place on the mattress.

I sat next to her.

She began to unbutton my shirt. "I haven't been the warmest creature on the planet lately, have I."

"You've had a rough go," I said.

"You, too."

"I'm fine. Don't feel as though you . . . ."

She pulled me down to her.

"What about the Careys' party?"

"Already called LuAnn. Said we'd be running a little late. Business."

"I suppose they'll just have to start without us." I reached for her.

"Not so fast, buster." She shifted around on the bed and snuggled her way into my arms. "What was it Bone said that you found so amusing?"

"You mean . . . the thing about not being able to hurry a pretty woman any more than you can a good pig?"

"Yeah. That. And I know one woman who plans to make this last a long, long, time."

ABOUT THE AUTHOR

JJ BRINKS is the author of the acclaimed new mystery, MURDER ON THE WHISKEY GEORGE, the premiere novel in a new series now available in both ebook and print formats from Amazon. com.

An independent writer for the television series, SILK STALKINGS, airing on the USA Network, Brinks followed his long-time passion to become a novelist when the series ended. In the course of developing and writing MURDER ON THE WHISKEY GEORGE, the author was introduced by the Editor-in-Chief at William Morrow to Richard Marek, a legend in New York literary circles who among other accomplishments in an illustrious career served as editor for nine Robert Ludlum bestselling novels.

Marek and Brinks worked together for over a year in what Brinks describes as an "amazing experience; an intense, indispensable education for which I am deeply grateful. Dick's sense of character development and his ability to drive plot and pace are unbelievable."

JJ BRINKS is a graduate of Syracuse University where he studied drama and creative writing at the School of Speech and Dramatic Art, and television at the Samuel I. Newhouse School of Communications.

The author is a member of the Writers Guild of America/ East.

MURDER IN BIG HOPE, the second installment in this compelling new series, is now available in ebook format at Amazon.com. Coming to paperback Fall 2015.

For more information about the author, visit JJBrinks.com.

NEXT IN THE ACCLAIMED NEW SERIES

BY JJ BRINKS

MURDER IN BIG HOPE

A Cage Royce, Luke Carey, Wesley Harland Novel

E-BOOK VERSION AVAILABLE NOW AT
AMAZON.COM

COMING TO PAPERBACK FALL 2015

Turn the page for an exciting preview!

MURDER IN BIG HOPE

A Novel by

JJ Brinks

ISBN 978-0-9836784-3-4

Copyright J.J. Brinks 2012.

All rights reserved.

Empire Mystery Press

This novel is a product of the Author's imagination. Any resemblance to any person, living or dead, is coincidental. Names of characters, places, and/or other incidents or events that may exist or have taken place are used fictitiously.

Any reproduction, re-publication, or other use of the material contained herein, either in whole or in part, is expressly prohibited without the written consent of the author.

PROLOGUE

HIS SENSES SENT confirmation racing to his brain although he'd never heard it before, never *felt* it, his ear and nerve endings instinctively identifying the sound and tremor of flesh against metal.

Robby Cain brought his truck to a skidding stop fifty yards past the point of collision, the beam of the aging Silverado's right headlight angling skyward through the ground fog like a lazy eye while the left shot a straight path along the obscured stretch of roadway.

He sat in the darkened cab for a minute, brooding. It wasn't the damage to his vehicle; it was the idea of death that weighed him down each time he drove to Atlanta and visited the nursing home where his grandmother fought the pain of her last days.

Robby switched on the overhead light and opened the glove box, pulling out a flashlight and automatic pistol. If the animal he'd hit had survived it would be badly injured. He wouldn't let it suffer.

He left his truck and walked slowly back along the edge of the Alabama road that ran between Phenix City and Eufaula, sweeping the ground with the flashlight as he went, cutting deeper into the scrub at the first traces of blood.

Thirty yards further on, the deer lay on its side, bloody foam coating its muzzle, its exposed flank rising and falling in labored breathing. Robby shined the flashlight over the animal's heart and fired a single shot through its hide.

As he returned to his truck, the shape of a man leaning against the front fender stopped him in his tracks twenty yards short. The hour was late, the road deserted. "Something you need, mister?"

"Deputy Sheriff," the figure said. "What say you move this way. Hold that light over your head with both hands. I'm not mistaken, that was a gun shot I just heard."

Robby stood his ground. "How about some identification? I don't see a cruiser anywhere."

The figured straightened. Robby heard a chuckle. "Smart one, aren't ya. That's good on account of I'm in no mood to deal with drunk and stupid." The officer walked to the front of Robby's truck. "Ridin' a cycle. See?" A beacon began to rotate, sending out a blue pulse of light.

In the staccato flashes Robby saw the officer clearly and did as instructed, noting that the sheriff's holster was unsnapped and his hand rested on the butt of his revolver. "The pistol," Robby said. "I have a permit for it. Gun's tucked in the back of my jeans."

"Just leave it where it is, boy, and tell me what this is all about—although from the looks of your Chevy I got a pretty good idea."

Robby explained what had happened while the deputy checked his driver's license and the pistol permit, then pulled the handgun from Robby's belt and examined it.

"Damn things scoot out of the dark like bad dreams, don't they?" the deputy said. "I'll call the boys at Highway to come cart the carcass off before the meat goes bad. There's folks around here can use all the help the law allows and the Good Lord provides. Now why don't you sit in your truck while I wander up the road and check this thing out."

Robby got back in his truck as ordered; the deputy sheriff started up the road and disappeared into the dark.

This, he flat out didn't need. He'd had a few beers along the way to help pass the miles—enough so that he might not walk the straightest of lines or touch his nose squarely on the first try. What if the cop had looked in the truck and seen the empties on the floor? One more ticket and he'd lose his license for sure. And that would put him out of work. Then what? How would he support his grandma?

Without giving himself a chance to think it through, Robby made an impulsive decision. He started the truck, and took off.

The deputy heard the engine turn over and the sudden screech of spinning tires. "Shit," he muttered. "Here we go."

He jogged back to his motorcycle. The truck had no more than a minute's head start on him by the time he mounted the Harley. Where the hell did this kid think he was gonna go? He turned on the beacon and the siren; a sharp twist of the throttle sent the bike up over seventy. The ground fog had thickened. He never saw the armadillo that lay dead in the road until it was too late. When he came to, he was lying in a ditch, gravel embedded in his skin, the truck long gone.

TWENTY MILES OF highway remained before the road would bring him north of Eufaula. To Robby, it felt more like a hundred.

His one good headlight cut a narrow path that traced the ribbon of road as it wandered through the rolling countryside, curving left and right in a series of turns. He'd seen nothing of the motorcycle cop in his rearview mirror. Good. The lazy bastard hadn't bothered. He knew it had been a stupid move taking off like that, but he was home free. Chalk one up to luck.

He slowed as he came to a patch of mist gathered in a deep hollow, then pulled the truck off the side of the road and stopped, badly needing to relieve himself. He got out and started for the tree line. Forty feet in from the road's edge, he came to three waist-high markers—simple white crosses made of wood and placed in memory and in warning that recklessness carries a penalty far greater than the laws of man.

Thin clouds lay across a harvest moon like gauze on a wound, playing amber light off the vapor that swirled around him as he walked, making him think of ghosts—as though he'd chanced on a cemetery and interrupted a gathering of spirits.

He passed the markers and headed toward the woods, aware of the coolness of the night air against his skin, a sensation that brought on a sudden shiver.

When he'd emptied his bladder he walked back by the crosses, stopping for a second to have a closer look—a man regarding Calgary, the bodies of the Innocent, the forgiven, and the non-repentant long since removed. It struck him as an odd thought; he was not by nature what his grandma would call a *true believer.*

"So who died here?" he asked in a curious whisper, not sure that he really wanted to know.

In reply came a throaty sound at his back. Startled, he spun on his heels. His eyes widened at what he saw: A large buck stood pawing the earth with its head lowered.

Robby took a cautious step backward. It was January; the animal was in rut. A dangerous time. Sweet Jesus, he thought. The buck's after me for hitting that deer. It couldn't be, but the ironic thought scared him badly and set his heart racing.

The animal reared, eyes intent; Robby backpedaled, struggling for balance.

The deer dropped its forelegs to the ground and advanced; Robby frantically groped the small of his back for the pistol. In a flash he saw the motorcycle cop stick the handgun in his waistband as he'd headed up the road. *Shit, man, is this bad!*

Then he saw a chance. The buck retreated a few feet to mount a full charge. As he did Robby made a blind dash to his left, only to collide with the markers, an arm of the center monument burying in his groin. He crumpled to the ground in agony.

The animal stood motionless, its eyes on Robby. With a violent shake of its antlers the buck raised its head to the sky, its shoulders tensing.

Robby drew himself into a ball, expecting the worst. But nothing came. When he finally opened his eyes and looked up the buck was slowly moving away, melding with the darkness until it receded into the night.

As the pain lessened, Robby got to his feet, listening for anything that might signal that the animal was still out there waiting in the darkness. Cautiously he began walking back toward his truck.

Damn things scoot out of the dark like bad dreams, don't they?

He shook the thought from his mind as he picked up his pace.

From behind him, came a heavy thud.

Robby froze, blood pumping. What now? He turned warily, his skin shrinking in patterns of gooseflesh on his bones. The center cruciform had fallen to the ground, a smoky light rising upward from the spot where it had stood. He watched transfixed as the light gathered into what might have been a human shape, or the shape of nothing at all.

Nothing, until it spoke to him. *Who's going to bear the weight of the sin, Robby? Can you tell us that? Can you please just tell us that?*

And then as the deer, the image slowly vanished until the light was extinguished.

HE DROVE ON through the night with his internal systems charged and his mind in overdrive. He'd imagined it, had hallucinated the whole thing. Too much stress for one day.

With the first rays of dawn showing on the horizon, Robby reached Panama City Beach. As he pulled into his trailer park he should have felt relief. He was home. But he knew he was in trouble. Big trouble. You don't run from a cop. And the handgun. Now, how totally dumb was that?

As he dragged himself from his truck, he tried to figure out how he could set it straight. But he was too exhausted to think. He'd need help on that issue, anyway. Christ, he thought as he put the key in the door, if I could just start this damn day over.

And get that creepy image and that weird question out of my head.

ONE

None speak false, when there is none to hear.

—*James Beattie*

CHAPTER 1

"ASPIRING TO FOUR hundred dollars per hour in this Godforsaken trade, Cage my boy, calls for the padding of one's won-loss record. A matter of avoidance, really. Allow controversy and the crassest criminals a wide berth. Forage instead in the troughs of the industrialists. Boring, but far safer. Forget all the other cockywaddle I've babbled on about over these past months. The money, lad. Head straight for the money."

Inspired words spoken years ago in a smoke-filled pub in Boston's Back Bay by an aging law professor, four Beefeater Gibsons bolstering his cynicism, a twice-removed subject of the Crown who at one time swayed jurors with his manufactured British accent, but in the end used its flavor to shield his ego.

He'd been a celebrated trial attorney until he'd stood in defense of an accused cop killer, a black youth whose arrest and confession seemed too convenient. He'd prevailed on defense, but not in the press. Tenure was all that saved him at Boston University.

As a yearling lawyer, I took his advice and abandoned any thoughts of a career built on trials with Perry Mason endings, opting instead for a shot at the big bucks that lay within corporate coffers.

Billing four hundred an hour, it turned out, was not my calling nor ever my fee. Half was more like it, the boredom double the professor's dispirited calculations.

I reached my late-thirties as a partner in a respectable New York corporate law firm where I slogged along day to day.

Bored but making a good buck. Until Billy was murdered—shot in the head and dumped like garbage on a patch of Florida swampland.

It took a year but I'd found my brother's killers where the authorities hadn't, and in the process unearthed a desire to live a freer life where I'd soon learn to regard the rules of law in a slightly different light.

So, here I am, transplanted and transforming, on most days practicing a simpler brand of law with my partner, Luke Carey, whiling away the sunny days amid DUI defenses, divorce decrees, personal injury claims, the structuring of wills and the filing of bankruptcies—the lot of man, not corporations; in part running *The Ship's Hatch Cafe*, a beach bar inherited from my deceased brother whose continued success I credit in my truest moments solely to my beautifully Irish, unwedded love, Jamie.

JANUARY ON FLORIDA'S Panhandle is a pleasant blend of cool days and cooler nights. The earth has moved to a point along its orbital path so that the sun sets well off shore in the Gulf of Mexico, setting fire to the sky by late afternoon.

I sat at a table on the deck of *The Hatch* near the outside bar beneath the warmth of a pole-mounted gas heater that Friday, blissfully sipping Ketel One on the rocks, watching in silence as the big orange ball slipped below the surface of the darkening water.

At four, Luke had shown up. He ordered a beer in clipped words, then drew deeply on the last of his cigarette and tamped it out in a glass ashtray as twin flumes of smoke streamed from his nostrils like a bull snorting a warning on a cold winter day.

I turned my attention from the palate of colors spreading slowly across the horizon and fixed my eyes on Luke. "Something bothering you?" I asked.

"Robby Cain. He's in some kind a' fix."

"Not surprising," I said.

Luke rested his tree trunk-sized forearms on the table. He flicked the top open and closed on the old dented Zippo lighter that seemed his talisman. "Had a run-in with a cop up on 431 near Big Hope last night. Messed up pretty good, he says."

"In jail?" I asked.

"Might a' been, he said, if he'd a' stuck around."

I sipped my vodka. "Charged with . . . ?"

"He didn't say much on the phone. Sounded shook, though. That much came through."

Robby Cain worked for the contractor who'd renovated *The Hatch* shortly after Jamie and I had taken title and moved in. He was a skilled framer and accomplished drinker, a redneck prone to participate in the local chapter of the Friday Night Fights.

Luke lit another cigarette. "He's not bad a kid, Cage. Works a full day. Most times, anyway. Takes care of his grandma. He had a rough go of it early on. That's all."

"And how many times have how many lawyers heard that excuse?"

"Not everybody's daddy in the Gulf War caught a bullet in the spine courtesy of some hopped up enlisted felon posin' as a regular troop and had the gears stripped on his legs and his nuts ."

"In war, not everyone's father *comes* home," I said, sorry that I had as soon as the words passed my lips.

Luke glared at me. He'd done two tours in the Army to my none. Timing. Age. The Lucky Sperm Club. Pick one. "It's true. Difference is, I didn't know 'em like I did Robby's daddy."

AT FIVE-THIRTY, ROBBY came through the wooden door with the brass portal and worked his way through the crowd to where Luke and I stood at the bar.

Robby was built like a middle-weight, every ounce as hard as the nails he pounded for a living, his brown hair shaggy, his face marked by sun damage that had aged him beyond his late twenties.

Luke watched him closely as he approached.

"I need a beer," Robby said. "And a lawyer. And my head shoved up my ass." He stuck out his hand. I shook it. "Cage, what's up?"

"My question," I said.

He bummed a cigarette from Luke. "It's not good. I freaked out and left a motorcycle cop with his dick in his hand. I'd had a few and, well, you know what my sheet looks like."

"Doesn't sound terminal," I said. "I think we can handle it. You sure he got your license and all that before you eighty-sixed him?"

The bartender brought Robby his beer. He took a long pull. "Doesn't matter. I gave him a gift to remember me by. My pistol. It's registered."

"What the *hell*?" Luke said.

"I hit a deer. Went looking for it and finished it off. Guy seen my truck sittin' there and heard the shot. I get back, he wants answers. He takes the gun and goes up the road for a look see and I take off. Brilliant, huh?"

Luke knuckled him on top of the head. "You'd had more than a few. Anything else, Einstein?"

Robby looked out the wide window, across the deck to the waters of the Gulf of Mexico, eyes narrowed as if the images of the previous night had followed him here and now floated somewhere on its black surface. He turned back to Luke. "Like that's not enough?"

"No," Luke answered, "like, if you hold anything back—anything at all—I'll put my boot up your scrawny ass."

Robby finished off his beer, then set the bottle on the bar and picked at the label. "Shit. Alright. But you're gonna want me committed," he said. "Deal is, I stopped to take a leak. It was near some a' them crosses—the ones for roadkill? Anyway, I finish up, then nearly get attacked by a horny buck. I run balls first into one a' them things tryin' to bolt and end up on the ground with my scrot in my throat. He finally wanders off, I haul ass for my truck, and guess what? Cross that took out my joint hits the ground behind me. Then— Come on Luke, this is as embarrassing as hell and don't mean squat."

"Size thirteen, and it's got a reinforced toe, Robby."

He signaled for another beer. "Goddamn if you ain't worse than my old man was."

Luke waved it off. "Son, if you haven't figured that out after all these years then I truly do give up."

"Fine," Robby huffed, his finger tracing a line of rivets in the copper top bar. "So, if ya gotta know, this . . . this light 'er smoke 'er somethin' farts up outta the ground and wants me to tell it who's gonna bear the sin. For what the hell, I have no idea. There. Happy?"

"More than a few," Luke said. "Sounds to me like you drank the whole friggin' case."

PRESCIENCE TO MOST people is the stuff of King novels. To me, it's all too real—a micro-burst that blows a hole in your vision and gives you a glimpse of something you'd rather not see. I've experienced it twice: the death of my parents by plane crash; the murder of my brother by gunshot. But we had blood-ties. If what Robby had witnessed was fact or fiction was beyond me.

Luke would chalk it up to beer and fatigue. He defines the world in terms of blood, bone, and supportable fact. For me, it's not that easy. The dead speak in too many ways.

I'd left Luke with Robby and gone out to the deck. Jamie was drawing a draft, the fluorescent light under the bar top painting her face with an iridescent glow, a pale hue set against the blackness of her thick, cropped hair.

She motioned me over with a quizzical expression. "You guys looked awfully serious in there."

I gave her a recap and asked her to apply her psychologist's brain to the mystery.

"As far as an hallucination," Jamie said, "it's chapter one stuff. Seeing his dying grandmother . . . killing the deer . . . the crosses . . . being tired, drunk—all of it. As for the sheriff? That's your area, Counselor. But this kid's going to end up in big trouble one of these days. "

"I'd say this qualifies, wouldn't you?"

"Can't save them all, sweet cakes."

"We can try, can't we?"

"As lawyers? Sure. But that's all you owe, him, Cage. That's the extent of it." With that she turned away and went to the aid of a customer who'd signaled his urgent need for more alcohol.

CHAPTER 2

WESLEY HARLAND SHOWED up at *The Hatch* a few minutes later, the bulk of his heavy muscle tight against the confines of his sweats, a white bandana stretched across a forehead as dark as coal.

Wes had been the Chief of Police in Panama City Beach, a good cop who'd grown tired of the increasing restrictions placed on his ability to deal with situations that required him to jump through too many procedural hoops.

Billy's murder had pushed him over the edge.

While my brother hadn't been a complete innocent, he was far from a hardened criminal. He'd made one mistake, and in the end received the death penalty at the hands of some truly bad guys while the law kept Wes's trussed firmly behind his back. He resigned shortly after the mystery finally unraveled and came to work in our law office as an investigator.

"Who called in the heavy artillery?" I asked Luke as Wes joined us at the bar.

"Nobody," Wes said. "But we need to talk. And I do mean now. In private. I came lookin' for the two of you. Havin' Robby here's a bonus—kind of."

We crammed ourselves into the small office off the kitchen.

Wes closed the door behind him and leaned against it. "I just had a talk with one of my old charges over at the station." He turned his eyes on Robby. "Good thing I got contacts. You're knee-deep in shit, sonny."

"We know," I said.

"How much of it you tell 'em?" Wes asked Robby.

"All of it. Everything."

"Everything you *know*. Assumin' you didn't totally lose your goddamn mind last night."

Robby looked confused. "But, you couldn't know about . . . . What the fuck?" he said to me. "You go and call Wes? Think my brain fart was that funny?"

"I didn't call anyone, Robby."

"Pardon me, gentlemen," Wes said, "but what the hell are y'all jawin' about? Trust me, there's nothin' funny about it."

"About what?" I asked.

"About a shot in the heart."

"The deer, you mean," Robby said.

"*What* deer? I'm talkin' about a man. Guy name of Raymond Lintz."

Robby turned pale beneath his tan, his eyes nearly doubling in size. "What the hell you tryin' to say? You think *I*—?"

"Slow down," Wes said. "I don't think anything. You go ahead and tell me your side, but then you're gonna need to hear me out."

Wes's former subordinate, also a friend of Robby's told Wes that the Sheriff's Department in Big Hope, Alabama, had made an urgent request of the Beach P.D. to pick Robby up and hold him pending extradition proceedings. They wouldn't say why.

The young duty officer called Wes who tapped his sources and uncovered two bits of disturbing information: a Missing Persons Report for a Raymond Lintz had been filed with the Fulton County Sheriff's Department in Atlanta on Tuesday; a body had been found early this morning near the town of Big Hope, Alabama.

"The body is that of a white male, approximate age, thirty. The description given by Holly Rhetman, twenty-eight, girlfriend of Lintz, thirty-four, when she filed the report, fits." Wes flipped open a spiral-bound steno book. "With a couple of notable exceptions. She described what Lintz had been wearing when she'd last seen him on Sunday, but the body had been stripped naked. The second point of interest is the bullet hole in his chest—a distinguishing mark we can assume was *not* known to her at the time she filed her report, if in fact the body is that of her boyfriend."

Robby shifted a nervous gaze from Wes to me. "And they're thinkin' they can pin this on me? I'm serious as I can be when I tell y'all I had not one goddamn thing to do with this other than bein' a dumb shit. Period."

"What caliber is your pistol?" Wes asked.

"Nine millimeter," Robby answered.

"Same as the slug they cut out of Lintz," Wes said, paying the words out like links in a heavy chain.

"The fuck am I gonna do now?" Robby said, struggling to keep his composure.

"I might have a suggestion," I said.

At nine that evening we parked in the lot at Destin Harbor, several miles west of Panama City Beach, and made our way along the dock.

The Free Spirit sat in her slip, her sleek white hull floating in the glow of footlights. She's a fifty-two foot Hatteras Convertible that had been owned by my brother—the spoils of his crime—fittingly named for his outlook on life. Now she operates as a fishing charter captained by Brian Martin and his girlfriend, Deanne.

The night air was crisp, scented by the thin smell of diesel fuel mixed with the stronger essence of steaks cooking close by on a stainless steel grill clamped to the stern rail of a handsome sloop, the water below her dark as pitch.

I introduced Robby as we boarded and went into the salon. Deanne and Brian live aboard and have added those personalized touches to the interior that convert space into a home.

"So I'm just 'sposed to take off on this luxury liner here like nothin's happened?" Robby said as he popped open a can of beer.

"We need time, son," Luke said. "Couple days and we'll know more about what we're dealin' with. If you were nothin' more than a person of interest and they wanted to fire a few questions your way, okay, we could go with that. But that deputy knows what really happened. So you're bein' set up by these characters and they're plannin' on closin' the lid down tight, seems to me. Why, is the question. We're gonna need that answer. You got the truth workin' your side, but they got timin', a body, and your gun."

"Thanks for the pep talk," Robby said.

"Our job now idn't about bein' cheerleaders," Luke said.

Brian went topside and started the engines; Luke and I helped with the lines, then watched *The Spirit* ease out of her slip at idle and turn to starboard, heading for the East Pass. From there she'd enter the Gulf of Mexico—destination, nowhere in particular beyond the jurisdictional limit.

TRAFFIC ALONG ROUTE 98 was light for a Friday night, and we were back at *The Hatch* by ten-fifteen.

We had a good crowd both inside and out, the deck-dwellers huddled together at tables under the glow of the propane heaters.

I skipped out on my usual late shift at the bar and accompanied Luke on the fifteen minute walk west along the beach to his Gulf front home, kicking off my shoes and leaving them at the bottom of the stairs that lead down from the deck. The sugar-white crystals felt cold underfoot and looked like snow in the pale moonlight.

While I trusted Wes's judgment in things connected to badges and warrants, I kept turning corners in my head and colliding with the same nagging thought: What if Robby *had* murdered someone? He was a hothead. Pour booze on a fire and funny things can happen.

"What's your gut tell you, Cage?"

"That the Red Sox will win it all again next year."

"You know damn well what I'm askin'."

"That he's innocent, I suppose."

"But you can't accept it on simple faith."

"It's not so much a matter of faith," I said, "as it is ignoring the circumstance."

Luke extracted a cigarette from a near-empty pack, produced his old Zippo and lit up in a flame that bent and danced like a miniature shaman in the faint breeze blowing in from the Gulf. In the flicker of light, I saw his familiar, crooked grin.

"Well, you can't just dismiss it, for Chrissake," I said.

"No, you can't. But if you dwell on it for too long it'll fuck with your head 'til you freeze up and don't know *what* to believe. You'll end up bein' no damn help to anybody."

We walked without words for several minutes.

"So then," I said finally, "I take it you're settled on his innocence?"

"Yep."

"And if you're wrong?"

"Partner, I been a one-man Boy's Club to that pup ever since his daddy passed when Robby was fifteen. I'm not wrong. But if it turns out that I am . . . ? Why'd you suggest sendin' him off on The Spirit?"

We stopped at the foot of the deck stairs. "For his benefit— so no one can get to him before we're ready."

"And . . . ?"

"And, *what*?"

"Oh, I don't know . . . maybe so he couldn't run out on us? Just in case?"

"That's . . . bullshit."

"There's nothin' wrong with doubt, Cage, so long as you don't allow it to get in the way to where you go and trip over it."

"What's that supposed to mean?"

He turned to face me. "It means that after your own flesh and blood got caught up on the wrong side of the law, to you the word *trust* doesn't have the same ring to it."

Part of me found Luke's insight intrusive, wanted to tell him to fuck off. But I let it go.

He started up the stairs to the house then stopped and turned toward the darkened water. I watched the arc of his cigarette trace a path against the lightless sky as it tailed to the sand below.

"Life's a Petrie dish, Cage. Whole goddamn thing's an experiment. That's the fun of it, and that's the hell of it. Now that you're witness to it, keep your eye on the glass. Study what's under it 'til you can pick out the good from the bad on your own. Otherwise one day you'll find yourself knocked flat on your ass and never know which mutant on this crazy fucking planet it was punched your ticket."

I jogged toward *The Hatch* along the tide-pack, dodging small waves that lapped the shore with a tongue of winter-cold water, upped the pace until my heart pounded and my breath ached in my chest; until I felt I could outdistance the ghost of my brother and the obsessive thought that I'd mortgaged a measure of my mortal being in seeking vengeance for his murder.

On the night breeze came the haunt of Billy's voice. *Tell me big brother, who'll bear the weight of the sin? Can you tell me that?*

A NOTE TO MY READERS

I HOPE YOU ENJOYED reading MURDER ON THE WHISKEY GEORGE, and meeting Cage, Jamie, Luke, Wes and the other players who made up the cast.

Many people offered their incredible insight and support during the writing of the book. I make note of their contributions in an interview on my website, and in part dedicate my first novel to each and every one of them. To all, my thanks and unending gratitude.

A special note to my wife: Thanks, babe, for everything, and for always.

And to each of you, my deepest appreciation for allowing me to become part of your entertainment world. If you'd like to ask a question or leave a comment, I can be reached at **jjbrinksbooks@gmail.com.** I promise to respond as quickly as possible.

See you again, soon, and I hope often, at *The Hatch*.

With warm regards,
JJ Brinks

23940276R00178

Made in the USA
San Bernardino, CA
05 September 2015